THE
GREAT
RESCUE

THE
GREAT
RESCUE

*American Heroes, an Iconic Ship,
and the Race to Save Europe in WWI*

PETER HERNON

HARPER

NEW YORK · LONDON · TORONTO · SYDNEY

HARPER

A hardcover edition of this book was published in 2017 by Harper, an imprint of HarperCollins Publishers.

The author would like to thank the following individuals and organizations for permission to reprint excerpts from the following:
Donald Smythe, excerpts from *Pershing: General of the Armies*. Copyright © 2007 by Donald Smythe. Reprinted with the permission of Indiana University Press.
Noelle Braynard for *The Story of the Leviathan: The World's Greatest Ship*, by Frank O. Braynard, South Street Seaport Museum, NY, 1972.
Dwight R. Messimer for *Escape*, Naval Institute Press, Annapolis, Maryland, 1994, and for an email July 18, 2015.
The Jesuit Archives: Central United States for the Donald Smythe Collection of Micheline Resco Material.

HarperCollins books may be purchased for educational, business, or sales promotional use. For information, please e-mail the Special Markets Department at SPsales@harpercollins.com.

FIRST HARPER PAPERBACK EDITION PUBLISHED 2018.

Designed by Fritz Metsch

Library of Congress Cataloging-in-Publication Data
Names: Hernon, Peter, 1947- author.
Title: American heroes, an iconic ship, and saving Europe during WWI / Peter Hernon.
Description: First edition. | New York, NY : HarperCollins Publishers, 2017. | Description based on print version record and CIP data provided by publisher; resource not viewed.
Identifiers: LCCN 2017012596 (print) | LCCN 2017014624 (ebook) | ISBN 9780062433886 (ebook) | ISBN 9780062433862 (hc) | ISBN 9780062676917 (audio) | ISBN 9780062433879 (trade pb)
Subjects: LCSH: Leviathan (Steamship) | World War, 1914-1918—Naval operations, American. | World War, 1914-1918—Transportation.
Classification: LCC VM383.L3 (ebook) | LCC VM383.L3 H47 2017 (print) | DDC 940.4/5973--dc23
LC record available at https://lccn.loc.gov/2017012596

ISBN 978-0-06-243387-9 (pbk.)

18 19 20 21 22   LSC   10 9 8 7 6 5 4 3 2 1

To Peter J. Connolly, Joseph E. Connolly, John Christian Schulte, and all those who wore the American uniform during the Great War. And in memory of Dennis Hernon.

CONTENTS

CHAPTER 1

Trapped in New York 1

"All the Best Pictures of the Ruins" 10

CHAPTER 2

"You Will Never Run Her" 21

Voting No to War 26

CHAPTER 3

Monster of the Deep 33

The General and the Mademoiselle 38

CHAPTER 4

Dead in the Water 51

"I Am Not Joking" 59

CHAPTER 5

Missed Rendezvous 63

"An Admiring and Jealous White Audience" 73

CHAPTER 6

A New Skipper 79

"The Tuscania's Been Hit" 82

CHAPTER 7

Steaming for "Rendezvous A" 89

Two Dead Nurses 95

CHAPTER 8

The Orphans of Brest. 101

A Promise of Help—and Micheline's Kisses 105

CHAPTER 9

POWs and Icebergs. 113

Lessons in Trench Warfare. 117

CHAPTER 10

Lost in the Fog 125

Hand Grenades and Brownings. 131

CHAPTER 11

"Blitzkatarrh," or "Flanders Fever". 137

An Even Better Target 141

CHAPTER 12

U-Boat Attack. 147

"Don't Lose Hope—I Beg You" 153

CHAPTER 13

Submarines and the Sky Pilot 161

"Another Way of Spelling the Word 'American'" . 166

CHAPTER 14

40 Hommes/8 Chevaux 175

The King of Gasses. 182

CHAPTER 15

Two Men Overboard 187

Visiting the Front with FDR 192

CHAPTER 16

A Near-Death Experience 197

Moving Up to the Front 201

CHAPTER 17

"Everyone Attack" 215

Fear of a "Flu Trip" 220

CHAPTER 18

A Bad Wound 223

The Eve of the Flu Voyage 230

CHAPTER 19

"Kamerad! Kamerad!" 233

Pandemic at Sea 240

CHAPTER 20

"Funny Little Smile" 247

Burials at Sea 252

CHAPTER 21

The U-Boats Go Home 257

The Eleventh Hour of the Eleventh Day of
the Eleventh Month 260

CHAPTER 22

Partying in Liverpool 273

A Sailor Named Bogart 279

CHAPTER 23

Journey of the Survivors 283

A Famous Shoreline 288

CHAPTER 24

"Amid a Silence That Hurt" 293

CHAPTER 25
Farewell to Arms 297
"I Have Made Plans for Us" 299

EPILOGUE 305
ACKNOWLEDGMENTS 311
NOTES 315
SELECT BIBLIOGRAPHY 335
INDEX 339

THE
GREAT
RESCUE

CHAPTER I

Trapped in New York

THE LARGEST, MOST luxurious ocean liner afloat was two days out of New York and steaming to the southwest at a steady twenty knots. It was July 28, 1914, and the SS *Vaterland*, Germany's newest superliner, was making her fourth round-trip from Hamburg, carrying 720 first-class passengers and another 1,200 in steerage, most of them German and eastern European immigrants on their way to the New World. After encountering icebergs on her maiden voyage two months earlier, the giant ship had taken a more southerly route across the North Atlantic on this trip. Icebergs were the terror of the sea. Barely two years earlier, on April 15, 1912, the *Titanic* had sunk within two short hours of ramming a floating mountain of ice in a disaster that claimed the lives of all but 705 of the 2,228 passengers and crew.

The German owners of the *Vaterland*, which set a new standard for luxury and size after the loss of the great White Star liner, were taking no chances. The *Vaterland* was equipped with one of the largest spotlights ever made, a six-foot-wide, 34,000-candle monster that could bore two miles into the darkness, its bright shaft of light probing and sweeping the surface of the water for these drifting ship killers.

But it was late in the iceberg-calving season, and the ship had encountered no such dangers since steaming out of Hamburg three days earlier. In fact, it had just finished another remarkable run, covering 540 miles in one day at an average speed of nearly twenty-two knots. The seas were glass smooth, the wake a white furrow trailing out a mile to the stern. Passengers by the hundreds, many decked out in upper-class finery—the latest summer seersucker, silk, or light tweeds—strolled the enclosed promenade reserved for them, or lounged on canvas-backed deck chairs. Newsboy-style caps and straw boaters were plentiful. The ship was designed to minimize rolling, the prime cause of seasickness, but with the ocean so calm, few such cases had been reported.

While the gravest questions of war and peace were casting disturbing shadows across the European landscape, aboard the *Vaterland*, the pride of Germany and the flagship of the Hamburg-American Line, the mood was far from glum. The world had never seen a luxury ship built on the scale of the *Vaterland*, at 950 feet the largest vessel afloat, nearly 300 feet longer than the mightiest English or American dreadnought, and 67 feet longer than the *Titanic*. It had eleven decks and soared twelve stories above sea level, with the bridge nearly ninety feet above the water.

The liner's distinctiveness started with her three canary-yellow sixty-four-foot-tall funnels and continued far below deck, where forty-eight coal-fed boilers turned four propellers that were each eighteen feet high. The real beauty, style, and lavishness of the ship were displayed throughout the eight main passenger decks. First-class passengers such as Paul J. Rainey, an American multimillionaire playboy and African big-game hunter, the German ambassador Count Heinrich von Bernstorff, and Adolph S. Ochs of the *New York Times* enjoyed luxurious trappings that rivaled the world's best hotels. The two imperial suites on C deck each had nine rooms complete with a private patio overlooking the ocean; one of the suites included an upright piano with inlaid wood specially designed for the kaiser. The sumptuous first-class staterooms had marble washstands and private baths with toilets, features unheard of on other liners.

The seven hundred first-class passengers enjoyed the run of

nearly 60 percent of the *Vaterland's* public spaces. The wealthiest among them had entrée to the opulent Ritz-Carlton restaurant and the equally regal Palm Court. Located on B deck, the Ritz-Carlton was the elegant twin of the New York restaurant by the same name. With fluted Doric columns and a wall of colored-glass windows that soared two decks high, it was operated by the Swiss hotelier César Ritz and decorated with walnut paneling. A single day's menu, under the title "Bold Dishes," included: "Pork Chops in Jelly; Duck a la Montmorency; Leg of Pork with Cold Slaw; Beefsteak Tartare; Roast beef; Roast veal; Smoked Ox Tongue; Smoked Ham; Boiled Ham; Various kinds sausages." The magnificent Palm Court, also called the Winter Garden, was located a mere six steps from the Ritz-Carlton and featured mature palm trees, a twenty-one-foot-high ceiling, gilt latticework, and oils by Giovanna Battista Pittoni, a seventeenth-century Venetian painter known for his florid rococo style.

The other first-class travelers, for whom dinner jackets, tuxedos, and formal gowns were de rigueur, ate in the dining saloon, which rose to a twenty-eight-foot-high cupola and included a balcony for the orchestra and two private dining rooms. A triple-tiered central staircase allowed guests to make a grand entrance as they descended from the upper deck. Four enormous oil paintings depicting scenes from the myth of Pandora by the seventeenth-century Flemish master Gerard de Lairesse and donated by the kaiser decorated the social hall, where guests gathered to dance to Strauss or the latest jazz. The kaiser had also donated a bronze statue of Marie Antoinette cast by Houdon in 1780 and a marble bust of himself with helmet and mounted hawk, which stood outside the hall.

The library on B deck featured a castle-size fireplace. The smoking room on A deck had a massive three-paneled stained glass window overlooking the bow, oak wainscoting, a beamed ceiling, and another impressive fireplace made of white stone with a wooden mantel. Paintings of Bismarck, members of German and English royalty, and other notables, including Washington and Lincoln, were mounted in the Ritz-Carlton and the Palm Room and in the other public spaces. The frescoed swimming pool was a must-see. Depicting scenes from Pompeii, it was dominated by a black marble statue of a winged, phallic cherub that sent long arcs of water splashing into the pool.

Second- and third-class accommodations included berths for up to 1,600 passengers. These guests weren't allowed in the swimming pool, but had their own elevator along with a gymnasium, dining saloon, and smoking room.

The steerage staterooms on G, H, and I decks were located just above and below the waterline and accommodated anywhere from four to eight people, who slept on bunk beds. Crammed into the bow section was enough space in steerage for 1,700 passengers, who shared a dining room on F deck outfitted with long wooden tables and bench seating. Although the space lacked the embroidered linens, sterling silver, Limoges china, and fresh flowers that graced dining tables in first class, it was staffed by attentive waiters in uniform, and for most of the immigrant passengers, many on their way to New York and points beyond, steerage must have seemed heaven sent. They even had a spacious area where they could do their wash in large enameled tubs with hot and cold water. Many of these passengers were couples with young children who were bundled in thick wool clothing and caps even in the bright July sunshine. Deck space was reserved for them in a long, narrow area just forward of the bridge, where they could enjoy the sea air, read, or play shuffleboard and other games. Steerage was a major money-maker for the owners, who charged $29.50 for passengers traveling from Hamburg to New York. For reasons that aren't clear, Russians were required to pay $1.25 extra.

All told, the ship had room for just over 4,000 passengers and a crew of 1,200. After the *Titanic* disaster, the German line made sure the *Vaterland* had enough lifeboats to carry 5,300 people. As another consequence of that deadly sinking, the *Vaterland* was also equipped with the most up-to-date wireless room in existence. Three operators on duty round-the-clock were in steady communication with shore-based radio stations. And on Thursday, July 30, as the ship approached Ambrose Channel and the entrance to New York's Upper Bay, these operators continued to handle a stream of ever-worsening news. It had started a month earlier, when an ominous story had broken during the *Vaterland*'s maiden voyage to New York: Archduke Franz Ferdinand, the heir to the Austro-Hungarian throne, had been assassinated with his wife by a Serbian nationalist in Sarajevo. Europe had exploded in war hysteria, and now Austria-Hungary had taken the first major step off the edge into the abyss. As many of the *Vaterland*'s passengers knew all too well, this meant that Serbia's close ally Russia would almost certainly declare war on Austria-Hungary.

As recently as July 28, the ship's newspaper had grimly reported that Austria-Hungary, the corrupt, worn-out dynasty aligned with Germany, had ignored Kaiser Wilhelm's frantic effort to defuse the time bomb and declared war on Serbia. On that same day, Winston Churchill, the first lord of the admiralty, had ordered the British fleet to put out from Dover and steam for its harbor at Scapa Flow on the northern tip of Scotland. Under bleak skies, the English armada sailed northward at dawn through the Strait of Dover, a line of battleships, cruisers, and destroyers that stretched across the horizon for eighteen miles.

THE ECONOMIC PANIC that ignited in New York with Austria's declaration of war on Serbia was spreading across Europe and closing financial markets. Germany, with over two million men under arms, was poised for mobilization, which had already been ordered in Russia and Austria. The peace that had lasted nearly half a century in Europe after the Franco-Prussian War ended with a German victory in 1871 was starting to unravel. War was certainly on the lips of many of the passengers as they lined the decks the morning of July 30—their bags packed or nearly so—to watch as the *Vaterland* steamed into the Narrows and passed the dim lights of Coney Island and Sandy Hook. The pilot had to take care that the ship hugged the main channel as she headed up the Hudson, which was dredged constantly to provide the forty-foot depth needed to accommodate big vessels such as the *Vaterland* and the *Lusitania*, a Cunard liner due in port the following day. The German ship drew thirty-six and a half feet and had little margin for error, especially as it battled the strong currents and wind that often blew down the Hudson. The Woolworth Building, the tallest skyscraper in the world, was soon visible on the Manhattan side of the river to everyone on deck. Many of the passengers had received illustrated brochures that depicted the *Vaterland* upended on her stern and standing next to the granite-fronted Woolworth. The ship towered over New York's most famous building by two hundred feet.

A flotilla of fourteen tugs with names like the *Johnny N*, all of them pouring white smoke from tall, thin stacks, helped nudge the big ship toward her pier, which jutted like a long finger into the harbor on the Hoboken side of the North River. The Brooklyn shore was lined with spectators who'd turned out by the thousands to watch as the liner slowly approached her mooring. Reporters from all the major New York dailies were on hand to cover the arrival as a matter of course, but they were also aware of the potential for disaster and the unexpected. It had almost happened before, twice.

On her maiden voyage in May, the *Vaterland* had had to cut power to avoid running into a tug pushing a tow of barges that unexpectedly veered in front of her as she was approaching the pier. Caught in the wind and drifting sideways downriver, the big liner required fifteen tugs to turn her around. A worse incident had occurred when the ship departed from New York later that same month. A headline in the *New-York Tribune* told the story: "*Vaterland* Terror of North River: Big Liner Sinks Coal Barge and Causes Panic in Sailing from Port." Somehow the ship's reverse engine jammed as she was slowly backing away from the pier. Shooting backward across the river, the *Vaterland* got stuck in the mud and silt just off Greenwich Village. When the engines were shifted into forward and powered up to pull her free, the ship's tremendous wash tore two small freight steamers and a pair of coal barges from their moorings.

This time there were no problems, and the hardworking tugs maneuvered the *Vaterland* into her slip, where she was tied up at a wharf as long as a city block, her smokestacks towering over the New Jersey shoreline. Passengers clutching jackets and umbrellas soon began to pour down the six gangways. Unlike at previous arrivals, the liner's band didn't break out in a brassy medley of German and American anthems. With the news from Europe growing more disturbing by the hour, perhaps no one was in the mood. The ship emptied quickly as the passengers, many with somber faces, hurried off to reclaim their baggage and confront whatever was coming next.

The next day, July 31, the crew hurried to prepare the *Vaterland* for a quick turnaround. They wanted to get out of New York and back to Germany before war broke out. Wispy trails of white steam rose from her stacks as the boilers were stoked. Mountains of baggage were sorted along with several tons of mail bound for Europe, and five thousand tons of coal were shoveled into the bunkers. Tickets had been sold for 720 first-class passengers; 420 in second class, and 2,500 in third class and steerage.

Then all preparations for departure came to an abrupt halt. A cable from Germany ordered the ship to remain in New York, warning that French and British warships were poised offshore to seize her if she tried to sail on August 1, as scheduled.

The morning dawned with the darkest news flash yet: Germany had declared war on Russia. The czarist government had ignored the imperial government's demand that the Russian army stand down within twelve hours. General mobilization orders were soon splashed across large posters that went up in cities throughout Russia. The kaiser immediately instructed the German mobilization to proceed after having earlier issued a *Kriegesgefahr*, or "danger of war" alert. It was the start of four tumultuous days.

Within hours, chaos broke out on the *Vaterland*'s pier, as hundreds of angry and frightened passengers, many of them German citizens, rushed through the gates and tried to board. Hoboken police officers had their hands full as they struggled with the mob. Amid the pushing and shoving, blows were thrown and scores arrested. The police called for backup, and a patrol boat soon arrived with fifty officers armed with billy clubs, who scrambled up on the pier to help restore order. The launch's spotlight was trained on the liner at night, and a net was later strung across her stern to thwart anyone from trying to attach a bomb to the hull. The newspapers were already reporting a conspiracy by French and Russian secret agents to blow up the *Vaterland*. Another story detailed how the kaiser had ordered the ship to flee New York under cover of darkness and make a run for home.

Nearly ten thousand German army reservists, many of them sailors on German ships like the *Vaterland*, descended on their country's consul office in Manhattan, demanding that they be sent back to Germany so they could join their units. The police braced for riots, but there were no demonstrations, and the crowd dispersed peacefully. Besides the *Vaterland*, eight other of Germany's largest ocean liners were tied up in Hoboken: the *Prinzess Irene*, *President Lincoln*, *Friedrich der Grosse*, *Pennsylvania*, *Barbarossa*, *Prinz Joachim*, *George Washington*, and *Martha Washington*. As many as thirty-five German passenger ships were trapped in American ports when the war started.

On Monday, August 3, another hammer blow fell when Germany declared war on France. The news was delivered to the French prime minister by the sobbing American ambassador in Paris, who announced that he'd been asked to take over the German embassy and raise the American flag over the premises, which he declined to do. The German ambassador arrived "in visible distress" moments later to deliver the message personally; pulling himself together, he then walked back to his carriage with his French counterpart. Before parting, the two men bowed to each other in silence. In New Jersey, crew members from the interned ships gathered at night for a mass meeting at the Atlantic Garden, a popular bar on the Hoboken waterfront, where the war was discussed amid cheers, patriotic songs, and music from the *Vaterland*'s brass band, all of it washed down with steins of pilsner. The main question on everyone's mind: How would they get back home? Hundreds of sailors and other reservists were already filtering off their ships and booking passage for Germany on vessels from neutral countries, as were most of the ship's stranded passengers.

The talk also focused on what England was going to do. Would it support France, which had already declared war on Germany in support of its Russian ally?

The world didn't have long to wait for an answer. Late in the night of August 4, after Germany ignored a British ultimatum and invaded Belgium, the British government issued a war telegram to its armed forces declaring that England was at war with Germany. Earlier on that hazy summer's day, German cavalry armed with carbines and twelve-foot-long lances crossed into neutral Belgium seventy miles east of Brussels. What had been unthinkable for a generation was rapidly starting to unfold. The evening before in Whitehall, Foreign Secretary Sir Edward Grey was standing with a friend at the window as the streetlamps were being lit and made his famous prediction: "The lamps are going out all over Europe; we shall not see them lit again in our lifetime." In New York, English passenger ships including the *Lusitania* and two other White Star liners, the *Adriatic* and the *Olympic*, were moored on the Manhattan side of the river. On August 5, the *Adriatic* was the first British steamer to depart for England after the declaration of war. Spectators jamming the pier broke out in "God Save the King" as the sleek two-stacker pulled into the Hudson and headed downstream, while across the river on the Hoboken side, the *Vaterland*'s crewmen watched in silence.

The *Vaterland* was about to begin a nearly three-year slumber tied to her pier in Hoboken, and few would have guessed that the next time she sailed it would be with American sailors aboard. The country's mood when war broke out favored strict neutrality. The *New York Times* editorialized that as the storm broke over Europe and the *Vaterland* entered "her terribly expensive rest, there is nowhere even a suspicion that the United States can be drawn into the savage quarrels."

"All the Best Pictures of the Ruins"

ON AUGUST 18, TWO weeks after the outbreak of hostilities, a frightened Belgian taxi driver pulled to the side of the road not far from Louvain. Smoke rose above the wooded hills that shrouded the famous medieval city, and there was an unmistakable rumble—faint, then becoming louder as the wind shifted. A late-summer thunderstorm? It rained nearly every day in this part of Belgium, and it seemed as if nearly all the fleeing residents of Louvain who passed by on the narrow road—thousands of men, women, and children—were armed with rolled-up umbrellas.

Irvin Cobb and the three other American journalists in the rickety, dust-caked cab—Will Irwin of *Collier's*; Arno Dosch of *The World's Work*, and John McCutcheon of the *Chicago Tribune*—soon realized this was something they'd never heard before: the sound of artillery fired in battle, large-caliber guns, and a lot of them. They'd set out that morning from the Palace Hotel in Brussels determined to find the war, and it looked as if it was waiting for them just up ahead.

Cobb, a hulking six-footer with thick black eyebrows and a taste for fancy clothes—he was wearing a silk shirt and a blue flannel suit—had been sent to cover the fighting for the *Saturday Evening Post*. But now the cab driver stood on the brakes.

"Boom! Boom!" he said, turning to his passengers, a worried look on his broad, red face.

"Nix on the panic, brother," said one of Cobb's companions. "What's a little boom among pals?"

The American handed the driver a ten-franc note and offered a pull from a quart bottle of brandy, and so they kept going for another mile, slowly weaving through the lines of refugees until another cannon blast rattled the windows of the cab. The driver would go no farther, promising through choppy gestures and the few words of French that Cobb and the others understood that he'd wait there for them while they found out what was happening in Louvain.

Leaving their raincoats in the cab—a big mistake; they never saw the driver again—Cobb and the others started walking against the flow of humanity that was fleeing the ancient Belgian city, some pushing carts, or carrying suitcases or bundles of clothing and food. The line of refugees stretched for miles along a road flanked by green fields of ripening cabbages sprinkled with the red caps of Belgian soldiers, who were crouching with rifles as they watched the black smoke rising over the spires and chimneys of the doomed city. Cobb started to hear the patter of machine gun fire.

Just eleven days earlier he'd been vacationing with his wife and daughter at a rented farm in southern Quebec. He had been fishing for bass on a small lake when a messenger paddled out in a canoe and handed him a telegram that read: "Seems like this here war has done busted right in our face. Your ship sails Thursday." It was signed by George Lorimer, the editor of the *Saturday Evening Post*.

Cobb, who was then one of the most well-known journalists in America, caught an overnight train to New York City, where he was given a passport, a stack of travelers' checks, a black handbag stuffed with six thousand dollars in gold coins, and an automatic pistol. He sailed for England aboard the SS *Saint Paul* on August 7.

Ignoring the artillery fire, Cobb and his three companions walked to Louvain, a city of fifty thousand residents with world-famous architecture and a renowned university. They arrived just as the invading gray-clad Germans were pouring through the cobbled streets. Rounding a corner, an open car carrying two English cameramen raced toward them, heading in the opposite direction. The car slowed just long enough for one of the passengers to shout, "The Germans are coming!"

Cobb and the others ducked into the courtyard of the Church of Saint Jacques. Four priests sitting at a table beneath pear trees bending with fruit offered the journalists a bottle of red wine brought up from the cellar and got a map for them. One of the priests spoke English and told the visitors that Belgium was a small country that had no quarrel with Germany. "You Americans, you come from a very great country," he said, his voice quivering with emotion. "Surely if the worst should come, America will not let our country perish from off the earth. Is not that so?"

Cobb's account, written soon after his return to the United States, doesn't mention how he or his companions answered, but the four of them quickly found themselves back on the street, where they encountered nearly fifty Belgian soldiers running down the sidewalk. Minutes later, they stopped in their tracks when a man on horseback rode slowly around a corner. Cobb and the others realized at the same moment that he was wearing German gray. He swung a carbine in their direction, then slowly passed them, "a tall, lean, blond young man with a little yellow mustache and high cheekbones." Within moments, the German and another soldier riding a bicycle were gone.

A group of residents crouched in their doorways and pointed toward a small park, where more Germans were emerging through clouds of dust. The soldiers were singing a marching song and were followed by a squad of cavalry, uhlans with death's-head insignia on their fur caps, then more infantry and troops on bicycles, hundreds of them. Shooting broke out in the distance, and the uhlans peeled out from the line, drew their carbines in a fluid motion, and galloped forward.

Cobb was one of the first witnesses to the violent unfolding of the Schlieffen plan. Devised by Count Alfred von Schlieffen, chief of the German general staff from 1891 to 1906, it was designed to crush France with one powerful blow. The plan called for sending the entire right wing of the German army—sixteen corps, or some 700,000 men—through Belgium in a sweeping arc that extended to the English Channel. At the same time, the left wing of 320,000 men would block any French attack on Alsace and Lorraine; the German center, nearly 400,000 soldiers strong, would then smash into France through Luxembourg and the Ardennes. The right wing was meant to provide the coup de grâce as the German army executed a massive pincer movement aimed at enveloping the French army before it could respond.

The finely honed German plan was based on the presumption that the small, poorly equipped Belgian army wouldn't put up a fight. The Germans were mistaken. Border guards began firing at the invaders. Small squads of soldiers dug in at crossroads and key railroad junctions and refused to surrender.

For the next three days, until they found a driver willing to take them to Brussels by side roads, Cobb and his friends took rooms in a small hotel in Louvain and watched in amazement as part of the largest, most powerful army in the world marched by their front door. He later remembered how he and his three companions were sitting at a sidewalk café on August 21 watching the unending line of soldiers pass when the sky slowly darkened.

"The sun," he wrote, started dimming "in eclipse like a copper disk."

Was it an omen, he wondered, some foreshadowing of cataclysmic events to come? Cobb wasn't superstitious or even religious, but he couldn't help being struck by the massive scale of what was unfolding before his eyes. "We watched the gray-clad columns pass until the mind grew numb at the prospect of computing their number. To think of trying to count them was like trying to count the leaves on a tree." Several hundred thousand men and over one hundred thousand horses strung out for miles in a long, dusty line. "They came and came," he wrote, "and kept on coming, and their iron-shod feet flailed the earth to powder and there was no end to them."

BY THE TIME Cobb and his colleagues returned to Brussels, the German army had already occupied the city. The four American journalists were stopped several times and accused of being British spies. They eventually talked a German general into giving them a safe-conduct pass, which they doctored to omit the crucial phrase "in Brussels and its suburbs," then set out on Saturday, August 23, in two horse-drawn carriages to find the front lines. It didn't take long.

One of their first stops was the town of Montignies Saint Christophe, forty-five miles from Brussels, where they exchanged their decrepit carriages for two bicycles and a cart drawn by an aging horse. The small, abandoned town was shot to pieces, and they had to force the mare pulling their cart past dead horses lying stiff-legged in a road littered with abandoned knapsacks, caps, and jackets—all of them French. The soldiers were gone, but the Americans encountered three men wearing Red Cross armbands helping pull a wagon that carried two dead French infantrymen; the face of one was shot away. Without ceremony, the bodies were rolled into a shallow trench cut into a field of red poppies—the flower that would become the symbol for a generation of war dead.

Later that day they visited another village, La Buissiere, where each of the tall, slate-gray homes that lined the twisting streets was a shattered ruin. The day before, German infantry had driven the French from a hill overlooking the town in a bayonet charge. The Germans were camped nearby, their large yellow turtle-shaped tents pitched for the night, cookstoves burning. A young lieutenant took Cobb to the hill where the fighting, often hand to hand, had raged earlier that morning. A steep climb to the top offered a post-card view of the town below and the Sambre River winding in from the north. The French had occupied the trench, which was now filled with discarded equipment—knapsacks, red caps, water bottles, broken guns. Surveying the scene, the officer quietly said they'd sustained casualties taking the town. Over five hundred German soldiers charged up the hill under fire.

"The enemy lost many men here before they ran," he said in broken English. "So did we lose many." The garish French uniform—bright red trousers and blue coats—was shameful. The gray German uniform faded into the background, but "a Frenchman in his foolish monkey clothes is a target for as far as you can see him."

Crossing the border into France before nightfall, the Americans caught up with the rear of the advancing German Seventh Army at Beaumont. Approaching in their creaking cart and on bicycle, their clothing dirty and all of them badly in need of a shave, they made their way through ranks of gawking troops to staff headquarters.

An officer stopped them and in perfect English asked, "Who are you?"

"A party of American war correspondents," Cobb said, prompting a ripple of laughter. The pleasantries didn't last long, and the reporters were promptly ordered back into German territory. The officer who escorted them to the train smiled and shook their hands, but as he left he whispered a warning to one of their guards: "If one of those journalists tries to slip away, don't take any chances—shoot him at once!"

On August 30, the reporters arrived in Aix-la-Chapelle on the German border in a slow-moving train crammed with wounded soldiers and French prisoners. For the first time in days, they were able to eat a full meal and take a bath. They were also allowed to meet the American consul, who had to work hard to convince the suspicious Germans his visitors weren't British spies. Kept under house arrest for several days, they finally wrote a letter to the kaiser at Cobb's prodding, "a business proposition" suggesting it would be a smart and prudent move to let them inform the American people—many of whom were of German ancestry—about how Germany was conducting the war and what it was fighting for. Their argument in a nutshell was that the kaiser needed some good publicity.

They were told repeatedly that sending such a message was a serious breach of etiquette and that the kaiser wouldn't even look at their letter. Three days later, a German officer, "a gorgeous military figure wrapped in a magnificent long gray coat with medals on his chest," arrived with a document written on parchment and decorated with seals and ribbons; signed by the kaiser, it allowed them to travel where they pleased and even provided a car.

FOR THE NEXT three weeks, Cobb and the others were allowed to tour military operations, visit the trenches, and even go up in an observation balloon. Climbing into the small, waist-high basket, Cobb and a German officer were let up five hundred feet by cable, high enough to see the Eiffel Tower in the distance and the cathedral at Reims. German batteries below them blasted away at the French lines across a long valley, and from his precarious vantage point, Cobb followed the trajectories of the big shells. He noticed "a row of tiny scarlet dots" moving slowly across the battlefield and saw through binoculars that they were men crawling on their stomachs. Puffs of black smoke from high-explosive shells burst over the heads of these ant-size French soldiers. When the smoke cleared, "those ants were not to be seen. They had altogether vanished."

Cobb and the artillery spotter with him were brought down abruptly when a French plane dove in and was driven off with antiaircraft fire. The bursting flak "looked like a bed of white water lilies and [the plane] like a black dragonfly skimming among the lilies," he wrote later.

During a dangerous stop in Reims, Cobb watched from a trench as the great gothic cathedral burned in the distance. One of its spires had been truncated by artillery shells, and he couldn't make out whether the intricate carvings over the door or the great rose window had survived. Minutes later, he had to flee the trench when a bomb exploded nearby and bullets began thudding into an earthen mound that provided cover.

At Cerny, forty miles from Paris, the journalists watched a German battery open up on French positions nearly two miles away, the long-barreled guns firing over a line of trees so that it was impossible to see what they were shooting at. The location and distance to the targets were called in by telephone from a spotter aboard one of the tethered balloons. "Remember to keep your mouth open to save your eardrums from being injured by the concussion," their guide warned repeatedly.

The fighting in this sector had been intense for two days, the French and English facing the Germans across a front four miles long, with the no-man's land between the lines nearly half a mile wide. While there, Cobb and his colleagues visited a field hospital where a German doctor who had an American wife worked in an improvised operating room set up in a former schoolhouse. Whenever the orderlies set down a stretcher in the courtyard after carrying a man into surgery, a dark brown stain was left on the stones. The doctor told Cobb about a soldier who'd lost both feet and still managed to crack a joke that it could have been worse; he was a tailor and could have lost his hands. As they left the schoolhouse, a breeze carried a sharp, pungent odor from the battlefield. Their German escort said that the men at the front were sent as much tobacco as they wanted. As long as they could smoke, the officer said, "they can stand . . . that."

Reaching Maubeuge a few days later, Cobb watched as hundreds of wounded soldiers arrived aboard trains that banged hard at their couplings when they rolled to a stop, jostling their suffering cargo. The men lay on matted straw in the filthy freight or cattle cars. Four French surgeons who were prisoners of war helped a handful of exhausted German doctors deal with the carnage in a hospital way station for trains headed into Germany.

Cobb and his companions started assisting the overwhelmed orderlies carry the wounded into the first aid rooms, where they removed bloody dressings, cleaned wounds, and performed minor surgery. A German surgeon too worn out to move was stretched out on a table and gave them instructions. "I aided at setting a cracked shinbone," Cobb wrote. "And from the shattered hand of a young Hessian private two of us sheared away three fingers so far gone from gangrene they looked like rotted bananas; and the soldier stood there while we were doing it and made little whimpering sounds . . . like a complaining sick kitten." For the most part, Cobb recalled, the wounded kept silent no matter how badly injured they were or how hopeless the prognosis. Lifting one of the men, Cobb suffered a hernia that would require surgery in the United States and nearly killed him.

A few weeks before leaving the war zone, Cobb revisited Louvain. Barely a month had passed since his first trip to the city. His hotel had vanished, shelled into oblivion, along with the sidewalk café where he and his friends had enjoyed a glass of wine as the eclipse darkened the sky.

The heart of the city, once known as the Oxford of Belgium, had been destroyed, and with it an incalculable number of Renaissance paintings, fine buildings, and furnishings. The university, founded in the fifteenth century, and its library, with 250,000 priceless volumes, were in ruins; so was the cathedral, the picturesque business district, the town hall, and long rows of medieval homes. The historic center of the city had been hollowed out by six days of shelling and fires.

Strangely, tourists from Germany and even Belgium had started descending on Louvain, many eager to buy postcards depicting the appalling damage. A woman wrapped in a shawl approached Cobb and the others.

"Please buy some pictures," she said in French. "My husband is dead."

"Who killed him?" one of the reporters asked.

"They did," she said, pointing to a square where German soldiers were burying nearly eighty of their dead comrades in two large trenches cut through a flower bed.

"They killed him," she repeated in a monotone. "Will you buy some postal cards, monsieur? All the best pictures of the ruins."

American embassy officials had reported the destruction as it was occurring, news that became part of what would be known as "the rape of Belgium." Over two hundred civilians were killed in Louvain, but that was just the beginning. As noted by the English historian John Keegan, "Within the first three weeks, there would be large-scale massacres of civilians in small Belgian towns. . . . The victims included children and women as well as men and the killing was systematic; at Tamines [where 384 were killed] the hostages were massed in the square, shot down by execution squads and survivors bayoneted." Priests were among those ruthlessly gunned down.

Cobb sailed back to the United States in late October on the *Lusitania*, a Cunard liner that would be famously torpedoed six months later. What happened in Belgium put the scope and savagery of the war into sharp focus and convinced some observers—Irvin Cobb among them—that the fighting wouldn't end anytime soon.

CHAPTER 2

"You Will Never Run Her"

At 4:00 A.M. on Thursday, April 5, 1917, four harbor-patrol boats pulled up at Pier 4 in Hoboken, one of a dozen major wharves along the Hudson River on the New Jersey shoreline. They'd shoved off an hour earlier from Governors Island and crossed Upper New York Bay in a driving rainstorm—two hundred soldiers and customs agents led by John Baylis, a thirty-three-year-old lieutenant in the Revenue Cutter Service, soon to be renamed the US Coast Guard.

"It was raining like the devil," he recalled. "It was a vicious, bitchy night."

Nearly three years had elapsed since Irvin Cobb reported on the opening weeks of a titanic struggle that still showed no sign of ending. Worse, the war was going terribly wrong for the Allies, but with their backs to the wall, they were about to receive a lifesaving boost from the United States.

As his boat bucked in the current, Lieutenant Baylis and his small fleet slipped past the Statue of Liberty and Ellis Island, both dimly illuminated and hard to see in the darkness, then passed a destroyer, no. 533, a low-slung, two-stacked warship. Although Baylis couldn't make her out clearly in the rain, he knew she was rocking at anchor somewhere off the *Vaterland*'s stern, her two mounted guns trained on the big ship. The destroyer had arrived five days earlier to make sure the captains of the interned superliner and eight other German passenger ships tied up at the Hoboken piers wouldn't be tempted to make a run for open water and Germany.

Baylis, a veteran of a sixteen-month around-the-world cruise on a four-masted British sailing ship and a graduate of the Coast Guard Academy, had prepared hard for this morning. His men were also well trained—and well armed—for what had to be done. The lieutenant, who was from Jamaica, New York, and acquainted with the Hoboken docks and the layout of the *Vaterland*, hustled his squad out of the patrol boats and marched them by twos down the pier alongside the German ship, which towered overhead.

Climbing up the main gangway, Baylis headed for the bridge as soldiers armed with carbines and shotguns fanned out along the decks. The German crew—at least those who still remained on the ship and happened to be awake—understood what was happening and stayed out of the way. The New York papers had been buzzing for weeks with stories and news bulletins saying that the ship would be seized any day. Treasury agents joined the soldiers, along with nearly four dozen New York City reserve police officers, who took up positions on the pier.

When Baylis approached the bridge, one of the *Vaterland*'s officers was waiting for him. The lieutenant curtly told him the US government was taking over the ship and that he needed to vacate the vessel immediately.

"I protest," the officer said in stiff, clear English.

His objection was a formality. The officers from all the interned ships had agreed weeks earlier on what to do in case they needed to surrender their vessels. Leaving the bridge, the German joined a handful of other officers and about 300 sailors who remained from the *Vaterland*'s original crew of nearly 1,200. Most of those men had managed to get back to Germany on ships from neutral countries. Several hundred others had opted to apply for US citizenship, some taking jobs in the many German restaurants in New York City and

Hoboken, or working as electricians or in other skilled trades. None of the remaining crew members offered resistance as they were led off the ship under guard and taken to Ellis Island, where they were given a choice to apply for citizenship or be sent to a federal prison in Georgia.

The details for the surrender of the most prized ship afloat had been worked out the night before aboard the *Vaterland*, when three American officials met with the commanding officers of the nine German ships interned in New York Harbor. The captains were cautioned not to resist or damage their vessels.

Everyone in the room that evening understood that America was about to declare war. The critical moment had been coming for weeks, gathering momentum ever since Germany had unleashed unrestricted submarine warfare two months earlier, sinking an average of fifty Allied ships a week and pushing England to the edge of starvation and defeat. Less than two hours before Baylis and his men boarded the *Vaterland*, the US House of Representatives had approved a war declaration after a similar overwhelming vote in the Senate. President Woodrow Wilson was expected to sign the document later that afternoon. Similar scenes were playing out in other American ports, as treasury officials and soldiers seized 103 German and Austrian ships over the perfunctory protests of their commanders.

Baylis and the others who boarded the slumbering giant on that dismally wet morning couldn't help being impressed, but after her long, enforced stay in Hoboken, the once magnificent liner was in miserable shape.

The *Vaterland*'s chief engineer offered a warning as he was led off the ship. "You will never run her."

THE *VATERLAND*'S GAME-CHANGING potential as a troopship had been evident to American naval strategists from her first voyage to New York City in May 1914. Albert Gleaves, the commandant of the US Navy Yard in New York, was one of the luncheon guests who boarded the ship that afternoon to celebrate her arrival. The German ambassador Count Bernstorff, who would soon direct his country's espionage network in the United States, was there, along with representatives of the ship's owner, the Hamburg-American Line.

Gleaves, who later became a vice admiral in charge of American troopships during the war, couldn't resist asking an official from the shipping company how many soldiers the huge liner could carry. With the outbreak of fighting rapidly approaching in Europe, his question was prophetic.

"Ten thousand," the official said, smiling. "And we built her to bring them over here."

"When they come, we will be here to meet them," Gleaves said, also smiling.

Now, as Lieutenant Baylis took control of the *Vaterland* and her remaining crew members were led away under guard, the effects of the vessel's long stay in Hoboken were dismally apparent. The lower decks were a mess, especially the "engine room, fire room and dynamo space [where] much deterioration had taken place." Also, the German officers had managed "to remove and probably destroy her operational manuals, machinery plans, and virtually all blueprints." Some of the missing manuals and blueprints were tracked down when Secret Service agents raided the Hamburg-American Line's office on Broadway a few days later, but the most important documents, including schematics of the wiring and plumbing systems, were never found.

Nonetheless, the new masters of the *Vaterland* were dazzled by the ship's incomparable style.

The skeleton crew that had stayed aboard during her internment had done its best to maintain at least a semblance of the ship's status as the world's most renowned luxury liner. The *Vaterland* had become an unofficial hub for many Americans who favored Germany in the war over England and France. Even after a German U-boat sank the *Lusitania* off the southern coast of Ireland on May 7, 1915, with a great loss of life—1,198 men, women, and children, including 128 Americans, a large, affluent, and often vocal segment of the population continued to back Germany. On November 4, 1916, barely six months after the *Lusitania* went down, a charity ball on Germany's behalf was held aboard the *Vaterland.*

William Randolph Hearst and his wife, Millicent, were among the guests; the newspaper mogul detested England, opposed America's entry into the war, and supported Germany on his barbed editorial pages. His presence helped guarantee the event's success.

As the war in Europe dragged on, the *Vaterland* largely dropped from the news pages, with only occasional stories, all of them untrue, that her turbines had been damaged or dismantled, or that her crew members were involved in wide-scale sabotage. There was good reason to be suspicious. German secret agents operating with the knowledge of Count Bernstorff were involved in smuggling bombs into the holds of freighters, timed to explode while the ships were at sea. German agents also blew up several factories on the East Coast and likely caused a spectacular explosion in 1916 that destroyed a munitions plant in Jersey City, killing five and shattering windows across the Hudson River in Manhattan. Aboard one of the interned ships in Hoboken, the *Friedrich der Grosse*, the crew systematically manufactured bombs, "which were carried off the ship in separate parts and assembled at the main factory in Hoboken, which was disguised as a fertilizer plant." The ring was broken up and those involved sent to prison.

None of these clandestine activities—and there were many others—were traced to crewmen of the *Vaterland*, at least not before America's entrance into the war.

Voting No to War

WHEN ROYAL JOHNSON, a young congressman from South Dakota, arrived at the Capitol on the evening of April 2, 1917, the chamber of the House of Representatives was brilliantly lit and bedecked with red, white, and blue bunting. It was already crowded with fellow legislators, members of the Supreme Court sitting in a half circle in front of the Speaker's dais, military leaders, other dignitaries and their guests, and the wives of public officials lucky enough to get a ticket, including Eleanor Roosevelt, whose husband, Franklin, was the assistant secretary of the navy.

Johnson was handed a small American flag as he entered the chamber. Less than two months after President's Wilson's inauguration to a second term, the patrician Virginian was going to urge Congress to do what he had promised to avoid at all costs: enter the war. Clusters of peace advocates had elbowed their way into the packed corridors at the capitol, where Senator Henry Cabot Lodge of Massachusetts, his steel-gray Vandyke beard neatly trimmed, traded insults, then blows, with an antiwar protester from Boston.

Johnson, a Republican serving his first term, was still learning the ropes, preferring to follow the lead of Joe Cannon, the legendary former Speaker of the House and the titular head of the GOP. Johnson had recently moved to Washington with his wife, Florence, whom he'd met at the University of South Dakota while he was in law school, and their two young sons, Everett and Harlan.

At thirty-four, Johnson was a shade over six feet tall and still had the wiry, muscular build that had helped him stand out as a catcher for a semiprofessional baseball team back in Aberdeen. He had an almost swarthy complexion, with thick black hair and deep-set gray eyes. Nearsighted, he'd worn glasses since high school, but that hadn't stopped him from playing football and basketball for

Yankton College, a small liberal arts school perched on a high bluff overlooking the Missouri River.

Shortly after Johnson took his seat that evening, the president entered the emotionally charged chamber at 8:32. It took nearly three minutes for the ovation to die away to silence. Wilson looked pale and even slimmer than usual. "I have called the Congress into extraordinary session," the president began, "because there are serious, very serious choices of policy to be made, and made immediately." His most recent effort to stay out of the war in Europe by arming merchant ships—it was called "armed neutrality"—had failed, he admitted, before zeroing in quickly on the depredations of German U-boats. "Vessels of every kind, whatever their flag, their character, their cargo, their destination . . . have been ruthlessly sent to the bottom without warning and without thought of help; or mercy."

Johnson listened intently as Wilson, his voice rising in pitch, ticked off the reasons for the path the president was going to ask the country to follow. Just two months earlier on February 1, Germany had announced unrestricted submarine warfare, which meant that any ship heading to an Allied port was subject to being torpedoed without warning. Three days later, the *Housatonic*, an American freighter out of Galveston carrying wheat, was sunk by the *U-53* off the English coast. Other ships soon followed, including the *Illinois*, a tanker attacked in the English Channel; the *Vigilancia*, the *Algonquin*, and the *City of Memphis*, all sent to the bottom on March 18 with the loss of American lives. Wilson had polled his cabinet two days later on whether or not to declare war. To a man, they favored belligerency, even the pacifist Josephus Daniels, Wilson's secretary of the navy, who broke down in tears when he announced his vote.

Germany's all-out submarine warfare was "a warfare against mankind," Wilson said. The country could submit, of course, and keep its merchant ships in port, or paint them with bright red-and-black striping as Germany demanded and avoid any French or English ports, but that was a decision "we cannot make." The time had come to fight for "peace and justice," and to assure that the world was "made safe for democracy." Wilson then asked Congress to declare the recent acts of the German government "to be in fact nothing less than war against the Government and people of the United States," and that this nation "formally accept the status of belligerent which has thus been thrust upon it." The president called for a national draft of half a million men, with similar-size calls to come if needed, and for fully equipping the navy, with a special focus on submarine defense.

The chamber erupted in wild cheering and applause as nearly all those in attendance rose to their feet. Johnson watched as Wilson stood grim faced on the dais, waiting for the clamor to die down before proceeding. Then came his final sentences, words that Johnson would take home that evening to share with his wife.

After declaring that the United States had "no quarrel with the German people," Wilson said, "It is a fearful thing to lead this great peaceful people into war, into the most terrible and disastrous of all wars, civilization itself seeming to be in the balance." He admitted there would be grievous sacrifices, but optimistically assured his listeners that in the cause of a just peace, "America is privileged to spend her blood and her might for the principles that gave her birth and happiness and the peace which she has treasured."

Head high, staring hard at something distant and unseen, Wilson concluded with a paraphrase from Martin Luther: "God helping her, she can do no other."

An outpouring of lusty approval rocked the chamber. Congressmen and senators rose as one, stumbling out of their chairs, shaking hands, pounding each other on the back, as spectators in the galleries waved flags and cheered.

There were a few notable exceptions to this roar of support. Across the aisle from Johnson stood one of his mentors, "arms ostentatiously folded high across his chest, a 'sardonic smile' upon his face." Senator Robert La Follette of Wisconsin, the most outspoken opponent of American entry into the war, was also one of the founders of the Republican progressive movement of which Johnson was a member. "Fighting Bob" was sure to come out swinging when the Senate voted on the war resolution. Debate was set to begin on Wednesday, April 4; then it would be his own chamber's turn to take up the issue.

ROYAL JOHNSON WAS conflicted about his vote. The constituents in his Second Congressional District, which included much of the eastern third of South Dakota, were overwhelmingly opposed to war, a sentiment shared by many representatives from the far western states. Although he didn't take those antiwar feelings lightly, Johnson was also a patriot enraged by the German U-boats' sinking American ships without warning. Like so many of his colleagues in the House, he was shocked when news broke of what came to be called the Zimmermann telegram. The previous January, British intelligence decoders had intercepted a copy of a dispatch that German foreign minister Arthur Zimmermann had sent to his country's ambassador in Mexico. The note, which President Wilson alluded to in his speech, informed the ambassador that unrestricted submarine warfare was about to begin on February 1, and that if this pushed the United States into the war, an alliance between Germany and Mexico was to be proposed. In exchange for coming in on Germany's side, Mexico would receive the kaiser's help in winning back "by conquest" its lost territory in Texas, New Mexico, and Arizona.

Johnson understood what his constituents thought about this outrage and what they expected of him. They knew him well, just as they'd known his father, Eli, a newspaperman who had moved his young family from Iowa to Highmore in 1883. The tiny but growing community of tar paper and sod shacks was spread out

along newly laid railroad tracks in the heart of central South Dakota just east of the Missouri River. The wide, muddy waterway
that Lewis and Clark had ascended nearly eighty years earlier on
their way to the Pacific split the state in two, the high plains grass-
lands on the east river side giving way to the rugged Black Hills and
the scoured, lunar-like Badlands on the west river side.

Eli and his family had arrived in Highmore from Cherokee,
Iowa, a railroad town on the extreme western edge of the state
where Royal was born in 1882 and where Eli had a printing business. They were riding a wave of immigration in what was very
much the Wild West. Barely six years earlier, in 1876, Sioux and
Cheyenne warriors had wiped out Custer and the Seventh Cavalry
a few hundred miles to the west at the Little Bighorn.

Eli's father started a newspaper in Highmore and became a
county judge and state's attorney of Hyde County, a position later
held by his son. Royal's mother, Philena, was a teacher. The son
followed his father's footsteps into the legal profession, graduat-
ing from law school in 1906, and quickly won election as state's attorney in Hyde County. Royal soon made his reputation when he
targeted a band of horse thieves who operated in the Ree Hills,
a rugged, canyon-riddled backwash forty miles east of Highmore.
Shortly after he was elected as a prosecutor in 1907, Johnson went
after the gang, which for years had raided ranches and farms, often
selling the stolen cattle and horses in Canada. According to one
newspaper account, Johnson spent six months on the case, playing
detective at some personal risk as he tracked down railroad and
banking records, following clues through Illinois, Iowa, and Ohio
before locating horses that had been stolen in Hyde County. He
charged three men, who were convicted and sentenced to time in
the state penitentiary.

Riding the heels of that victory—the fate of horse thieves was
big news in South Dakota—Johnson was elected the state's attorney general, serving through 1914, when he entered Congress. The

war and whether the United States should get sucked into a fight that was achieving new heights of barbarism quickly became a major issue. Few in South Dakota wanted anything to do with the bloodletting, and they let Johnson know their views whenever he visited his home and law office in Aberdeen. The progressive movement was strong in South Dakota, a Republican stronghold, and noninvolvement in the war was a bedrock belief. A sizable number of western progressives had voted for Wilson's 1916 reelection when the Democrat promised not to send American boys to fight in France. For many of these Republicans, Wilson's call to war was a betrayal.

WHEN ROBERT LA FOLLETTE took the floor of the Senate on April 4 to argue against the war, the new congressman was eager to hear the man's unmistakable eloquence. La Follette didn't hesitate to get down to business, and there were protests from the gallery as soon as he began to attack the president's call to war. The insults didn't slow him down, and he spoke for nearly two hours through the late afternoon and into the evening, assailing Wilson's arguments point by point, punctuating his remarks by slamming his fist against his open palm. He expanded on a criticism that a fellow progressive, Senator George Norris of Nebraska, had already leveled—namely, that it was hypocritical to blame the Germans for the submarine campaign while America had done next to nothing to object to Great Britain's blockade of Germany. The German people were being threatened with starvation just as the British were, La Follette charged, yet the United States meekly went along with England's illegal maneuver while labeling the German submarine campaign a war against mankind.

The Wisconsin senator read into the record reports that tens of thousands of Americans had expressed their opposition to the war in letters and postcards. When he finished speaking, his face was wet with tears.

It was a tremendous, courageous speech, but it didn't matter. Shortly after he sat down, the Senate voted 82 to 6 in favor of the war declaration. The issue went to the House, where twenty representatives rose to speak against the resolution. The prowar advocates included Joe Cannon of Illinois, who sharply bit off each syllable as he declared his support. Jeannette Rankin of Montana, the first woman elected to Congress, sat speechless for a long moment before slowly rising to her feet to deliver the first vote of her career—no to the war—then sinking back into her seat in tears.

The final vote, which came in the predawn hours of April 6, Good Friday, was 373 to 50. Royal Johnson, who didn't speak, voted with the minority. The war resolution was rushed by courier to the White House, where President Wilson signed the document with a gold pen. Within minutes, the news was flashed to navy ships around the world.

With his no vote, Johnson supported his conscience and the will of his constituents, along with other western progressives who cast over half the nays. But he wanted to stand with his country in an hour of great trial and may already have been thinking about taking a radical step suggested a few hours earlier during the angry debate in the House, when a flummoxed representative railing at an antiwar colleague shouted that there was a simple way for the man to prove his patriotism: he could enlist.

CHAPTER 3

Monster of the Deep

TWO HARD HAT divers tethered to air hoses and lifelines were gingerly lowered from Hoboken's Pier 4 into the dark water of the Hudson River. Hired by the navy, the commercial divers wore copper helmets, each with four vision ports, or "lights," wet suits woven from thick cotton twill that wouldn't tear easily if they brushed against sharp metal, padded rubber gloves, and weighted boots. Their lead belts weighed nearly fifty pounds, and lead weights also hung from their chests and backs. Their helmets were equipped with telephone lines to the pier, a recent innovation. Their mission: check for bombs that might have been attached to the hull of the giant ship.

The water was freezing that April morning and so black they couldn't see their hands a few inches from their faces forty feet below the surface. Working by feel and instinct in the strong current, they told their handlers over the telephone line when to lift them by rope so they could make their way along the submerged sides of the ship. It was painstaking, dangerous work, the divers constantly at risk from cut air lines or, when they surfaced, from the bends.

The divers would return to their search over several days before they gave the all clear.

Although nothing was found, there was abundant reason to be cautious. Within days of the *Vaterland*'s seizure, saboteurs made several "attempts to smuggle small bombs and explosives" on board, slipping them onto the long, conveyer-belt-like coal chutes, which were loaded from barges tied up alongside. Guards spotted the explosives, and vigilance was increased aboard the ship and on the pier.

Sabotage was a major concern, especially in New York City and Hoboken, both of which had sizable German populations and where undercover police officers and federal agents had been battling a well-funded, well-organized German spy network from the earliest days of the war. Cigar-shaped bombs ingeniously fashioned from lead and designed to ignite into a fireball when acids ate through a copper disk and mixed with other chemicals had been smuggled aboard freighters that caught fire a few days after sailing. During the last six months of 1915, thirteen ships burned or were rocked by explosions at sea. The spy ring that operated out of New York City with money and instructions from the dapper and wily German ambassador Count Bernstorff also targeted railroads and bridges, some of them in Canada, as well as powder mills and factories along the East Coast that were blown up, often resulting in casualties.

The attacks went on for months before the United States entered the war, culminating with the massive explosions that rocked Manhattan early on the morning of July 30, 1916. On that Sunday, the "Black Tom" munitions plant across the Hudson in Jersey City went up in flames, igniting warehouses and railcars packed with bombs and ammunition and casting an eerie glow against the sky. Investigators had no doubt that the perpetrators were German.

The search for submerged bombs wasn't the only focus for the divers. It was also their mission to find the precise location of the *Vaterland*'s four massive propellers, which had sunk deep into New York Harbor's silt. Each giant propeller, or "wheel," had four blades, but without blueprints it wasn't clear where they were positioned on the stern. As they were hoisted and lowered along the murky river bottom, the divers had to find them by hand. They were also tasked with locating the ship's rudder, the largest in the world.

In the meantime, work began to clear the ship's bottom of barnacles. For this laborious but crucial operation, navy engineers made the ship list, first on one side, then on the other, by pumping water from her ballast tanks, exposing large sections of the hull to light and air. Sailors dangling from bosun's chairs or leaning out from a web of rope ladders and planks swarmed over the raised sides, scraping off barnacles and giving the hull a fresh coat of gray paint.

As for the interior of the ship, without blueprints and confronting miles of uncharted plumbing and electrical wiring, the navy could pinpoint damage only by an inch-by-inch check of lines and circuitry often hidden behind the wood paneling in the passenger compartments. The ship's turbines as well as the navigational and steering equipment and radios also had to be inspected, a monumental task. As they looked for damage and broken equipment, scores of sailors armed with flashlights fanned out through the cold, dank compartments, working cautiously amid concerns that the engine and fire rooms had been booby-trapped. It took days to get some of the electrical power back on so fans could pull fresh air into the ship's lower decks.

Bernstorff, the German ambassador, admitted that as early as January 1917 he'd ordered "the engines of all German ships lying in American harbors . . . to be destroyed." Every passenger ship turned over to the navy for conversion into a troop carrier had sustained significant damage. "Cylinders had been broken, throttle and engine valves destroyed, pipes cut, fittings smashed," wrote the former navy secretary Josephus Daniels. Parts were often tossed overboard, and much of the damage was cunningly concealed. "Important parts were cut in half, then replaced so the cut would not be discovered," Daniels wrote. "Obstructions were placed in cylinders to wreck the engines as soon as steam was turned on."

In the *Vaterland*, some water lines installed behind the paneling were found cut, the ends squeezed together to disguise the damage so that when the water was turned on "numerous floods were caused throughout the ship." Connecting rods in the machinery rooms were severed, steam pipes plugged with chunks of metal, and telegraph and radio systems smashed. Navy technicians determined that the most serious damage to the engines wasn't the result of sabotage, however, blaming instead carelessness and just plain bad luck. Blades in the four turbines used for going in reverse, thousands of them, had been overheated and ruined during the *Vaterland*'s last trip when the ship had gotten stuck in the mud backing away from the pier. All those steel blades had to be replaced, a major repair job.

YET NONE OF this compared in scope with the wholesale transformation of an incomparable luxury liner into the largest troopship afloat. The bow-to-stern overhaul was carried out by hundreds of men armed with sledgehammers, crowbars, and cold chisels, who worked in shifts around the clock. The official navy history includes a description of this wreckage from a German newspaper: "The big ship was never built to carry troops and ammunition, and to make it fit for such uses the thieves tore out all of our beautiful art and all of the fine woodwork, regardless of all feeling. Twenty freight cars full of wood and furnishings were . . . loaded in Hoboken to be burned." Many of the *Vaterland*'s finest artistic touches as well as "the vast accumulation of . . . stores and provisions, the high class wines, the magnificent table linens and china and glassware and about $150,000 worth of silverware were placed on the pier" and carted off to warehouses.

In a startling blend of wholesale destruction and refitting, navy workmen reduced the 1,500 staterooms to 300 first-class cabins, which remained on the largely unscathed A, B, C, and D decks, to be reserved for officers and VIP passengers. On the four lower decks, starting with E, the wreckage was appalling. "Bathtubs were broken with sledgehammers to get them out of the way. Cushions and chairs were often just tossed overboard. Wall fixtures were ripped out of their sockets. Porcelain and rubber tiling were painted over and ruined. Leaded-glass windows were removed and packed away in boxes but the work was done so carelessly that three-fourths of them were broken in the process."

The football-field-size spaces that were opened in the lower decks as a result of this assault were crammed with "standees," iron-frame bunks with canvas bottoms, stacked four high. By putting every inch of available room to use, the US Navy hoped the ship could carry up to seventeen thousand soldiers and crew members.

As the renovations proceeded, the gigantic four-paneled painting of Pandora was loaned to the Metropolitan Museum of Art. The portraits of Washington, Lincoln, Bismarck, Roosevelt, and assorted royalties were placed in storage, along with some of the ship's most elegant furnishings—chairs, cabinetry, and a gold table service. The Ritz-Carlton restaurant was left largely intact, along with the decorative paintings by Giovanna Battista Pittoni that flanked the entry. The adjoining Palm Court also escaped the wreckers. But the spacious dining saloon, with its recessed, brightly colored ceiling mural of an eighteenth-century hunting scene, was converted into a mess hall for troops, the beautiful furnishings replaced with wooden tables arrayed at waist level so that the soldiers could eat while standing, a thousand at a time.

Space also was found for the prodigious quantities of food that would be needed for each round trip: 200,000 pounds of flour; 60,000 pounds of tinned meats; 120,000 pounds of smoked meats, 260,000 pounds of fresh meats, 25,000 pounds of turkey and fowl; 30,000 dozen eggs, 175,000 fresh fruits, and thousands of pounds of other stores—enough food to feed 10,000 troops and 1,400 crewmen for twenty-five days.

As the summer progressed, the social hall was converted into a hospital, and the gymnasium on A deck, an isolation ward. The swimming pool with its Pompeian frescoes became a baggage room that was soon brimming with olive-drab duffel bags; the real baggage room was turned into a brig and partially used to store ammunition.

The ship was also armed. The top deck, which still included the enclosed promenade where first-class passengers once strolled in their finery, was outfitted with eight six-inch naval guns—two on the forward deckhouse, two on the forward well deck, and four more arrayed along the stern. The guns fore and aft were seven hundred feet apart, a distance longer than any battleship the United States had in commission. Other armaments included two "Y" guns for firing depth charges; a pair of machine guns; one Lewis gun; and two Bausch and Lomb range finders. The shipboard arsenal also consisted of 150 Springfield rifles and seventy-five .45-caliber pistols.

As the work continued, the *Vaterland* soon required a different name. As it was an American ship now, its former German name wouldn't do anymore, and Edith Wilson, the president's wife, was invited to come up with something new. Uncertain about which name to choose, she asked the president one evening as he was concentrating on paperwork at the White House.

"That's easy," he said without looking up from his desk. "Leviathan. It's in the Bible, monster of the deep."

The General and the Mademoiselle

As WORKERS SWARMED over the newly renamed *Leviathan*, a White Star liner cast off her mooring lines and backed away from the docks almost directly across the North River. The SS *Baltic* was shorter than the *Leviathan* by over two hundred feet and could accommodate only 2,800 passengers, but on this foggy morning in late May she would carry the most important passenger in her history—General John J. Pershing, the recently appointed commander of the American Expeditionary Force, which would soon follow him to France. At the moment, however, the robust former frontier cavalry officer was a fifty-seven-year-old general without an army. That still needed to be assembled, and largely from scratch, and so he was sailing to France on the *Baltic* with only his staff of 191 officers and enlisted men, all of them handpicked veterans.

The plan was for Pershing and his sizable entourage to come aboard the ship shortly after it cast off, part of a not-so-carefully orchestrated effort to keep their movements secret. The men had arrived at Governors Island on May 28, far from any prying eyes farther up the river at Pier 60, where the *Baltic* cast off. Every member of the advance party was supposed to wear civilian clothing to help keep the general's presence under wraps, but about thirty men apparently didn't get the message and showed up in their uniforms; others wore ill-fitting civilian suits along with their army boots. There were other glaring miscues. Pershing and his aides were supposed to mark their baggage "D.E. McCarthy," but an orderly had slapped large red tags on the general's bags and trunks that bore the words "General Pershing, Paris France." And there were all those hard-to-miss bags, boxes, and crates that had been stacking up at the pier for days, each of them clearly marked "S.S. Baltic, General Pershing's Headquarters." Reporters contacted the transport officer at Pier 60, asking when the "big fellow" was going to sail. Pershing later complained that an "artillery salute fired from the batteries on Governors Island made the announcement of our departure complete."

A side-wheeled harbor tug carried the lantern-jawed, rarely smiling general and his party out to the Lower Bay and maneuvered alongside the *Baltic* with difficulty in the teeth of a stiff wind. As the tug pitched and rolled in the whitecaps, the ship lowered a narrow gangplank. Carefully timing his move, Pershing was the first to cross, then the others came, one or two darting across at a time until everyone was safely on board. There were shouts of farewell and good luck from both ships as the *Baltic* began to pull away, and a little after five o'clock, the first detachment of the American Expeditionary Force that would later number over two million men was off for France.

During the nine-day crossing to Liverpool, Pershing huddled with his senior officers about the organization and training of an army that didn't exist even on paper. When America declared war, its pitifully small military force numbered only 127,588 officers and men; another 80,466 were in the National Guard, but their fighting quality was considered questionable at best. Pershing thought it suitable, at least initially, to plan for an army of one million men, and he wanted to get them to France as quickly as possible.

Other questions included: Where could the army have its best chance for decisive action? How would the Americans get along with the French and British, who were already ratcheting up the pressure to have a few US regiments or even an entire division placed under their command? And where would the Americans find the shipping necessary to carry all those troops to France? Helping fill the crowded hours were lectures on German military tactics, French culture, and one of the general's pet subjects: preventing venereal disease.

The *Baltic*'s captain held abandon-ship drills two or three times a day, and when the ship began zigzagging through the three-hundred-mile submarine danger zone that extended into the North Atlantic from the coasts of Ireland and Britain, Pershing and his staff put their civilian clothing back on. U-boats sometimes opened fire on any lifeboats carrying soldiers, and the German submarines were on a tear. "Hardly an hour passed without an SOS from a sinking ship or from one fleeing a submarine," wrote Pershing biographer Donald Smythe. "The *Baltic* responded to none of them, fearing that they were fake distress signals sent by a waiting sub. Fifteen ships went down in British waters while Pershing crossed the Atlantic."

The liner reached Liverpool on June 8, and the next morning, after a train trip to London, Pershing met privately with King George V at Buckingham Palace. Dressed in the uniform of a field marshal, the king mentioned the tremendous losses his army had suffered and "severely condemned the German submarine atrocities," Pershing later recorded in his diary. "He was not optimistic over the outlook and expressed the hope that we 'would send over a large number of destroyers.'" At their next meeting two days later for lunch, the king and Pershing stood near a window overlooking the Buckingham gardens and the soaring monument to Queen Victoria, the grandmother of both the king and Kaiser Wilhelm. Abruptly turning the conversation to the nightly air raids on London, the English monarch launched into another attack on the "inhumanity of the Germans," Pershing recalled. German bombers and zeppelins had been bombing the city for weeks, attacks that killed comparatively few but steeled British resolve. The king gestured to the statue of the queen. "The Kaiser, God damn him," he said, "has even tried to destroy the statue of his own grandmother."

Focusing again on the transport issue, the king said "it was entirely out of the question," for the British to provide the hundreds of ships needed to ferry an American army to Europe, when shipping losses to German submarines were threatening his country's very existence.

Pershing received a similar response when he raised the subject with Prime Minister David Lloyd George at a state dinner at Lancaster House on Tuesday, June 12. After the inevitable toasts to the king and to President Wilson, Pershing found the British leader pleasant enough and was pleased he "expressed a desire to help us in every possible manner," but behind a veneer of cheerfulness, Pershing detected the prime minister's "serious apprehension." The dimensions of the impending disaster were spelled out to him in hushed tones: There'd been an appalling increase in shipping losses to U-boats, news that hadn't been made public for fear it would shock the war-weary population. Over the last two months, these losses had doubled from 1.5 million to 3 million tons. Great Britain was rapidly running out of food.

Lloyd George pressed Pershing on when American troops would be ready and how many could be expected. But when the general pushed back on the critical need for transport help, the prime minister "did not seem to be particularly interested and offered little hope that the British would be able to furnish us any shipping whatever."

After five exhausting days in London, on June 13 Pershing and his party crossed the English Channel by steamer, reaching Boulogne at about 10:00 a.m. Every member of the French honor guard that greeted them wore a field uniform decorated with insignia that indicated service at the front, and many had wound stripes on their sleeves. Seeing all the men, women, and children who poured into the streets clutching American flags, Pershing felt a pang of regret. "I am sure," he wrote later, "that each one of us silently wished that our army might have been more nearly ready to fulfill the mission that loomed so large before us."

THIS WAS PERSHING'S first time back in France since the autumn of 1908, when he and his wife and their two small children—they were to have two more—visited the country. It was a lovely and beguiling interlude for Pershing after his second tour of duty in the Philippine Islands. He spent several months in France, studying the language and taking motor trips to Versailles and other historic places with his family.

He had met Helen Frances Warren in 1903, when he was forty-three. She was the daughter of the US senator Francis E. Warren of Wyoming, who had made a fortune in ranching and real estate in Cheyenne. Twenty years younger than Pershing, Helen was a recent graduate of Wellesley College. Raised in Washington and on her father's spacious ranch out west, where she became a skilled rider, "Frankie" Warren had an engaging smile, dark hair that she liked to cut short, and a slender build. Completely swept off her feet by the dashing officer, she wrote in her diary after a party in Washington: "Danced every dance but one, and have lost my heart to Captain Pershing irretrievably." They married two years later with President Theodore Roosevelt in attendance and spent their honeymoon in Tokyo, where Pershing had served as an observer during the Russo-Japanese War.

By then he was a seasoned, well-respected cavalry officer who'd helped put down the Indian Ghost Dance uprising. Behind his back he was sometimes called "Black Jack," because he commanded African American troops on the frontier and later in the Spanish-American War, where he was "cool as a bowl of cracked ice" under fire, according to his commanding officer. When he married Frankie Warren, he was still only a captain after twenty-one years of service and seriously thinking about leaving the army to practice law. With some help from his influential father-in-law, Pershing was promoted quickly to brigadier general, leapfrogging 835 officers who had more seniority and triggering complaints of favoritism.

Assigned to command the Eighth Brigade, Pershing moved to the Presidio in San Francisco, and when trouble broke out along the Mexican border in 1915, he and his troops were ordered to El Paso, while his wife and family remained in California.

Pershing was in Texas when the great tragedy of his life occurred. On a cool August night, coals from a hearth ignited the freshly waxed floors at his two-story Victorian home on the army base in San Francisco, the flames racing upstairs. Helen and the three girls suffocated. Warren, five years old, was saved when a soldier saw the smoke and flames, scrambled up on the porch roof, and pulled him out from a second-story window. Devastated by the loss, Pershing retreated into his work. "As he told a friend when promoted to major general in 1916: 'All the promotion in the world would make no difference now.'"

That year and into the first few months of 1917, Pershing led eleven thousand troops into Mexico in search of the bandit Francisco "Pancho" Villa after his gang shot up Columbus, New Mexico, during a raid that left sixteen Americans dead. Mounted on horseback, but also making early use of trucks and airplanes, members of the so-called Punitive Expedition never caught the elusive Villa, but they broke up his band of marauders and gave young officers such as George S. Patton a chance to show their stuff. Pershing pushed himself and his men relentlessly.

At the same time, he pulled strings to become the commander of the American forces that he knew would soon be sent to France. After crossing the border back into Texas, Pershing gathered some of the news reporters who'd accompanied the expedition, making no secret of his desire to lead the army that would go abroad. "Each of you must know some way in which you can help me," he told them. "Now tell me how I can help you so that you can help me." One of the reporters was Damon Runyon, Hearst's top writer. Runyon had already met privately several times with the general in Mexico, agreeing not to print a story he'd uncovered about an American plot to poison Villa. More than once, a grateful Pershing privately thanked Runyon, urging him to let him know "if I can be of help sometime." Runyon wouldn't have long to wait. The occasion for a major payback would come barely a year after Pershing's dramatic arrival at the Gare du Nord in Paris.

FROM THE MOMENT his train pulled into the station late on the afternoon of June 13, the crowds that greeted the small band of Americans were delirious with joy and hope, many weeping openly as they waved handkerchiefs, hats, and American flags. They threw flowers into streets festooned with red, white, and blue bunting and kissed the Americans whenever they could get close enough. "Women climbed into our automobiles, screaming, 'Vive l'Amerique,'" Pershing recalled. The two-mile trip from the station to the

Hôtel de Crillon next to the American embassy on the Place de la Concorde took over an hour as the frenzied crowds pressed against the convoy of cars. Pershing found the scene touching and also pathetic. "It brought home to us as nothing else could have done a full appreciation of the war-weary state of the nation and stirred within us a deep sense of the responsibility resting upon America."

Later that evening at a dinner in his honor, the general was jolted when the American ambassador, voice trembling, summoned up the nerve to express his deepest fear.

"I hope," he said, "you have not arrived too late."

After three years of war, the French were emotionally and physically drained. Their armies had lost nearly one million men out of a population of twenty million males since the fighting began, losses that continued during a catastrophic offensive that April and which soon ground to a halt against the Hindenburg Line. The price tag was horrendous: another 120,000 men sacrificed by an arrogant commander who bragged that he'd break the German front within "twenty-four to forty-eight hours."

Mass slaughter from repeated suicidal attacks ordered against fortified machine gun positions triggered the mutinies that pushed almost half of the French army's 113 divisions to near collapse. A cry spread from regiment to regiment across the western front: "We have had enough! Down with the war!" Entire units declined to fight or showed up in the trenches drunk and without their weapons. When Pershing arrived in France, the mutinies and nearly four dozen executions that had rocked the French army—all of it kept secret—were still occurring, though by June the worst of them were over. France was all but eliminated from the war, and the generals knew it. "I shall wait for the Americans and the tanks," confessed the newly appointed French commander, Philippe Pétain.

The mood was no better in the English army, where military bureaucrats came up with an inspired phrase for the enormous casualties from German bombardments: "normal wastage." One year earlier during the opening day of the four-month Battle of the Somme, July 1, 1916, the British lost about sixty thousand men, "of whom twenty-one thousand [were] killed, most in the first hour of the attack, perhaps the first minutes," wrote the English historian John Keegan. After a bombardment that began a week earlier and had dropped nearly 1.5 million artillery shells on the German lines, the signal whistles blew, and the Tommies went up the ladders and out into no-man's land at zero hour, 7:30 a.m. on Z-day. Keegan describes the "long docile lines of young men, shoddily uniformed, heavily burdened, numbered about their necks, plodding forward across a featureless landscape to their own extermination inside the barbed wire." Keegan, whose father fought in the war, wrote that there was something "Treblinka-like" to the killing. The methodical slaughter and the trenches have been likened to the concentration camps of the war that followed.

Conditions had only worsened by 1917. Around the time of Pershing's arrival, British field marshal Sir Douglas Haig, convinced that the French army was a "broken reed," launched possibly the most futile and controversial offensive of the war, the three-month Battle of Passchendaele in Flanders, Belgium. Prodded by Haig, arguably the best army England had ever assembled fought to exhaustion during repeated assaults against the strong German lines in some of the wettest, ugliest weather in decades. For all the blood and sacrifice, the offensive gained virtually nothing and cost 310,000 men, over half of them killed. Orders went out for the ambulance trains to arrive late at night in London so the wounded could be unloaded without anyone seeing the consequences of the carnage.

The battle was actually the third of the costly English offensives fought around Ypres and across the fields of Flanders that cut through the top of Belgium. The second battle, in May 1915, inspired probably the most famous World War I poem. Written by the Canadian doctor and soldier John McCrae, "In Flanders Fields" was meant to mark the death of a friend whom McCrae buried on the battlefield but became synonymous with the suffering of an entire generation. The poem opens with the famous lines: "In Flanders fields the poppies blow / between the crosses, row on row."

The historian William Manchester wrote that it was "quite simply, the worst thing that had ever happened. . . . The insanities of World War II, Korea and Vietnam never quite matched the madness of World War I."

And now, at the very moment that defeat seemed so near for the Allies, the United States was all in, though virtually unprepared. The Germans also continued to press their unrestricted U-boat campaign. The German High Command's gamble that their weakened enemies could be forced to surrender before American troops arrived in any meaningful numbers looked better by the day.

In London, Fleet Admiral John Jellicoe confessed to newly arrived US admiral William Sims that England was on the verge of collapse, as U-boats prowling the North Atlantic and the approaches to the English Channel continued to send frighteningly large numbers of Allied ships to the bottom. During one three-week period that spring, 152 British merchant ships were sunk.

"It looks as though the Germans [are] winning the war," Sims said.

"They will win, unless we can stop these losses—and stop them soon," Jellicoe said.

"Is there no solution for the problem?"

"Absolutely none that we can see now."

Sims was soon prodding the British to assemble their merchant ships into convoys, a safety-in-numbers approach long supported by President Wilson that the Americans considered the best way to counter the U-boat menace. Long disdained by the British admiralty and especially by its naval chief, Winston Churchill, the tactic eventually achieved dramatically successful results, but the turnaround remained months away, and meanwhile the situation on the ground was dire. There was no question that the German army, strengthened by its divisions from the eastern front no longer needed after the Russian Revolution, was going to try for a breakthrough in the west. They'd come dangerously close to achieving that goal during the opening weeks of the war, when they pushed to within twenty miles of Paris, and Irvin Cobb glimpsed the Eiffel Tower from a German observation balloon.

With another blow certain to fall, it was no surprise that almost from his first moments in France, Pershing was confronted by desperate English and French generals and politicians who wanted to know: When will your soldiers arrive and when can we use them as we see fit?

THE DAY PERSHING arrived to delirious crowds in Paris, he met a charming young woman who'd come to the Hôtel de Crillon in hopes that he would agree to let her paint his portrait. Micheline Resco, who had been hired by the French minister of war to complete her task, watched the general as he strode into the brightly lit reception room flanked by Marshals Joseph Joffre and Ferdinand Foch. Members of the American diplomatic corps and other dignitaries hovered nearby, waiting to introduce themselves to Pershing. Micheline thought the American general had an instinct for the beau geste, or dramatic gesture, as he moved among all the lofty dignitaries with an easy confidence. A few hours earlier, he'd caused the crowds in the Place de la Concorde to erupt in cheers when he stepped onto the balcony of his apartment at the Crillon and kissed the French tricolor.

Micheline stood in a corner of the glittering room by herself, studying her subject. She found him to be a fine-looking man, just under six feet tall, who exuded physical strength. For her part, she wasn't the most elegant woman at the reception that evening, but she was undeniably appealing. Petite and blond with large, expressive brown eyes, Micheline was "attractive but not beautiful" and bubbling with winsome charm, according to historian Donald

Smythe, who met her. "Very soft and feline, she was a person who delighted in being waited on . . . and a person who needed someone to cling to."

Pershing caught her eye, walked over to her, bowed, and introduced himself. The young artist smiled when he shook her hand. From that moment both were smitten. "Later they were to tell their friends that each had felt that this was no ordinary meeting."

CHAPTER 4

Dead in the Water

THE *LEVIATHAN'S* THREE-YEAR slumber ended at nine thirty on a bright November morning with a terse command from Captain Joseph Oman on the ship's bridge. Up before dawn, he'd been nervously asking himself whether the ship could free herself from the deep bed of silt that had encased her keel since her internment began. Would the turbines start? Would the propellers turn? Could they get up enough steam? The previous day, Oman had received a report from the engineering officer, Lieutenant Vincent Woodward, who concluded that "this vessel is in all respects ready for sea," though he knew such a bold expression of confidence wasn't universally shared by other officers or the crew.

Oman glanced at Captain Allan Howell, the chief harbor pilot, who stood next to him near the helm. Getting away smoothly from the dock wouldn't be easy after such a long mooring. With all harbor traffic halted, Oman gave the order through the funnel speaker to the engine room eight decks below him.

"All reverse slow."

Steam flowed into the four high-pressure reverse turbines, the great ship quivered, and the four massive propellers began to turn, churning the river in a hundred-yard mud slick, the bubbling, oily water washing up against the six tugs poised to help the *Leviathan* back away from her pier. Twelve other harbor tugs, their funnels pouring smoke, were poised in midchannel ready to nudge the ship downstream. As the four-bladed propellers made their slow revolutions, the *Leviathan* throbbed with the sound penetrating into her deepest recesses.

Deep below in the engine room, Lieutenant Woodward studied the pressure gauges arrayed in clusters on the control panel while Captain Oman watched tensely from the bridge. The *Leviathan*, recently painted gray from top to bottom, slid stern-first into the Hudson River, her three towering stacks belching clouds of white smoke. Someone on the bridge pulled long and hard on the whistle cord, and a shrill blast washed over the bars and marine supply shops that lined River Street. Spectators poured onto the wharves and piers for a look at the giant as the tugs, their own whistles chiming in, pushed her tall bow downstream toward the Battery and the Narrows. As the ship slowly turned and her overhanging stern swung into view, many spectators could see the gilded German eagle and the seal of Hamburg, and VATERLAND etched into the ship's bell.

The ship's departure on November 17, 1917, came as no surprise. The German and American press had speculated that the *Leviathan* was getting ready to sail, and German sympathizers in Hoboken were certain to have reported the coaling and arrival of a full contingent of sailors—hundreds of them, carrying their white canvas sea bags aboard on their shoulders. Interest in the famous ship had been building, and on October 20 the *New-York Tribune* ran a story about Captain Hans Mortensen of the American freighter *Paolina* sunk one month earlier by a U-boat. When Mortensen was pulled from the sea, the paper reported, the first question the submarine captain put to him was: "When will the *Vaterland* go?" Mortensen warned that the Germans "have set a trap for her and are eagerly awaiting her first voyage as a troopship."

Well aware of this, Captain Oman had devised some diversionary tactics. Only a few of his officers knew the final destination for this shakedown cruise: Guantánamo Bay in Cuba. The passengers included 241 marines who were scheduled to relieve another marine detachment stationed at the US naval base on the island. A few days earlier, hundreds of bales of hay were loaded aboard and left on deck where they could easily be seen from the pier. Oman also ordered the marines to stand in conspicuous positions on the upper decks as the ship departed, to suggest that the *Leviathan* was loaded with a full detachment of troops and cavalry bound for Europe.

Oman was from rural Pennsylvania and had graduated from the Naval Academy in 1883 and served with distinction in the Spanish-American War. Following a typically slow trajectory through the ranks, he made captain in 1913 and took command of the *Leviathan* in July. In a contemporary fitness report, the fifty-three-year-old captain was rated as calm, even tempered, and painstaking. Short and balding, he cut a dapper figure in uniform, looking "more like a Methodist minister than anything else," and for reasons that aren't clear was nicknamed "Buggs," possibly because of the way his prominent eyes bored in if he thought someone had fouled up.

He made sure the first day's cruise was short. Barely an hour after departing Pier 4, the ship dropped anchor on the eastern edge of Staten Island's green hills so the engines could be thoroughly reinspected. After spending the night moored in the channel, the ship caught the high tide in the morning, slowly steamed out of the Narrows, and headed east toward Nantucket, a route that was designed to suggest the ship was making for France. A stream of New York–bound freighters got a close look at her long silhouette as the new troopship built up speed to a respectable eighteen knots and held to an easterly course. Crewmen aboard those ships could confirm rumors that the *Leviathan* was heading toward the North Atlantic and were certain to recount what they'd seen at the waterfront bars later that night, reports likely to be passed along by German spies or sympathizers. They wouldn't witness what happened later that day, when Oman ordered an abrupt change of course for the warm Gulf Stream waters off Florida and then Cuba.

During the early stages of the voyage, the crew got acquainted with their new accommodations, and a ship of such colossal size offered a great deal to see and learn. For starters, sailors were ordered not to wear white or light-colored clothing on deck after sundown because of the submarine threat. The Leviathan ran blacked out at night, her portholes also darkened. The green lights that glowed on her bridge were visible for only a few feet. Smoking was not allowed on deck, a rule strictly enforced with severe punishment, and sailors were warned repeatedly that a lit match could be spotted half a mile at sea.

Facing the almost certain prospect of submarine attacks when the ship started carrying troops, the captain ordered gunnery practice as soon as they turned south. Voice tubes and telephone lines linked the guns to the fire control officer, and spotting stations and salvo warning bells had been installed. The second day at sea, Oman directed the gun crews to fire at barrels with red flags attached that were dropped over the side. All veterans, they quickly scored a succession of near hits as clouds of gunpowder laced with the strong odor of sulfur drifted across the decks. The concussion of the firing broke some of the topside portholes.

The Leviathan still carried traces of her former ocean liner grandeur that couldn't fail to impress her new crewmen.

Sailors were given color-coded maps of the troop compartments and taken on orientation tours. During one of the early abandon-ship drills, many of them had trouble finding their assigned lifeboats in the labyrinth of passageways, often getting lost or arriving at the wrong station. The drill was repeated at night until the men could reach their boats quickly and in the dark. The inflatable lifeboats were lashed to the exterior of the ship, twenty-five to a side along the two upper decks, and dozens of others were tied down wherever a patch of space allowed. The larger wooden boats— seventy-two of them—were covered with canvas and stacked by twos along the top decks, each rigged for immediate lowering by hydraulic hoists.

The wisdom of making a trial run became obvious the fourth day out, when the *Leviathan* suddenly lost her steering. As the ship started drifting off course, Captain Oman grabbed the speaker funnel and called below: Stop all engines!

Lieutenant Woodward got on the tube with bad news. They'd blown a valve stem on the port steering engine.

The engineering officer hesitated when Oman pressed him on how long it would take to make repairs. Woodward had recently discovered an assortment of broken valve stems in a storage room, which indicated that the Germans had struggled with the same problem. The captain's immediate concern was that the ship was dead in the water and drifting in the Gulf Stream, a helpless target for any passing enemy submarine. If this had been the North Atlantic, he would have immediately put the crew on battle alert and made sure the lifeboats were manned. German submarines were rarely reported this far south, but the newer, bigger, and better-armed Type-151 U-boats easily had the range to cruise in these waters. Worried that the *Leviathan* was a sitting duck, Oman increased the watch, made sure the blackout was in effect, then hurried below deck, where he learned that Woodward and his engine crew were uncertain how to fix the problem. Hesitant to interfere, the captain headed back to the bridge, telling the lieutenant to report within one hour on any progress.

For the next day and a half, Woodward pored over blueprints and studied from top to bottom the engine steering compartment and its maze of steam pipes. He tried some jury-rigged repairs with improvised parts, but every time the engines were started up and the ship began making headway, the valve stem broke under the increased steam pressure. After working on the problem nonstop for over thirty-six hours, Woodward looked so haggard that the ship's doctor ordered him to lie down and rest. Still wearing his greasy, oil-stained dungarees, the lieutenant tossed restlessly for an hour on the couch in his cabin, then sat upright and hurried back to the engine room. He had an idea for a fix, which he explained to his equally exhausted engineering crew. "The machine shop was invaded and a new valve stem of heavier design and altered pattern was fitted," according to the ship's history.

When they were ready to test the retooled part, Captain Oman went below to watch for himself along with his executive officer. Every face in the steering compartment was taut from nervous exhaustion and strain, and no one wanted to guess what would happen or what they'd do next if this didn't work.

Oman gave the order: Start the engines, all full.

The throttle was opened wide, allowing the steering turbine to race hard. Oman and Woodward said nothing, holding their emotions in check as they focused on the valve and gauges. The test continued for one anxious minute after another, and after twenty minutes, the captain smiled and congratulated Woodward and his crew and gave orders for the *Leviathan* to get under way again. The redesigned part would remain in place for the duration of the war.

THE NEXT MORNING the *Leviathan* steamed past San Salvador, the island where Columbus had landed on his voyage of discovery. Hours later, as the ship neared Cuba, crewmen on deck picked up a strong, unmistakable scent, the pungent aroma of tropical vegetation. Seven days after leaving New York, the *Leviathan* anchored at the mouth of the harbor at Guantánamo Bay, where the detachment of marines was taken ashore. The men they replaced came aboard along with some other navy personnel from the American base.

While the ship was anchored, the chief butcher went out on the stern deck and stared hard into the bay's shimmering blue water. A newly enlisted sailor asked him what he was looking for so intently.

His answer quickly drew a crowd: sharks.

He'd been there before and had seen plenty of the beasts—huge sharks, dozens of them, their long bodies and tails flashing in the sunlit water. He suggested trying to catch a few of them, explaining that shark steaks weren't bad to eat and he could throw them on the grill that evening.

The captain gave the go-ahead. The butcher fetched a double-pronged hook that he baited with an entire cow's liver tied to a long piece of one-inch hemp line and tossed it into the bay from B deck nearly fifty feet above the water. The bait was visible thirty feet below the surface. "In a short time," according to the ship's history, "a large black body with a white belly swam with lightning swiftness past the line several times, darting back and forth, but [all of] a sudden it turned, seized the bait and tried to make off with it." Forty sailors grabbed the line, which was attached to a stanchion, and began to slowly pull the monster up the side and over the railing. As soon as it hit the deck, everyone scattered as the big fish—it was over ten feet long—started lashing its tail from side to side and snapping its huge jaws. When the beast was finally exhausted and unable to move, the butcher drove a cleaver into its skull.

The same baited hook snagged three more sharks of similar size, all of them hauled onto the deck and dispatched after wild, thrashing battles. The line finally snapped under the weight of a tremendous shark that disappeared into the depths with the hook, bait, and thirty feet of line. After the fun was over, grilled shark steaks were prepared, and the backbones were saved for some of the old hands who used them for scrimshaw carvings.

The *Leviathan* got under way again the next day to complete the second half of her shakedown cruise. On the trip back to New York, Captain Oman put her through a speed trial, the most important test of the voyage. He'd held the ship's speed to a leisurely eighteen knots on the cruise down to Cuba, well below a top luxury liner's performance for a normal Atlantic crossing. But now he wanted to push the *Leviathan* beyond that, knowing the ship would have to make well over twenty knots as she passed through the submarine danger zone. During a U-boat attack, speed would be her best weapon. No enemy submarine, not even the newer, larger class with a maximum surface speed of fifteen knots, could hope to keep up with her. The *Leviathan's* speed could mean all the difference between escape and disaster.

On her maiden voyage from Hamburg to New York in May 1914, the *Vaterland* nudged over twenty-two knots, deliberately holding back from trying to set a record even though many thought she was easily capable of doing so. During extensive sea trials off Norway in April 1914, the liner averaged twenty-six knots and still had plenty of steam left to spare. The Cunard liner *Mauretania* held the famous "Blue Riband" at that time for the fastest transatlantic crossing, averaging just over twenty-six knots, and before the war broke out the *Vaterland* was widely expected to break that mark.

On a beautiful sun-streaked dawn one hundred nautical miles off the coast of Florida with the seas running smooth, Oman ordered the speed increased. The "firemen's crew" picked up their backbreaking cadence of shoveling coal into the *Leviathan's* boilers, and the entire ship started to shake as engines capable of 90,400 horsepower drove her forward, the vibrations rattling plates and cups in the galleys. From the open bridge Oman could look behind at the *Leviathan's* turbulent wake as a thick line of black smoke trailed far behind the stern. From his vantage point high above the bow, he put the largest passenger ship afloat through her paces and felt her respond to the challenge.

The captain instructed Woodward to increase the propeller revolutions. Gulping 138 shovelfuls of coal every three minutes, the *Leviathan* was doing 22.5 knots, a speed she held for well over two hours, and her boilers hadn't come close to running at full throttle, but Oman wasn't going to push it.

When the ship reached port again in Hoboken on November 29, the captain had excellent reason to be pleased with the performance of the ship and her crew, especially the successful speed trial. It wouldn't be long, he realized, before they'd try again, but the next time would be under war conditions in the North Atlantic. He'd received word while still at sea that the *Leviathan* was scheduled to shove off in a few weeks with nearly eight thousand doughboys aboard.

"I Am Not Joking"

B Y THE FALL of 1917, the assistant secretary of the navy, Franklin D. Roosevelt, had become obsessed with U-boats. Working late into the night in his office in the ornate State, War, and Navy Building across the street from the White House, Roosevelt had privileged knowledge of the frightening toll German submarines were taking on Allied shipping. He also knew about the critical shortage of food and war supplies in Britain.

The data was nightmarish: submarines had sunk 50 ships in all of 1915, but by 1917, the numbers had exploded—250 sunk in February, 330 in March, and 430 in April. Roosevelt feared that a rogue submarine might penetrate New York Harbor, or even attack Campobello Island on the edge of Maine's extreme northeastern coast, where his wife, Eleanor, and their five children had spent the summer and much of the fall at the family compound. In a letter to Eleanor, he warned her that if a submarine started to shell the island, she should "grab the children and beat it into the woods. Don't stay to see what is going on. I am not joking about this."

The youngest assistant secretary of the navy in the nation's history—just thirty-one when he was appointed in 1913—Roosevelt was a tall, blond, Harvard-educated aristocrat who'd proven himself an effective administrator. A lover of military pageantry, Roosevelt appreciated the seventeen-gun salutes he received during visits to naval yards, or when he boarded a US warship for an inspection. If they ran up the snappy flag he'd personally designed for the office he held, so much the better.

His "Cousin Theodore," former president Teddy Roosevelt, had held the same position nearly twenty years earlier. But unlike President McKinley, who allowed TR to resign and organize the Rough Riders and fight in the Spanish-American War, President Wilson declined to let Roosevelt quit his post and take a commission in the navy when America declared war on Germany. Thwarted from his dream of military glory, Roosevelt reluctantly stuck to his position as a desk warrior. While the *Leviathan* was undergoing her long refitting in Hoboken, Roosevelt concentrated on the submarine threat and the need to extend a curtain of mines across the North Atlantic.

He was sympathetic to concerns about the ship voiced by several senior admirals, including a scathing report by Admiral David Taylor, chief of the Navy's Bureau of Construction and Repair, a highly respected expert who concluded that the *Leviathan*'s great size would make her especially vulnerable to a submarine attack. Raising the specter of a terrible loss of life, Taylor openly asked what it would mean to the country's psyche if the ship were sunk while carrying thousands of soldiers. Roosevelt sent a copy of the admiral's report to the *Navy and Merchant Marine Magazine* and to one of his Harvard friends, a maritime writer named Ralph Cropley. Well connected politically and socially in Washington, Cropley began a letter-writing campaign against using the ship to carry troops, telling the secretary of the treasury, William McAdoo, that it "would end in the murdering of eight or ten thousand of our boys." Cropley was also convinced the former liner was dangerously unbalanced and that if she were torpedoed or hit a mine, the ship would, "like the rest of the gigantic liners . . . flop over on her side" within six minutes.

Critics such as Cropley urged that the *Leviathan* should be used strictly as a hospital ship or even as a brig for German prisoners of war, and that troops should be transported to Europe in smaller vessels. It isn't clear whether Roosevelt supported these suggestions, and the discussion quickly became moot. Whatever reservations he may have had during that long summer and fall were eclipsed by momentous events rapidly unfolding in Europe.

On November 7, less than two weeks before the *Leviathan* sailed for Cuba, the Bolsheviks seized power in Russia and began maneuvering for a quick end to the war with Germany. Now free to move hundreds of thousands of soldiers from the eastern to the western front, German general Erich von Ludendorff, the country's political dictator and supreme military commander, was building up strength for a resumed offensive early in 1918. For the first time in the war, he would hold a decisive edge in troop strength over the Allies.

Nine months after the United States declared war, the American army had only 175,000 soldiers in France, and the French and English were pushing General Pershing and the Wilson administration hard to dramatically increase those numbers. The American army had recently suffered its first combat deaths, news not widely reported, because of censorship.

The details were disturbing. In early November, a German raiding party had attacked an isolated outpost occupied by a First Division platoon in what had been a quiet sector of the front near Nancy. Facing Americans for the first time, the Germans decided to challenge them, and after a one-hour bombardment, over two hundred battle-tested raiders hit the First Division's soldiers from two sides, withdrawing after fifteen minutes of hand-to-hand fighting in the trenches. Five Americans were wounded, twelve taken prisoner, and three killed: one had his throat cut, another had his skull crushed, and one was shot. The deaths left the survivors shaken.

CHAPTER 5

Missed Rendezvous

THE DEPARTURE DATE finally arrived on Friday, December 14, 1917, almost a month after the successful shakedown cruise to Cuba.

Captain Oman watched closely from his windy perch on the *Leviathan's* flying bridge as the lines were cast off from the pier in Hoboken at 7:55 a.m. After months of refitting, repairs, and tests, the ship was finally ready to begin her second life as a troop transport, shoving off with thousands of soldiers bound for France by way of Liverpool, England. Snow had been coming down hard for four days, but no one seemed to notice or mind. The *Leviathan* backed away from the pier during the precise two-minute interval when the flood tide in the North River was running strongest, her huge props slowly churning the water in reverse. Helped by the tidal current and a flotilla of tugboats, the ship was soon pointed downstream and on her way.

With her nearly forty-foot draft, it was crucial that the *Leviathan* avoid the many shallows that littered the channel. Between the Hoboken docks and the Statue of Liberty there wasn't enough water in the middle of the river for the ship to float, so she hugged the eastern shore, where the deep "prehistoric gorge of the Hudson" flowed down through the Narrows.

Oman had received the final troop count only days earlier, and it was still hard to believe. The *Leviathan* was sailing with a record-breaking number of soldiers and crew members—nearly 10,000 men, including 7,254 from the 163rd and 164th infantry regiments. No vessel had ever carried more people, and the responsibility for getting all those badly needed soldiers to France was solely his. He'd issued strict orders to make sure passengers didn't rush from one side of the *Leviathan* to the other to admire the sights as they traveled down the magnificent harbor. It wasn't likely the ship would capsize, but she could list and run aground.

The excited doughboys jammed the railings shoulder-to-shoulder as the falling snow turned the brims of their campaign hats white. Joined by dozens of army nurses, they didn't let the miserable weather dampen their mood or their cheering as the ship passed the Statue of Liberty. Their spirits were high—at least until seasickness started to sweep through their ranks a few hours later, keeping many of them groaning in their bunks and staterooms for the duration of the ten-day voyage.

Oman had already opened his orders and reviewed their carefully detailed course headings. Dropping south from New York, the *Leviathan* would follow the Fortieth Parallel on an eastwardly route for approximately 1,500 miles to the first charted position, then veer northeast and steam another 500 miles to the second position, code-named "XYZ," roughly midway between New York and the English Channel. From there, the *Leviathan* would travel another 800 miles on a similar heading to her rendezvous point with seven navy destroyers that would sail out to meet her from Queenstown, Ireland. The warships would escort the ship through the submarine zone that extended into the Irish Sea as far north as Liverpool.

Known as Torpedo Alley, the Irish Sea had been the burial ground for the SS *Lusitania* in 1915 and for dozens of other ships since. It wasn't unusual for Irish fishermen to find bodies still in their cork life jackets, bobbing in the water. U-boats had torpedoed so many ships that the sea was strewn with their wreckage over three hundred miles from shore. During one three-week stretch in April, 152 British merchant ships were sunk in the Queenstown zone, an area covering twenty-five thousand square miles. As recently as December 6, an American destroyer, the *Jacob Jones*, was torpedoed on her way to Queenstown from the French port of Brest. Hit in her fuel tanks, the ship sank in eight minutes, her depth charges exploding like a string of powerful firecrackers as she rolled over and went down stern-first. Sixty-four men were lost.

Certain that submarines were hunting the *Leviathan*, Oman knew it was crucial to link up with the destroyers at the right time and place, but barely one day out of New York he was forced to delay their rendezvous. To his dismay, he learned that the ship had been loaded with an inferior grade of coal, which meant that more of it had to be burned to keep the ship's speed up. Worse, the bunkers contained about two thousand fewer tons than originally thought. Oman's executive officer double-checked his calculations and delivered the bad news—they had barely enough coal to reach Liverpool. With luck, they'd arrive with about five hundred tons to spare, barely enough for a half day's steaming. Trying to conserve precious fuel, Oman slowed the ship's speed, forcing her to reach the rendezvous a day late instead of at 8:00 a.m. on December 21, as originally planned. He radioed a message to that effect, but the officer in charge of the destroyer squadron sent to meet the *Leviathan* never received it, a breakdown in communications that would have serious repercussions.

Allowing himself plenty of time to reach the meeting place, Commander S. W. Bryant had shoved off on December 18 from Queenstown, a busy port on the eastern tip of Ireland. Conditions were miserable—gale-force winds and squalls that would soon get worse.

Nearly one thousand miles to the west, the *Leviathan* was also steaming into rough weather. After enjoying a few days of clear skies and warm temperatures in the Gulf Stream—remarkably good luck, considering it was the storm season—everything went off the rails. The ship began to roll badly in the huge waves, sending hundreds of already queasy men and women scurrying for the buckets strategically located for just such an emergency. The sick bay on E deck began to fill with scores of retching soldiers, and army doctors who were also fighting seasickness made the rounds of staterooms to treat nurses clinging to their bunks in misery.

Despite the storm, Oman ordered the gun crews to fire some practice rounds. Knowing the odds were good they'd run into a submarine, he planned to rely on the ship's speed to get them out of trouble, but if a U-boat suddenly surfaced and left them with no escape options, his gunners would have to shoot it out and wouldn't have much time to score a hit. He wanted to keep them sharp.

On December 22, the wind increased to sixty-five knots, Category 1 hurricane strength. The captain ordered the passengers and crew to wear their life preservers at all times and to sleep in their clothes. They were also repeatedly reminded not to smoke on deck when the weather cleared. Anyone caught violating that rule would be thrown into the brig and put on bread and water, no questions asked.

As the Leviathan neared the submarine zone, Oman ordered the helmsman to begin zigzagging, changing course every twenty-five to thirty minutes as directed by a special clock on the bridge. They kept it up until the next morning, when just before dawn a lookout spotted a slender band of white water far off the stern. Fearing it was the wake of a periscope, Oman called the gun crews back to their stations and put the ship on battle alert. Every man on deck, sailors and soldiers alike, was searching for a submarine when a light flashed in the twilight, a signal from one of the US destroyers. The gunships were about three miles off the Leviathan's bow. As the sky lightened and began to clear, Oman was both relieved and shocked by what he saw. The small "tin cans"—they were barely one-third the length of his ship—were taking a beating in the swells, rising high on the cresting waves, then crashing down in the troughs, their decks running with foaming water and all but disappearing from view.

The ships were struggling to keep up with the *Leviathan* as she continued her zigzag course, steaming faster now that they were in the U-boat zone. Trying to hold radio communications to a minimum in case the Germans were listening, the *Leviathan* signaled that she was making seventeen knots. Two of the destroyers, the *Downes* and the *McDouglas*, already had reduced their speed to sixteen knots because of the pounding they were taking. A sailor aboard one of the destroyers offered the following account: "Down below it seemed as if the entire ship would be pulled in two. She was bending and springing all the time, and the green seas were coming over the forecastle in a way that threatened to smash in the decks, but we stuck it out. . . . By night our charthouse was bent in, the forecastle gun out of commission, most of the ammunition had gone out of the racks, the machine guns stands were bent and the deck was leaking."

Five of the warships pushed their shuddering engines to the maximum, straining to keep up. Commander Bryant, aboard the *O'Brien*, had received a recent report that at least two U-boats were operating in the Irish Sea and that a submarine had been sighted on the *Leviathan*'s likely approach into Liverpool. Bryant instructed the troopship by blinker signal to change course immediately. The destroyers that could still keep up with her—at least one had fallen out of sight—took positions to the side and out in front of the big ship. One of them released a smoke screen across the *Leviathan*'s bow, obscuring the vessel in a low, thick wall of black clouds.

Bryant was seething that the transport had arrived a day late at the rendezvous, forcing his destroyers to hang around in rough seas until they were dangerously low on oil. And now the *Leviathan* was increasing her speed, making it even more difficult to keep up.

Didn't her captain know better? Why was he trying to outrun them in an area where U-boats were known to be operating?

Oman figured it differently. He wasn't about to slow down, and if one of the destroyers dropped behind, that was too bad. The faster he traveled through the danger zone, the more difficult it would be for a U-boat commander to get a shot at him.

Nearly everyone was jumpy. That afternoon, the *Leviathan's* gun crews were called back to battle stations when a submarine was sighted far off the ship's starboard beam. Fortunately, it checked out as a British sub. Then a strange-looking aircraft with a bizarre metallic sheen suddenly appeared in the distance, headed their way. It turned out to be a British dirigible patrolling for submarines.

Unwilling to chance a tricky approach up the river Mersey in the dimming light, Oman decided to drop anchor just outside the entrance to Liverpool's harbor. The destroyers continued circling the ship throughout the night, as enemy submarines were probably watching them.

The next morning, December 24, Oman ordered the anchors up, and the ship slowly headed into the Mersey, where the tidal rise and fall was a robust twenty-one feet. The navigator and pilot had to carefully time entering the channel to the precise moment of maximum tide to make sure the *Leviathan* had enough water under her to clear a sandbar.

By 6:00 a.m., the *Leviathan* picked up speed and safely entered the channel, passing the Bar Light Vessel, a lightship anchored where the river opened into the long, deep harbor of Liverpool. On the bridge, Oman heard a sailor on the lightship singing "We Wish You a Merry Christmas," his fine voice amplified by a large megaphone.

There was more tight-lipped apprehension than good cheer on display on the bridge. Oman still had to supervise maneuvering the ship to a tricky anchorage so that thousands of soldiers could disembark as quickly as possible. Dodging the many shallows in the Mersey was even more of a challenge than navigating the Hudson, and not trusting his charts, the captain had two sailors lowered from the bow so they could drop sounding leads and call out the depth as the ship moved slowly upstream.

One of the largest ports in the world suddenly spread out before them—gritty, smoke-begrimed Liverpool, with her notorious foul air, leaden skies, and foggy streets. The *Leviathan* was soon tied up at the Princess Landing, her long gangways quickly extended as troops carrying their sixty-pound packs and rifles started descending the narrow ramps single file, a process that took most of the day. The men formed up in squares on the pier, then marched away to cheers from crew members watching from the ship's upper decks. The soldiers, joined by nurses bundled up in their long blue cloaks, white caps, and black gloves, headed to the train station for the long trip to London, then to the coast to board the transports that would carry them across the channel to France.

Shortly after the *Leviathan*'s arrival, Oman had an unexpected visit from Commander Bryant. The two met on the bridge as troops were descending the gangways. His voice rising, Bryant blasted Oman for not showing up on time and then for outrunning the destroyers. Oman was having none of it—it wasn't his fault if Bryant hadn't been notified about the ship's coal problem or the need to delay the rendezvous, and he wasn't about to slow down in a submarine zone.

Bryant had reason to be angry, considering the beating his small ships had endured as they waited for the *Leviathan*. But Oman had been right in what he'd done—though he didn't know how much trouble it would cost him.

SO BEGAN A nearly six-week interlude for the ship, which needed to be in dry dock at Liverpool's massive Gladstone Dock, the only one large enough at the time to accommodate her. The *Leviathan*'s

bottom needed to be cleaned and repainted after the earlier mainte-
nance in Hoboken, and her keel outfitted with couplings to support
the paravanes, a pair of metal wings designed to flare out beneath
the surface of the water and ward off mines.

Oman and his crew had to wait nearly three weeks for the maximum high tide to fill the dry dock again, so they settled down for
an extended liberty in the dreary English port. The captain met
with the lord mayor and other dignitaries while his sailors visited
the city, where the reception was occasionally rocky, especially if
the men were drinking, which was usually the case. The first liberty party left the ship at 4:30 p.m. on December 24 and was due
back on Christmas Day. The sodden, gloomy weather seemed to
match the crew's mood in a city where some of the citizens, embittered by the appalling battlefield losses, food shortages, and air
raids, resented that the Americans had taken so long getting there.
Some of this pent-up anger spilled out when the *Leviathan*'s sailors insisted on riding in first-class train compartments. "It took our
bluejackets quite some time and cost a few black eyes and bumped
noses to convince some Englishmen that an American would not
stand for" second-class seating arrangements.

More happily, the musicals and vaudeville shows were numerous in Liverpool, and there was always the latest Charlie Chaplin
movie to catch. The sailors found the English girls more than willing to talk to them and admired how nimble they were at hop-
ping aboard moving streetcars. There were fights, too. Fights over
women, fights with fellow sailors, fights with the locals in bars,
all of it fueled by beer and whiskey—enough trouble to keep the
twenty-six-man shore patrol details busy from eight to midnight
every evening. The ship's log for the night of January 5 captures the
flavor: 9:12 p.m., a sailor brought on board "was helplessly drunk";
9:20 p.m., a straggler from another ship turned himself in and was
"ordered to be made a prisoner at large"; 10:12 p.m., a sailor carried
in by a shore patrolman and city policeman had fallen off a curb and

broken his left leg between the knee and ankle and "was in a state of alcoholic intoxication"; 11:45 p.m., a sailor was helped aboard "in a disorderly condition" triggered by "alcoholic intoxication."

Finally, on January 14, the tide was running deep enough for Oman to try to get the *Leviathan* into the dry dock, but the wind kicked up as they headed down the Mersey, pushing the ship like a kite and making it impossible to steer her into the dry dock's narrow entrance. Oman tried again the next morning, the last day the tide would be with them for another month. They had about one hour to get the ship downstream from her mooring and into the dry dock enclosure, a tight fit in the best of conditions for such a large vessel, but with a much higher degree of difficulty because of the current. There wasn't enough room to use tugboats, so the ship had to approach the dock at a crawl, cutting her power at the precise moment her forward movement let her slip through the massive iron gates.

Once the enclosure's steel doors were shut, the water was pumped out, and over the next three weeks, the *Leviathan* was propped up on steel and wooden chocks as her bottom was scraped clean and repainted. Working around the clock, a team of sailors and "English experts" applied camouflage, or "dazzle" paint, to her sides, an elaborate geometric design with lightning-streak slashes of blue, gray, and white several hundred feet long and a series of triangles and sawteeth, all designed to create a false bow wave. The hope was the visual illusion would make it difficult for a submarine skipper to get an accurate reading on the ship's course. It was mistakenly believed by the public and even by some sailors that the forbidding paint job would render the vessel invisible, while the real purpose was to make it appear from a distance that she was moving in the opposite direction.

Oman, who likely had his doubts as did many others about these camouflage tactics, watched as the painters dramatically changed the ship's appearance while it was propped up behind the dry dock's huge steel doors. More than anything, he wanted the work completed so that they could leave. After six weeks in Liverpool, he was eager to get back to Hoboken and pick up the next load of troops.

THE LEVIATHAN FINALLY put to sea on February 11. Like many others on board, Oman had had enough of the bleak English weather and long winter nights. He was even more on edge on the return trip. Commander Bryant's stinging allegations were still fresh in his mind, and his commanding officer had asked him to respond to them in writing. It didn't help his mood that shortly after they put to sea, the ship was rocked by an explosion.

A lookout on one of the destroyers that accompanied the Leviathan into the Irish Sea had spotted what he thought was a periscope. Turning about sharply, the small warship raced to the position of the last sighting and dropped a three-hundred-pound depth charge. The underwater concussion rocked the Leviathan from end to end, pitching glassware and plates off tables and sending most of the crew to battle stations or rushing to lifeboats. The periscope turned out to be a piece of driftwood that had been blown to bits. The destroyers shepherding the Leviathan once again had trouble keeping up as storm-tossed waves crashed over their bows, but the escort hung on for a full day until Captain Oman radioed that his ship was out of the U-boat zone and they could turn back.

The North Atlantic continued to boil, tearing gunwales apart and ripping lifeboats from their fastenings. The storm lasted five hard days, finally giving way to fog so thick off the Grand Banks of Newfoundland that Oman couldn't see the bow from the bridge. For the next eight hours, the Leviathan's foghorn sounded warnings at one-minute intervals in a densely fished area where trawlers were plentiful and could easily be run over. The transport finally emerged from the whiteout on the night of February 18, only to run into more fog the next morning at the entrance to New York Harbor. Proceeding at a crawl up the Hudson, the Leviathan was greeted by a noisy fugue of ships' whistles and horns as tugboats cautiously guided her into the slip at Pier 4. The mooring lines were cast down and Wilson's monster of the deep was tied up, her first voyage as a troopship successfully completed.

"An Admiring and Jealous White Audience"

FEBRUARY 22, 1918, three days after the *Leviathan* safely moored at Pier 4 in Hoboken, was Washington's birthday, and the citizens of Columbia, South Carolina, lined their famously broad streets (designed to be one hundred feet wide in the mistaken belief mosquitoes couldn't fly that far and would die trying to cross them) to watch a spectacle such as they'd never seen before. To help mark the celebration, three thousand African American soldiers from the newly formed 371st Regiment put on a display of marching that drew cheers from the spectators. The grim-looking soldiers, their faces shaded by the wide brims of their Montana Peak campaign hats, marched ten abreast. They wore khaki-drab uniforms and tight-fitting leggings that came to the knee. They looked proud, strong, and fit as they strode down the long streets after their six-mile march from Camp Jackson, a new military base that had been hacked out of thick forests of blackjack oak and loblolly pine.

Eager to join the fighting in France, many of these men had recently signed up for US government–backed $10,000 life insurance policies. The sales had gone slow until a noncommissioned officer told them it was the only way Uncle Sam would put them in "front-line trenches where the killing is the thickest." The town's jubilant reaction was surprising given that a few months earlier many in the community had angrily protested when they found out that black soldiers were coming to Camp Jackson.

They were led by white officers, nearly all of them from the

South—men who were bitterly disappointed when they had been assigned to the 371st in October, but who wouldn't trade their places now for any other regiment in the army. Among the newly promoted noncommissioned officers was Corporal Freddie Stowers, an African American with C Company. Stowers had risen quickly through the ranks during the four months since he was drafted, and like almost everyone else in the new regiment hailed from a rural community in the Deep South. Most of the men were illiterate, but Stowers could read and write, and he adapted quickly to military life and discipline. A twenty-one-year-old farm laborer, he was described on his draft registration card as having a slender build, no disabilities, and a wife.

Born on January 12, 1896, the fourth of ten children, Freddie Stowers was from Sandy Springs, a crossroads hamlet in the piedmont seven miles northwest of Columbia. His grandparents had been slaves on a plantation just across the Savannah River in nearby Georgia. When the Civil War ended, they remained on the farm as sharecroppers. After Mr. Stowers and his family, the owners of the farm, died from tuberculosis in the late 1870s, their property was sold, and the African Americans who worked for them moved to Sandy Springs in Anderson County, South Carolina, where they found jobs in the cotton mills or as farm laborers.

Freddie Stowers had married a woman named Pearl shortly before he was drafted. They were expecting their first child when he marched through Columbia in February with his regiment.

By the time Stowers reported in October with other African American draftees, their arrival had been delayed nearly a month so that the men, many of them farmhands, could help harvest the 1917 cotton crop. When they finally walked up to the entrance of the racially segregated camp, their sudden appearance triggered an uproar. "The first intimation we had that the men had really arrived was the sound of distant yelling, catcalling and laughter as our mob of embryo warriors was led up through the divisional area and through the crowds of convulsed white troops," the regiment's historian wrote later.

Arriving with Stowers that first day were men wearing their Sunday-best suits, overalls, or tattered clothing. Some were barefoot or carried their possessions wrapped in handkerchiefs. Others had guitars or banjos slung across their backs. The men bunked in tents in their own encampment, which was kept separate from the white troops who also trained there. Like every other military base in the country, Camp Jackson was rigidly segregated; whites and blacks didn't mingle in the barracks or mess halls or on the parade grounds. For weeks the African American soldiers had to drill in civilian clothes, unlike the whites, who received their uniforms first. The raw recruits were quickly transformed into spit-and-polish soldiers eager to show what they could do, and it wasn't long before the derisive laughter started to die away. Within a few months, the men were as good as any troops on the base and had received training in the rudiments of throwing hand grenades and using the bayonet. They were no longer, as their commander put it, "the laughing stock of the camp."

Desperate for platoon leaders, senior officers promoted Stowers to private first class and then to corporal. In an often chaotic atmosphere in which an entire army was being built from scratch, the best rose through the ranks quickly and had to develop the toughness and leadership skills required to handle men who weren't afraid to fight—either the enemy or each other. NCOs like Stowers had to know when to push someone or go easy.

The only likeness, a composite drawn decades later based on photographs of his two sisters, shows an intense-looking young man with a thin face, high cheekbones, and finely shaped eyebrows whose stare is all business.

The 371st Regiment didn't want to be assigned to a depot brigade, often the fate of African American troops, who frequently worked as stevedores, baggage handlers, or janitors. These men had an entirely different role in mind for themselves. They knew about the famous Buffalo Soldiers and the exploits of the Ninth and Tenth Cavalry at San Juan Hill. They also knew that 180,000 black Americans had fought for the Union in the Civil War. Their commanding officer was a West Point graduate who reminded them that African Americans had fought with Perry at Lake Erie and with Jackson in New Orleans during the War of 1812. Stowers and his fellow soldiers wanted a combat assignment and had no illusions about what that meant.

The former president William H. Taft visited Camp Jackson in late January during one of the coldest winters in memory to deliver a version of the same speech he was giving all over the country. Entitled "Why We Are at War," his remarks touched on international law, the U-boat attacks, and the German military machine's attitude toward Americans. Speaking of the kaiser's High Command, Taft said, "When it saw us, it said, 'There is a tango-loving nation, too fat to fight, too lazy to go into the trenches.'"

Taft shared recent military bulletins from England, where in one month the country "saw a loss of 114,000 in the British Army; 26,000 privates killed and 16,000 officers killed in action; 76,000 privates wounded and 3,600 officers wounded and 7,000 missing."

"My friends," Taft warned them. "We are going to make these [same] sacrifices."

IN EARLY SPRING, the men of the 371st learned they were going to be transferred to an army supply depot at Camp Jackson, exactly what they didn't want to do. The camp commander recognized the regiment's fighting potential and personally intervened, sending a long telegram to the chief of staff that asked him to reconsider. Within days he did, with unexpected consequences. The 371st was placed on the priority list for service overseas as part of the newly organized 93rd Division, composed of four African American regiments pulled together from different regions of the country.

The enlisted men and officers were elated, the regiment's history recounts. "Everyone simply 'knocked' you down with a salute: sentinels came to the 'present' with a slap that could be heard for yards; orderlies stood at statue-like attention when delivering messages, and about faced and stepped from the orderly room 'by the numbers;' N.C.O.'s and privates talking in a group bawled 'Attention' whenever an officer came anywhere near the prescribed distance." The regiment was the envy of the entire camp, especially "an admiring and jealous white audience" as the men started gathering their equipment and stenciling the three magic letters on mountains of packs, boxes, and crates—AEF.

On March 23, the adjutant general of the army wired the regiment's commander in code with a question that demanded an immediate answer: When could they move out? The men were urgently needed in France.

Freddie Stowers and the other NCOs had to wrap up the final days of training and finish all their packing. Their new Springfield rifles—the crates of weapons had arrived only a few weeks earlier—were double-and triple-checked. The men had had only a few chances to practice shooting at the camp's six-hundred-yard range and weren't even close to becoming proficient as marksmen, but that would soon change in France.

With the troops about to depart, all telegrams and mail were put on hold for security reasons. Bundles of clothing and other personal effects that were sent home were also delayed; it wasn't until the men reached their destinations that many families found out that their sons had departed for France. In late March, the regiment received postcards preprinted with the words: "I have arrived safely overseas." The men were told to address the cards, which would be mailed when they reached France.

After several days of mounting anxiety, Stowers received their orders: they'd shove off on April 5 for Newport News.

CHAPTER 6

A New Skipper

WITH THE *LEVIATHAN* tied up in Hoboken, Captain Oman learned more about the accusations leveled against him after the missed rendezvous on the way to Liverpool by Rear Admiral William Sims, the autocratic, white-bearded commander of American naval operations in European waters. In a confidential letter dated January 26, 1918, Sims wrote the chief of naval operations that "something was very wrong about the handling of the ship," and that the *Leviathan* "ran a very serious risk of being torpedoed and possibly losing a great many of the 7,000 troops she carried."

The commander of the destroyers insisted that the *Leviathan* had been far off course and Sims believed him. He'd known Oman for years and respected him, but he didn't hesitate to try to have him relieved. "While he may be a valuable officer in certain respects and for certain duties," Sims wrote, "I consider him a positive danger in his present position. . . . I should feel very anxious for the safety of the vessel, if he is left in command." Sims tempered his remarks only slightly by suggesting that Oman be removed "in such way as not to humiliate or discredit [the] officer concerned, who may be very able and capable, but is not suitable for his present duty."

His letter lit a fuse among many senior naval officers, many of whom liked and admired Oman. They agreed with the captain's argument that it would have been foolish to slow down and wait for the destroyers in the submarine danger zone and that "it was safer to continue zigzagging at high speed than to slow down." Oman also insisted that it was "entirely incorrect" to say, as Sims had, that the ship had only one destroyer with her when she passed through the Irish Sea, where submarines were operating. The *Leviathan*, he said, was surrounded by five destroyers and that only one fell behind and later caught up.

"Sims," he wrote in conclusion, "misunderstood conditions."

Oman was eventually cleared of even the slightest suspicion of dereliction of duty, and Josephus Daniels, the secretary of the Navy, later wrote him to say as much, adding that if all the facts had been known "the department would not have taken [such] drastic action" in removing him from command. But in early March, drastic action was indeed taken. Booted upstairs, Oman was promoted to rear admiral and put in charge of the Second Naval District in Rhode Island.

He was replaced by Captain Henry Bryan. A few years younger than Oman, Bryan wasn't especially well liked at first. Scholarly, well read, and guarded in his comments, he was uncomfortable with small talk and virtually lived on the bridge, where he made himself accessible to any sailor on the ship. The officers and crew quickly grew comfortable with his easygoing, just-don't-screw-up style of command.

His father, a native of England, had a small trucking business in Cincinnati, where Bryan, one of ten children, was born in 1865. He'd worked hard for everything in his life, including admission to Annapolis. Like Oman, the *Leviathan*'s new captain had paid his dues during a naval career that started in 1889 when he was assigned to the USS *Monacacy*. After serving on a succession of warships, he experienced a high moment during the Spanish-American War in 1898 when he was "present at the bombardment of [the] forts at Santiago." A year later, he was detached from his ship for fifteen weeks to command a landing party of seventy men assigned to guard a mountain pass in Luzon during the hard-fought Philippine Uprising, an assignment where he had a "daily expectation of meeting the enemy."

A gifted linguist, Bryan was fluent in French and Spanish and could read German and Italian, skills often noted in evaluations, along with comments that he was "a great reader," and "an accomplished officer and gentleman." After a brief posting in Naval Intelligence, Bryan was named head of the Department of Modern Languages at Annapolis in August 1907, a refreshing break from sea duty and where he would meet his wife.

Elizabeth Champlin Badger was the daughter of the superintendent of the Naval Academy, Charles J. Badger. She married Bryan at the Boston Naval Yard at the home of her grandfather Commodore Oscar Badger, who'd directed the Union blockade of the East Coast during the Civil War. At twenty-four, Elizabeth was eighteen years younger than her husband.

The couple soon had three children, two daughters and a son, Charles. As a young boy, Charles sometimes got a chance to follow his father aboard when he served as executive officer on the USS *Kansas*, a turn-of-the-century battleship. "He would show me around the ship," he recalled, "and how proud I was—nasty little brat—when we discovered something that called for a reprimand to some unfortunate sailor!" The family lived in a handsome two-and-a-half-story American Georgian home on Lowell Street in Washington, DC, while Bryan served as commander of the Second Naval District. That's where he learned he'd been ordered to take command of the *Leviathan* and that Captain Oman would succeed him in Newport.

Arriving on board March 3, the new captain learned that workers were racing to enlarge the troop capacity from 7,500 men to 12,500. Hundreds of new bunks that were little more than "rough bedsprings fastened to the bulkhead and made so they would fold out when in use" were jammed into the enclosed promenades. To handle all those extra soldiers, the crew would be increased from 2,000 to 2,500.

Bryan had no reservations about accepting command. The assignment was just what he wanted.

"The Tuscania's *Been Hit"*

D URING ONE OF the worst weeks of the war for submarine attacks, a convoy of twelve ships headed for Liverpool was ambushed at night in the Irish Sea by a lone-wolf U-boat that had been stalking them since dawn. The *Leviathan* would soon be heading in that same direction.

Irvin Cobb had a ringside seat that day. His own troopship, the SS *Baltic*, the same British-owned troopship that had taken General Pershing to Europe the previous May, was part of the convoy, sailing in the middle of three rows of ships that were being shadowed by six British destroyers. The weather was unusually fine for February 5, bright, cold, and clear, with none of the blasting winds and rolling seas that had made for rough going ever since the convoy had sailed from Halifax, Nova Scotia.

The first body from an earlier U-boat attack was spotted that afternoon floating several hundred yards off the *Baltic*'s port side. Some of the passengers who'd gone up on deck for fresh air thought at first that the dark object rocking in the waves might be a mine, but then another one appeared riding higher in the water, and there was no mistaking the head and upper torso. The two bodies, Cobb wrote, were "sustained in upright posture by life belts, so that those dead men seemed to be staring [in our direction] as they bobbed stiffly by." The bodies drifted out of sight as the ship veered away. Troopships were under strict orders never to slow down or stop to pick up the dead or even survivors from a torpedoed ship in case it might be an ambush. German submarines liked to lurk in the vicinity of a sinking and wait for another target.

Joining Cobb aboard the *Baltic* were several thousand soldiers and a few dozen VIP passengers. They were one day from their destination, and the captain, a legendary skipper named Tubby Finch (he had gotten the nickname because he stood five feet four and weighed nearly three hundred pounds) who'd already survived one torpedoing, ordered the engines slowed even though they'd entered the submarine zone.

The reason for such caution appeared obvious to Cobb. Wreckage was spread around them as far as he could see—pieces of wood, spars and rigging, and barrels—floating evidence that the *Baltic* was steaming through a ship graveyard as she zigzagged on a northeasterly course along the Irish coast, followed by the SS *Tuscania*, a smaller British ship that was carrying two thousand American soldiers, aviators, and military policemen to Liverpool. Both vessels had sailed from Hoboken late in January, then pushed on to Halifax to join the convoy.

The sight of the two bodies floating alone and abandoned in the sea was ghoulish enough, but equally chilling was the sudden appearance of a lifeboat that seemed to come out of nowhere and almost banged up against the side of the ship. Empty and without oars, the small boat pitched dangerously in the swells. Staring down at it from the deck, Cobb noticed "what looked like a woman's cloak lying across the thwarts" and wondered what had happened to her. As he stood at the railing, "a good many persons decided to tie on their life preservers."

Cobb wasn't unhappy when the small white boat slipped out of view and disappeared in the *Baltic*'s wash. He knew the risks he'd face on this trip; there was always the chance he could be killed if he tried to get as close to the fighting as he'd done in the summer of 1914. And this time, his health wasn't at its best.

A shade over six feet tall with the shoulders and thick neck of a football lineman, Cobb was badly overweight and out of shape. He had needed surgery in 1915 to repair the hernia he'd suffered helping unload wounded German soldiers from the troop train in France, and he'd almost died on the operating table. His recovery took months instead of the three or four days he'd been told to expect, an experience that provided a rich vein of sardonic humor for the most popular book he ever wrote, *Speaking of Operations*.

During the presidential election of 1916, Cobb barnstormed the country, giving a series of speeches in support of Woodrow Wilson's reelection and focusing his talks on the horrors he'd witnessed in Europe. After what he'd seen in France and Belgium, he appreciated Wilson's vow to keep the United States out of war, but now that the country had entered the fight, Cobb supported the effort wholeheartedly. He targeted the stridently antiwar senator Robert La Follette in a *Saturday Evening Post* article titled "The Thunders of Silence," published while Cobb was on his way to France. He even volunteered to enlist. He visited the White House to talk to President Wilson personally about a job in military intelligence. Wilson heard him out, then let him down easy, telling him he could help the cause more by going back to France as a reporter for the *Saturday Evening Post*. Wilson said he wasn't about to give him "one of those phony commissions."

"You can be of some account to your country over there," the president said, "writing about our effort, our spirit, our boys—most of all about our boys. . . . That's where I'm telling you to go. No, that's where I'm ordering you . . . to go."

His first crossing, in August 1914, had been something of a lark for Cobb, but his mood was markedly different this time with the signs of submarine warfare littering the ocean all around him. He was uneasy about visiting the front. He'd also been bothered by seasickness but after three days cooped up in his cabin was feeling well enough to go on deck for some air. As the sun went down, the white flashes from a lighthouse gave him "a feeling of security" because it meant they were only seven miles from land, a comfort if they were torpedoed. For a few minutes he watched the coast of Northern Ireland emerge from the darkness. The wind fell off and the sea was running in a moderate swell, and as the twilight deepened he lost sight of the other ships in the convoy, all of them running in strict blackout conditions. The *Baltic* was scheduled to veer northeast toward the English shore later that evening and arrive in Liverpool in the morning.

Cobb later joined five other travelers for a farewell card game in one of their cabins. The party included three Canadian soldiers returning to their regiments in France and a Canadian military surgeon. They'd gotten in a few hands of draw poker when something hard and metallic suddenly banged along the entire length of the ship just below the darkened portholes. The cabin was on a lower deck just above the waterline.

"What the devil was that?" someone asked.

"No doubt a torpedo knocking for admission," said another player.

A poor joke, thought Cobb, figuring that the ship had probably struck a piece of floating debris. Minutes later, an American officer stuck his head through the doorway.

"The *Tuscania's* been hit right behind us," he said. "Come along quietly. Not many on this boat know yet what's happened."

The torpedo had been meant for them. The biggest ship in the world when she was launched in 1903, the *Baltic* was 729 feet long and had a distinctive profile because of her four masts, two forward, two aft. She was the largest and most recognizable ship in the convoy. The German submarine UB-77 had spotted her shortly after dawn and had shadowed the slow-moving convoy all day, taking care to hang far behind to avoid the British destroyers that were flanking the transport ships. After night fell, the submarine surfaced in calm seas at ten o'clock and fired two torpedoes at the *Baltic*. The first shot missed. The ship's captain spotted the second torpedo and ordered his helmsman to steer straight for it at full speed. There wasn't time to turn or maneuver, and the captain figured their best chance was to take the torpedo in a head-on collision. The explosion might rip off the bow of the ship, but Finch hoped the watertight compartments in the main section of the hull would keep her afloat.

Instead, the torpedo grazed the entire length of the *Baltic*—the deep scars it left in the iron plates were visible in the morning—and slammed into the side of the *Tuscania*. The smaller ship was trailing the *Baltic* by several hundred yards and had started to veer away, turning broadside to the torpedo. When Cobb and the other card players got up on deck for a look, the stricken ship had started going down by the bow and was already half a mile to their stern and still aglow with light.

Cobb saw a red rocket go up, then another and another, hanging for long moments in the sky, then bursting in a cascading shower of red balls. A chorus of "Ahs" rose from the deck of the *Baltic* as he and the others took in the spectacle. Everyone realized the captain wasn't going to turn around to pick up survivors. Cobb wrote later that he felt like a coward as he watched the lights of the ship growing fainter behind them.

A young officer standing next to him finally broke the silence. Just before they sailed, he'd learned that his brother, who was also in the army, was aboard the *Tuscania*. If he had drowned, the soldier said, "it [would] only add a little more interest to the debt I already owe those damned Germans."

No one spoke. Another flare went up in a showering burst of red.

The *Tuscania* sank in 330 feet of water seven miles off the Irish coast. It wasn't the only ship torpedoed that night. Another ship in the convoy was sunk, and two others that were torpedoed managed to limp into port. A single U-boat had racked up a deadly tally. Of the eleven ships that sailed from Halifax, four were either sunk or damaged.

Soon after reaching Liverpool, Cobb learned that two British destroyers had rescued all but about two hundred of the over two thousand Americans and other passengers aboard the stricken *Tuscania*. As the soldiers gathered on the slanting decks of the doomed ship and went over the side into lifeboats, or more often than not straight into the black water, many of them were singing a popular war song: "Where Do We Go from Here, Boys?"

CHAPTER 7

Steaming for "Rendezvous A"

O N MARCH 4, BARELY one month after the U-boat attacks that had decimated Irvin Cobb's convoy, the *Leviathan* cast off from Pier 4 in Hoboken and cautiously backed into the Hudson. These were heart-pounding moments for her new commander, Captain Henry Bryan, who'd come aboard only one day earlier. He was perched on the open bridge as the lines were cast off and the gangways raised. Helped by a retinue of tugboats, the giant ship eased into the New York side of the channel, a tricky maneuver that kept Bryan and the ship's pilot on edge until she caught the current and headed downstream past Ellis Island, the Statue of Liberty, and the Battery. It was the first opportunity many New Yorkers had to see the big ship decked out in her head-turning dazzle paint, and throngs hurried to the waterfront to get a look or watched from the windows of the tall buildings along lower Manhattan as she headed for the Narrows and New York Bay.

Thousands of khaki-clad soldiers stood on the open decks, waving their hats and shouting their farewells into the wind, but this time no bands were playing to mark the ship's departure. Although the army was trying its best to keep the *Leviathan*'s departures as low key as possible, once she cast off it was impossible to miss the monster, her tall gray funnels rising high over the wharves and other ships as she glided by.

Bryan's first destination was the Ambrose Lightship. Anchored several miles off Sandy Hook, the aging copper-hulled Coast Guard vessel served as a floating lighthouse and was equipped with two powerful arc lamps that on foggy nights marked the entrance to the shipping channel into New York Harbor. The captain had been directed to proceed from the Ambrose Lightship to "Rendezvous A" at "approximately 17.8 knots, including zig-zag." The orders were precise, if spare: he was supposed to arrive at the rendezvous in the North Atlantic four hundred nautical miles off the southern tip of Ireland at 6:00 a.m. on March 11, where he would meet a destroyer escort, "weather and conditions permitting."

Bryan's sailing orders addressed his main concern. The first bulleted paragraph—"latest enemy information as follows"—warned that the greatest submarine activity was in the English and Irish Channels and that "within the past two days, submarines have been reported in approximately Longitude nineteen west Latitude forty-six north."

The coordinates marked where the *Leviathan* was headed with 8,242 soldiers and a navy crew of nearly 2,000 sailors. The German subs kept attacking with audacity and skill, often getting brazenly close to their targets before firing. During February and through the end of March, over fifty ships were sunk in the Irish Sea.

If the *Leviathan* arrived at the rendezvous and wasn't met by the destroyers, Bryan was to continue "at best speed" to Liverpool and hope that the destroyers would intercept him somewhere en route. He must have appreciated the irony in light of what had happened to his predecessor.

The weather turned ugly with squalls shortly after the ship reached the Ambrose Lightship and headed into the Atlantic. Bryan spent almost all of his waking moments on the bridge except for a few hours of sleep each night in his cabin. He liked to be available to his officers at all hours, and they were encouraged to approach him for one-on-one conversations, especially if they could suggest any improvements in how the ship operated.

One of his first orders of business was to provide a list of procedures to follow in case of a submarine attack. Six short siren blasts meant a submarine was off the bow; one long blast, off the starboard; and two long blasts, off the port side. A square green flag with a white diagonal line signaled enemy to starboard; a red flag with a white diagonal, to port. At sundown the ship went to "battle lights," dim blue lights that burned on the bridge and near all the watertight doors and stairways. Anyone who turned on an unauthorized light faced the risk of court-martial. The only exception to the strict lights-off policy was in the latrines, where lamps were left on around the clock, an arrangement that drew dice players at all hours. At Bryan's insistence, lifeboat drills were carried out night and day until every soldier on board could find his assigned boat in the dark. Each passenger was also given a life preserver and shown how to strap it on around the waist.

On the afternoon of March 7, when the *Leviathan* was nearly three days out of New York, a long smudge of black smoke was spotted trailing over the horizon. The gun crews hustled to their stations and started zeroing in their range finders, tracking the approaching ship as the distance rapidly closed. From all the smoke it was putting out, the vessel looked big. Bryan and others on the bridge kept their binoculars pressed to their eyes until they received a radio message that it was a British cruiser. With the German High Seas Fleet bottled up in the North Sea port of Wilhelmshaven, it wasn't likely they'd have to worry about an encounter with the enemy, but there was always the chance of running into a raider, one of the heavily armed merchant ships that had sunk so many vessels earlier in the war.

Even in rough seas, Bryan made sure his gun crews practiced daily, firing a few rounds from each of the *Leviathan*'s eight batteries. The gunnery officers were notified that flat-nosed, nonricocheting shells designed to bite into the water and hit a submerged submarine rather than skip along the surface were to be kept in the weapons at all times.

Bryan insisted on reading the war warnings dispatch the moment it came in by wireless six times a day at one thirty, five thirty, and nine thirty in the morning and evening. The bulletins notified ship captains of enemy cruisers, raiders, or submarines that might be prowling in their area.

On March 9, one of these messages reported that three Allied submarines were close by and heading to Bermuda. A day later, the *Leviathan*'s wireless room received a dispatch from the USS *Manley*, one of seven American destroyers sent out from Ireland to meet them. Bryan and the destroyer captain worked out the location and timing of the rendezvous, and early the next morning a lookout on the *Leviathan* spotted the ships approaching through weather that was "very thick, the visibility about one mile." Word quickly spread through the ship. Within minutes, hundreds of soldiers were on the decks cheering and roaring their welcome across the waves to the *Manley*.

They were soon nearing the mouth of the river Mersey, the gateway to Liverpool harbor and Gladstone Dock, where the ship would once again go into dry dock. The *Manley*, which was leading the convoy of destroyers screening the *Leviathan*, suddenly peeled off to port as her forward battery opened fire with a five-inch gun. Startled, Bryan couldn't see what the ship was shooting at. Neither could anyone else on the bridge. The destroyer cut sharply and dropped a depth charge.

Bryan ordered the helmsman to turn to starboard, an abrupt maneuver that sent china crashing below in the galleys. Moments later a powerful explosion rocked the *Leviathan* "from stem to stern."

"We've hit a mine!" someone shouted on the bridge.

Bryan knew better. Barely five hundred yards away from the destroyer, the ship had been rocked by the depth charge. A few months later, a story appeared in the *Chicago Tribune* that described a furious attack on the *Leviathan* by three submarines and the "destruction of two U-boats by U.S. destroyers." The "eyewitness account" that described how one of the submarines was "blown to atoms" was based on a letter an army officer on the ship mailed to his son in Michigan. Not a word of the story was true, and within days it prompted a scorching memo to Bryan and other captains from Admiral Sims. The subject: "Undesirable press reports."

The *Manley* and the other destroyers didn't slow down to go back and check whether a submarine might have been there. The convoy kept pushing ahead at high speed, nearly twenty-three knots, not slowing down until it reached the Mersey later that day. Taking advantage of the high tide, the ship promptly entered the harbor and proceeded straight to the dry dock where it had tied up during the last visit.

THE SOLDIERS IMMEDIATELY started to disembark, a process that continued throughout the night and ended the following morning. Many of the regiments marched off with their flags flying and bands playing as they headed to the railway station, where they climbed into trains bound for Winchester, the next stop on their journey to France. Some residents cheered as they watched the Americans pass, but for the most part the welcome in Liverpool was cool. There were even a few boos and hisses mixed in with the smattering of applause. The war had been going on for so long that many in the crowd must have wondered whether these Americans would actually make a difference. What could these men possibly do to affect the outcome?

Bryan was acutely aware of these sentiments, as was his commander, Vice Admiral Albert Gleaves, the Nashville-born sixty-year-old logistical wizard credited with devising the first workable system for refueling ships at sea. Gleaves was in charge of all the US transports carrying soldiers to France.

When the *Leviathan* dropped anchor in Liverpool on Tuesday, March 12, the German attack that the Allied high command had long feared was about to explode. In the predawn gloom of March 21, "the heaviest German bombardment of the war could be heard as far back as Petain's headquarters at Compiegne" where it was compared "to the roar of a distant surf." It was the first of three German offensives in the spring and summer of 1918, and when the first assault ended in April, the results were disastrous for the Allies. British losses numbered 164,000 casualties and 90,000 prisoners. Once again, the roads around Paris were clogged with refugees trying to flee the front in any truck, car, or cart that would carry them out of range of the guns. The German breakthrough threatened catastrophe.

Gleaves was concerned that the *Leviathan* had to be in dry dock in Liverpool for nearly a month because of an ongoing problem with unusually strong tides aggravated by wind and storm surges. The delay was totally unacceptable considering the critical need to get troops to France, with the outcome of the war hanging in the balance. So, shortly after the *Leviathan* arrived in the English port, Gleaves ordered Bryan to go to Brest and devise a plan for mooring the ship and unloading troops there. The admiral had visited the city several months earlier. A photograph showed him standing next to Pershing on the deck of a destroyer, Gleaves a full head shorter and more rumpled looking than the dapper AEF commander. The French port, which had been heavily fortified by Napoleon, had plenty of deep water to accommodate the *Leviathan* at any tide, but the ship was too large to tie up at any of the piers, which meant she'd need to anchor outside the harbor.

Bryan's mission gave him his first chance to see how the war was going in France and gather the latest intelligence from naval commanders on German U-boat activity. Enemy submarines were patrolling the approaches to Brest with deadly efficiency, and the captain was sure they'd be hunting for the *Leviathan*.

Two Dead Nurses

O N MARCH 4, THE same day that the big ship had swung out into the Hudson for the trip to Liverpool, a young woman who'd soon travel aboard her was starting another crowded day on Ellis Island, where she was training as an army nurse. Elizabeth Weaver had just finished roll call and a hurried breakfast when the *Leviathan*, in all her head-turning, war-painted glory, slowly passed the famous stopping place for immigrant families that recently had been transformed into a teeming military base. The men, women, and children from central and eastern Europe who made the island in Upper New York Bay famous as the gateway to America had been replaced by thousands of army and navy personnel, many of them, like Elizabeth, soon to leave for France.

Sharing space in spare twenty-person dormitories, Elizabeth and sixty-four other young nurses were members of an army hospital team organized by the University of Pennsylvania, where Elizabeth had attended nursing school. Other American universities were doing the same thing, supplying and staffing what were known as base hospitals. The Pennsylvania unit had been mobilized on November 30, 1917, and included 22 medical officers, 2 dentists, 153 enlisted men, and the nurses, who were getting their no-frills initiation to the army on the improvised parade grounds at Ellis Island.

A member of a well-known Mennonite family in Pennsylvania's Lancaster County, Elizabeth—she didn't like her first name, Emma—was one of five children. She was born near Blue Ball, a hamlet that got its colorful name from a Revolutionary War–era hotel in Earl Township, where her father, Moses, was a farmer and the county's deputy collector. Her mother, Anna, was from another prominent farming family. As a girl, Elizabeth grew up riding horses on her father's farm and sometimes set off at a gallop through his prized apple orchards. She was a spirited child who wasn't afraid to express her feelings and emotions in a rural community where men and women wore their best dark suits and dresses on Sunday and rode buggies or walked to church.

Elizabeth was barely thirteen when an older brother, a freshman at a state teaching college, came home for a short vacation and complained that he wasn't feeling well. He went to bed and died after a few days of intense pain from what was diagnosed as inflammatory rheumatism. Cortland Scott Weaver had been seventeen years old. Over one thousand family members, college students, and friends paid their respects at the family home, and two sermons were delivered at the service, one in German by the Mennonite pastor, the other in English by the Presbyterian minister. The teen was buried in the Weaverland Mennonite Cemetery.

Her brother's unexpected death devastated Elizabeth. She didn't understand how he could arrive home in seemingly perfect health and then suddenly die, and how no one could do anything for him, including the family doctor, who had initially told them the boy wasn't in any danger. She'd tried to talk to Cortland as he lay in bed, watching him suffer until he no longer seemed to recognize her.

For the rest of her life, Elizabeth was infused with the desire to help the sick, especially the seemingly hopeless cases. It was still rare in America then for women to become doctors or nurses, and their doing so was even considered scandalous in some families.

Elizabeth graduated from the University of Pennsylvania in 1904 and for the next decade worked in private hospitals in Philadelphia. Elizabeth's most attractive features were her smile and her thick brown hair, which she combed low in a wavy curl over her forehead. Her eyes were wide set and deep blue, and she had a finely shaped nose and dark eyebrows. If not a conventional beauty by today's standards, she was gracefully athletic and easy to be with.

Elizabeth Weaver's life changed forever when she enlisted in the Army Nurse Corps. There was a growing, soon-to-be critical need for nurses as the US Army started taking casualties in France. After discussing her decision with her supportive family—her mother gave her a charm bracelet to help keep her safe—Elizabeth joined the army on February 16, 1918, a cold Saturday morning in Philadelphia, where she was sworn in at the University of Pennsylvania. As she and the other nurses from Base Hospital 20 climbed aboard their train at the Broad Street Station, each one of them was handed a bouquet of flowers and a basket of fruit. Elizabeth, who was in her midthirties, was the oldest of the group. Their mood and morale were excellent, especially when the train slowly passed another one filled with khaki-clad recruits. "We flocked to the windows," Elizabeth wrote, "and there was wild cheering and waving and exchanging of salutes."

Arriving in New York City, the women took a ferry to Ellis Island, where they were quickly introduced to the organized chaos of their new military life. The island was crawling with thousands of soldiers and sailors and several hundred fresh-faced nurses attached to different base hospitals, who drew appreciative stares whenever they marched out onto the drill field. Instructing sixty-five women in the basics of marching, Elizabeth admitted, was a hard business, but they eventually learned to do "squads right," "column four," and "about face" without embarrassing themselves. They also received the first of a series of inoculations and vaccinations for smallpox, typhoid, and other diseases.

It wasn't long before the nurses were throwing parties in their dormitories, dancing to the Victrola, and enjoying ice cream and cake as the winter weather hardened. There were frequent snowstorms, and fast-moving ice floes filled the harbor. From her dormitory window, Elizabeth enjoyed a spectacular view at night of the illuminated Statue of Liberty, which glowed "clear and beautiful" over the water. "The Goddess of Liberty is our guardian angel," she wrote. "She will guard us and protect us while we are gone and until we again return to America."

Over the next few weeks, Elizabeth prepared a will and took out a $10,000 war risk insurance policy that she carefully noted would pay her $57 a month for twenty years if she were disabled. There were regular trips to New York for dinner or to see a movie—among them *Seven Days Leave*, and *Why Not Marry*. They also had daily French lessons in the chapel and on at least one occasion hosted a dance attended by officers and enlisted men—"good times," she noted.

During one of her visits to the city, Elizabeth and a friend attended a lecture by Ralph Connor, a bestselling Canadian writer and Presbyterian minister. Connor had served as a chaplain to a Canadian regiment during the Second Battle of Ypres, where he'd watched his closest friends die in the 1915 engagement. The Germans had released chlorine gas with hellish effect, sending the greenish-yellow clouds drifting over the trenches, where it asphyxiated thousands of unprepared soldiers within minutes. Connor, who'd witnessed the attack, was the pen name for the Reverend Charles William Gordon. He didn't mention that his views of the war had started to change as a result of what he'd experienced at Ypres and that he was leaning strongly toward pacifism.

Elizabeth attended other lectures on what to expect overseas and also served rotations at the Ellis Island hospital, one of the first stops for injured Americans returning to the States. One night in mid-March, a troopship arrived at the pier with one hundred critically ill soldiers on board. At least forty of them had tuberculosis—the often-fatal lung disease wasn't uncommon in the army—and twelve others had suffered mental breakdowns from what they'd experienced—bombardments, machine gun fire, and ghastly injuries that took away arms, legs, and faces. The rest had a variety of serious wounds.

Elizabeth wrote about one case she couldn't get out of her mind, a young soldier from Nebraska she'd helped treat for diphtheria. They gave him a shot of antitoxin, but it was too little, too late, and he died choking in agony in his bed. Elizabeth didn't want to leave him. The doctors insisted that she get an antitoxin injection, which knocked her off her feet for a day.

The instructors at Ellis Island didn't sugarcoat the risks of serving in France, where many of the nurses would spend weeks in frontline field hospitals, working under the constant threat of shelling, gas, and air attacks. So far no nurses had died from enemy fire, but everyone was aware of a freak accident that had killed two American nurses a few months earlier as they sailed for France. It had happened aboard the SS *Mongolia*, which was carrying members of Northwestern University's Base Hospital 12 to France. The women were on the promenade deck with other nurses as a gun crew fired a few practice rounds soon after the vessel departed from New York. The two nurses were sitting about 175 feet behind the gun when the brass casing from one of the fired shells "boomeranged" back over the deck and broke into fragments. A jagged piece struck one of the women in the head; the other was hit in the chest. Both were killed instantly, and a nurse sitting near them was badly wounded.

As the weeks passed, one of the nurses' commanding officers tried to raise $3,000 to buy them "safety suits," flotation devices that could be worn "for any length of time in coldest water" and had "lead in the bottom to keep you in an upright position and . . . other material in the chest to give buoyancy." Fortunately these cumbersome and probably lethal devices were never acquired, and Elizabeth was issued a more practical though still hopelessly inadequate cork life vest.

CHAPTER 8

The Orphans of Brest

CAPTAIN BRYAN'S SEA passage to Brest took him between the black cliffs of the twin Gibraltar-like outcroppings that marked the entrance to the narrow deep-water harbor first developed by Cardinal Richelieu. With its tight, steep streets and quaint Mother Hubbard stone houses, the city was built on the hills that swept up from the harbor. A seventeenth-century fortress with crenulated walls and a tower—the Tour Tanquy—dominated the western shore along with the arsenal and the tall brownstone wall that surrounded the oldest part of the city.

With the *Leviathan* still in dry dock, Bryan most likely arrived at the port aboard one of the American destroyers that were increasingly using the harbor as a base to protect the troopships making the dangerous passage from the United States. The rocky coast with its cliffs and sea-carved grottoes was famous for dense fog, but the hills surrounding Brest harbor—the Rade Abri—offered protection from weather and enemy cannon fire.

The harbor was jammed with shipping—two rows of camouflaged American destroyers swinging at anchor, a cluster of two- and three-masted schooners, as well as assorted freighters, fishing smacks, barges, and tenders, and two large repair ships. A pair of French submarines was also moored there. A gray observation balloon tethered to the stern of a ship swung one hundred feet over the harbor with a spotter aboard who searched for the periscope wash of German submarines. Two yellow French dirigibles slowly passed overhead, also prowling for U-boats.

There was a pocket of "dead water," meaning no strong currents, about one mile to the south. Several smaller troopships from the United States were anchoring there—the USS *Mount Vernon* and the USS *Lincoln* among them, both former German liners. Bryan planned to focus on that area as a possible mooring site for the much larger *Leviathan*. Over the next few days, he went out to the wind-swept location several times in a launch with the French officer in charge of the port, and working together in the evenings in the burgeoning American navy encampment, they designed a behemoth mooring buoy. Bryan, whose fluency in French was a great help, sketched a design in pencil that showed eight legs of chain, each 60 fathoms, or 360 feet, long and attached to an anchor that weighed 18,000 pounds. The chains were linked to a cylindrically shaped buoy the size of a water tower tank. The *Leviathan*'s bow would be chained to the buoy, which was large enough to support four sailors to handle the coupling. Once secured, the ship would unload her cargo of American doughboys, who would be ferried ashore on barge-size troop carriers. The design was quickly approved and sent to Boston, where the massive anchors and chains—each iron link was four inches thick—were fabricated. The buoy would be constructed in New York, and Bryan was assured that everything would be ready in time to load it aboard the *Leviathan* for the next sailing.

During his stay in the French port, the captain was surprised by the overwhelming scope and speed of the American expansion that had begun barely four months earlier after a military disaster. In early November, a German-Austrian surprise attack had annihilated an Italian army at Caporetto. Using shock troops and infiltration tactics improved upon later by one of the participants—a young combat officer named George Rommel—the "Alpenkorps" advanced eighty miles in less than two weeks, rolling up the Italians between the Tyrol and the Adriatic and capturing 275,000 prisoners. The panic of the Italian retreat and the shooting of stragglers by battle police was powerfully captured by Ernest Hemingway in *A Farewell to Arms*. In one of the Great War's few clear-cut victories, the Germans virtually pushed Italy out of the fighting and forced England to provide the troops to fill the void, creating yet another critical need for more men on the western front. Until then, the French had been reluctant to let the Americans use Brest as a debarkation site for fear that the massive influx of soldiers would overwhelm their already dangerously strained railroad system. Caporetto changed all that overnight.

Bryan had a remarkable chance to observe the scale of the buildup that was transforming the city. Work was under way wherever he looked. Navy engineers helped by German prisoners wearing their gray field uniforms and pillbox caps were raising the wooden framing for two large warehouses along the waterfront. The Germans were handy with hammers, saws, and shovels and didn't look all that unhappy to be out of the fighting. African American troops were also working on the waterfront as stevedores. Other black soldiers were helping construct the new US Army encampment just south of the city around the famed Pontanezen Barracks where Napoleon once was quartered.

There were so many odd sights and sounds to take in: the wooden shoes everyone wore that clacked on the paving stones, and the goat and donkey carriages that hauled passengers up and down the plunging streets. Older men favored wide-brimmed black hats that trailed long black ribbons. Women wore dainty caps made of white lace. But the most conspicuous sight for Bryan was something that he did not see: young men. As in so many other towns and villages in France, the overwhelming majority of men from Brest in their twenties and thirties were in the army; appallingly, over one million of them in France were dead and another four million wounded.

The city was filled with orphans. Tucked away on side streets or attached to churches or even private homes, the many orphanages cared for more children than they could handle. Newsreels from that period show American sailors and soldiers holding small children in their arms or playing with them in the parks, giving them chewing gum or toys, or letting them sit on their laps during band concerts.

With three young children of his own, Bryan was acutely aware of the needs of these often-overlooked casualties of the war. In a letter to his eight-year-old son, Charles, written around this time, the captain described a story he'd read in a French newspaper about children who were asked how the war was affecting them. One twelve-year-old girl said that life was bleak. "Mothers are no longer gay," she said. "The husbands of some of them are dead." Another child remembered the day when the war broke out and all the men who were working in the fields had to depart immediately and report for duty. "Everything is changed since that day," he said.

Bryan's two other children, Elizabeth and Helen, were five and two years old. Marrying late, he enjoyed being a father and wrote his son, the oldest, whenever he could, promising to buy him some French toy soldiers the next time he got to Brest and to look for dolls for his daughters.

When he finally left Brest, he was thinking about his return trip and the good chance they'd encounter a submarine. U-boats had sunk at least thirty ships on the approaches to Brest from November through January, and though the numbers had dropped off in February, the danger level remained high. The harbor and roadstead were patrolled by French torpedo boats and submarines, and US destroyers were now escorting troop transports into the port. Bryan knew the Germans would quickly learn from spies—the city was overrun with them—that the *Leviathan* would soon be using Brest instead of Liverpool.

Indeed, the kaiser had personally offered a handsome reward—nearly a quarter-million dollars in today's currency—to the U-boat crew that sank her.

A Promise of Help—and Micheline's Kisses

O N MARCH 11, THE day before the *Leviathan* arrived in Liverpool, German bombs fell dangerously close to General Pershing as he tried to grab a few hours of sleep at his quarters on the rue de Varenne in Paris. If Pershing had any doubts that the Germans were preparing a major offensive, they disappeared that evening, as Gotha and Zeppelin bombers flew over the city and London. In what he called a "severe air raid," the bombers caused few casualties but scored several direct hits nearby.

Earlier that day, Pershing had welcomed the US secretary of war, Newton Baker, to Paris, introducing him to French prime minister Georges Clemenceau and Marshal Joffre. They had a lot to talk about. The war wasn't going well, and the French and English were pressuring Pershing almost daily to let them use American soldiers wherever they believed they were needed. The number of available troops was still dismally low. Nearly ten months after the United States declared war, it had managed to field only five 25,000-man divisions, and only one of these, the First Division, had even limited experience in the trenches, a performance Pershing found depressing in the extreme.

And now the bottom was about to fall out.

The Germans were transferring hundreds of thousands of troops from the eastern to the western front. These divisions would give the German army numerical superiority on the western front—at least until the Americans could get more soldiers overseas, which didn't seem likely anytime soon. Big ships like the *Leviathan* were struggling to increase capacity and speed up their six-to-seven-week turnaround time.

On March 21, the Germans unleashed their heaviest bombardment of the war, a deluge of fire and iron that started at 4:40 a.m. and was heard thirty miles away at Pétain's headquarters in Compiègne. The shells fell constantly for five hours, often landing so close together the craters touched—trench mortars, howitzer and incendiary shells, eighteen pounders, seventy-fives, seventy-sevens, whizz bangs, flying pigs, Jack Johnsons, and gas. Bunkers, trenches, command posts, and gun emplacements were obliterated. Then, attacking out of the fog, 64 specially trained German divisions of the 192 on the western front slammed into 26 British divisions at a weak point in the Somme valley. The front extended about fifty miles between the Oise and Scarpe Rivers near the junction of the French and British lines. The danger was critical. If the Germans smashed the British right flank, they'd force them into Flanders and open a short, direct route to the channel.

The storm troopers came first with light machine guns, flame-throwers, and stick bombs. By nightfall, gaping holes had been punched through the English lines. The next day, the British fell back ten miles, opening a bulge that would soon extend forty miles deep and forty wide. On the sixth day, German artillery was shelling the outskirts of Paris and the strategic railway was cut between Amiens and the capital. By the seventh day, Pershing was ready to do something he vowed he'd never do—throw American soldiers piecemeal into the line to prop up an Allied army before it was overrun. When the attack finally ended—it would last nearly two weeks—the British had suffered 164,000 casualties and lost 90,000 prisoners. Paris, once again, was threatened. It was a catastrophe.

On the evening of March 27, Pershing passed the Gare du Nord in his black Rolls-Royce staff car after a long meeting with Secretary Baker, who encouraged him to use American troops to relieve French divisions so they could drop back and defend the French capital. The train station and the streets around it were jammed with terror-stricken men and women, many with small children, carrying suitcases and bundles, all of them fleeing their threatened farms and villages. Thousands were in the streets, jamming the sidewalks and train platforms. Pershing was deeply moved by the spectacle, which he found "most pathetic." Few of these refugees had any place to go, and he wondered how many of them had parents who'd similarly fled their homes not fifty years earlier when the Germans defeated the French in the Franco-Prussian War.

The next day, Pershing drove to Clermont-sur-Oise, fifty miles north of Paris, to deliver the good news to Marshal Foch. He got hung up in traffic for hours as slow-moving columns of trucks loaded with troops and supplies headed north along the muddy roads toward Montdidier, a city that predated the Roman conquest and where the French were making a furious counterattack. When he finally arrived at Clermont-sur-Oise, Pershing had to hunt for Foch's headquarters, a small farmhouse well off the road and screened by tall poplars. The American general and his staff cooled their heels outside for a few minutes, and Pershing took the time while he waited to admire a cherry tree in full bloom. The setting was picturesque and strangely unsettling, he wrote later, with no sounds drifting in from the desperate battle being waged just a few miles to the northeast.

Finally admitted to the house, Pershing found Foch, Pétain, and Clemenceau hunched over a table with a map spread out. The details of the still-developing battle were quickly pointed out to him. The shared opinion was the British Fifth Army was starting to fight back and that at least for the time being the lines would hold.

Indicating that he wanted to talk to Foch in private, Pershing and the general were quickly left alone. Speaking in French, what he said so moved the French commander that he grabbed Pershing by the arm and rushed him outside and across the lawn. His eyes blazing, Foch asked him to repeat for Pétain and Clemenceau what he'd just told him.

"I come to tell you that the American people would consider it a great honor if our troops were engaged in the present battle," he said.

"I ask you this in my name and in theirs.

"The only question that matters right now is the battle. Infantry, artillery, aviation—all that we have is yours.

"Use it as you see fit."

Foch's voice quivered with emotion and excitement. Nicknamed "Le Tigre," Georges Clemenceau, the French prime minister, also showed deep feeling, his face reddening. Everyone was touched, and Pershing quickly ordered the US First Division from Lorraine to the front in Picardy. At the same time, the Second Division extended its front while the Forty-Second relieved three French divisions in the Baccarat sector, so they could be diverted to protect Paris in case of a German breakthrough.

The Forty-Second was under the frontline command of Colonel Douglas MacArthur, who often found himself at odds with Pershing. At thirty-eight, MacArthur was already famous for his combat exploits. Colorful and fearless, he was known to go on raids wearing riding breeches, a turtleneck sweater, and a maroon-colored muffler knitted by his mother. He'd already received the first of seven Silver Stars he would earn during the war and had been awarded a Distinguished Service Cross for an engagement earlier that month. Climbing the scaling ladder when the whistles blew at zero hour, he went over the top as quickly as he could and "scrambled forward. The blast was like a fiery furnace. For a dozen terrible seconds I felt they were not following me. But then, without turning around, I knew how wrong I was to have doubted for even an instant. In a moment they were around me, ahead of me, a roaring avalanche of glittering steel and cursing men. We carried the enemy position." He'd already been gassed—MacArthur didn't carry a gas mask—and wasn't completely recovered when the unit was sent to Baccarat.

During a recent visit to the city famed for its glassworks and crystal, Pershing had dinner with a French family in their home, where he spent the night as a guest. A quarter of the buildings in the town had been destroyed during earlier fighting. At dinner and with the children seated around the table, the discussion turned to whether it was possible to put an end to war. The grandmother, the family's matriarch, slowly shook her head, he recalled later.

"No," she said. "That is not likely. We have had war here in this part of Europe every fifty years during the last thousand."

The general's greatest hope in the coming battle rested on the First Division, which had been the first in the AEF to go into the trenches, relieving Moroccan troops in January in the Saint Mihiel sector after marching overnight to the front during a sleeting rainstorm. A warning from Pétain that the Americans' presence might invite a strong German raid was quickly proven correct. The Germans hit them twice in succession on a miserably cold January evening, raiding a listening post and ambushing a patrol, killing six men, wounding four, and capturing three. Pershing was distressed by the news.

Now in late March he was eagerly waiting for his troops, still relatively few in number, to distinguish themselves as they learned the deadly business of trench warfare, often under French instructors. He was trying to come up with a breakout strategy, what he liked to call "open field" warfare. The defining moment would come soon enough, but the learning curve for the poorly trained American army was steep.

FORTUNATELY, ON MARCH 28, the very day the First Division went into the line at Picardy, the German offensive began grinding to a halt, the troops advancing too far for their supply wagons and artillery to keep up with them over roads cratered by some of the worst shelling of the war.

Taking advantage of the enemy's slowdown, Pershing returned

to his headquarters at Chaumont, a town of fifteen thousand inhabitants located 150 miles east of Paris on the upper Marne. A century earlier, in 1814, the monarchs of England, Austria, Russia, and Prussia gathered there and agreed to fight Napoleon, who was defeated the following year at Waterloo. Pershing had moved out of Paris the previous September to escape all the social distractions and uninvited visitors and to get closer to the sector that American forces likely would occupy.

His personal residence at Val des Ecoliers was a Renaissance-style château built in 1889 with a spire and turrets on each corner. The large house was "garishly furnished in the style of the nouveau riche," the walls decorated with animal heads and the front hall dominated by the skin of a fifteen-foot-long crocodile. Pershing's office contained little more than a narrow desk with a telephone and a shaded banker's lamp flanked by two tall windows. An oak table stacked with books was set against it at a right angle. Four chairs were positioned in front of a large map of France that filled an entire wall. A wooden stand supporting an oversize French dictionary was behind the desk, and a cuspidor was within spitting range. A smaller desk near the door accommodated an aide, and another large map of the western front was displayed on the far wall. Most mornings Pershing was sitting at his desk by seven o'clock, wearing his high-collared olive-drab tunic.

Throughout March and into early April, his main goal remained unchanged—to transport as many soldiers as possible to France. The German offensive found him with fewer than 320,000 enlisted men and officers, and about 100,000 of these were in supply operations. "There was a great danger," Pershing wrote, "that the enemy would be able to defeat the French and British armies before substantial aid could be brought from America. If our forces could not be put into the lines in sufficient numbers within the next few months it might be too late. The war was up to America to win or lose."

Pershing received a major assist from the new army chief of staff, General Peyton C. March, who'd taken over the job barely a month earlier and had already made troop shipments his only priority. An abrasive, spindle-thin officer, March could be arrogant and dictatorial. He feuded regularly with Pershing on other issues, but got results. Before he took over, the turnaround for troopships averaged as long as sixty-seven days. He cut the number to thirty-five. In February the United States sent 49,000 soldiers to France; in March, almost 120,000. During the crucial next three months, the numbers exploded: 245,000 for April, 278,000 for May, and 306,000 for June.

Pershing was delighted to learn in early April that the *Leviathan* would be operating out of Brest and that her capacity had been increased to over 10,000 soldiers. He needed every one of those men as soon as he could get them. Over the next few days, the Germans launched their second spring offensive, beginning on April 9 and falling once more on the British, who were again caught off guard. Hitting strongpoints and trenches, storm troopers attacked with poison gas, pouring through a hole that opened in the English lines and advancing along a twenty-four-mile front. In extremis, the British general Douglas Haig issued this order: "There is no other course open to us but to fight it out! Every position must be held to the last man; there must be no retirement. With our backs to the wall, and believing in the justice of our cause, each one of us must fight on to the end. The safety of our homes and the freedom of mankind alike depend upon the conduct of each one of us at this critical moment."

The pressure on Pershing was intense as the British and French renewed their demands that he release more American troops to them in the face of the German steamroller. During weeks of often hectoring attacks from allies who didn't hesitate to go over his head—both Clemenceau and Lloyd George played that game—Pershing remained steadfast. His objective was to assemble an army that would fight intact and under American command—although it looked as if they'd run out of time long before that happened.

SINCE BECOMING LOVERS in the months after his arrival in France, Pershing and Micheline Resco exchanged letters often—and would do so for the rest of their lives—Pershing almost always writing in French, usually late at night.

Her love helped sustain him in moments of great crisis. While he focused on trying to build up an American army that could stave off disaster for France and England, Micheline tried to ease his burdens, turning her lovely apartment and studio into a sanctuary. Pershing's biographer Donald Smythe interviewed Micheline in Paris in the 1960s and described how she and the general "sat in front of the fire, holding hands, neither saying anything, or saying very little, for long periods. When they talked it was of everything in general and nothing in particular . . . what they had done that day, what they'd seen or read or heard."

Although Pershing had moved his staff headquarters to Chaumont, he still made frequent trips to Paris, often finding a few hours to visit Micheline under the pretense of sitting for his portrait. He usually came at night in his staff car, riding in the front seat with the driver rather than in the back, to avoid being spotted, and removing the pennants on the fenders that bore the four red stars of the commander in chief.

Writing after the war, Douglas MacArthur mentioned the many "quips and ribald jokes about [Pershing's] conquests," adding, of course, that there wasn't the "slightest foundation for such talk," but mentioning the night he came upon Pershing's stalled car blocking a road. The general's chauffeur at the time was Sergeant Eddie Rickenbacker, a race car driver who became America's most famous fighter ace of the war. When MacArthur asked him what the problem was, Rickenbacker "squinted hard at me, then said, 'Don't know, General, but it might be a hairpin in the clutch.'"

CHAPTER 9

POWs and Icebergs

CAPTAIN BRYAN HAD one more reason to worry as the *Leviathan* moved slowly down the Mersey River: as the great ship steamed away from Liverpool and headed into the open sea on her way to New York, the passenger list included thirty-seven German prisoners of war. The men had been brought aboard under guard just before the ship shoved off, and the captain hadn't taken his eyes off them until they were all in secure quarters. The thirty-three enlisted men and four officers were from a U-boat that American destroyers had captured after a running battle nearly three months earlier. Bryan had strengthened the ship's security detail and armed them with sawed-off shotguns. Red patches were sewn on the trouser legs of German enlisted men to identify them as POWs, and they were kept in the aft brig. The officers, an arrogant group who were all fluent in English, were kept in staterooms on C deck, guarded by NCOs who'd recently served on a torpedoed ship. These men weren't happy to be anywhere near the prisoners, and it showed.

On April 11, the *Leviathan*'s second day out of Liverpool, one of the German officers curtly asked why his room didn't have hot water.

A navy guard gave him a cold stare and reminded him that Germans had built the ship.

Later that afternoon when the *Leviathan* was still within the U-boat danger zone, Bryan ordered the gun crews to fire one of the new antisubmarine rounds. At the sound of the first shot, the prisoners panicked, thinking one of their subs was attacking.

A German officer asked what would happen to them if they had to abandon ship.

A navy guard barked out they'd get the same treatment they provided "for the lost souls on the *Lusitania*."

The German was well aware that 1,198 passengers had drowned when a U-boat torpedoed the British vessel in water not far from where the *Leviathan* was currently sailing. The guard's barbed wisecrack wasn't true, of course, but no one went out of his way to offer words of encouragement to the German officers. The small group ate alone at a table reserved for them in the Ritz-Carlton dining room while two guards stood nearby with their shotguns at the ready.

The enlisted men were more friendly and weren't afraid to let it be known that they didn't like their aristocratic officers any more than the Americans did. One of them was a machinist who'd been a bartender in Boston before the war; another was in business in Cincinnati. They admitted they were grateful that American sailors had risked their lives to save them back in November.

After a lookout spotted the periscope, two US destroyers, the *Fanning* and the *Nicholson*, dropped depth charges on the submarine, the U-58, then opened fire with cannons when the damaged U-boat surfaced. The crew poured out onto the deck, throwing up their hands and shouting, "Kamerad!" Moving dangerously close, the destroyers took the men off in lifeboats and managed to get a line attached to the foundering submarine. They'd just started a tow when two German crewmen who were hiding opened up the flood valves and scuttled the boat, which sank within minutes. The men barely got off in time and were swept away. Two American sailors dived into the water and, fighting the current and waves, hauled both of them back to a destroyer, where one of the men died from hypothermia. Given warm clothing, hot coffee, sandwiches, and cigarettes, the prisoners told their captors they were glad to be finished with the war.

Bryan had bigger things to worry about. At 2:00 p.m., on their fourth day out of New York, a sailor with binoculars perched high in the crow's nest telephoned the warning to the *Leviathan*'s bridge.

"Iceberg!"

Next to enemy submarines, nothing was more terrifying than these floating mountains of ice that could slice open the side of a ship. With fog setting in, Bryan changed course to the south and increased the speed to nineteen knots to get far away from any icebergs or floes.

During the voyage, they passed the SS *New York* going in the opposite direction. Nearly everyone on the bridge instantly recognized the former liner, which had a distinctive pair of tall stacks and a "clipper ship" bow, as it crossed their path at a distance of five miles. A decade earlier, the five-hundred-foot-long *New York* would have been considered a big ship, but she could carry no more than two thousand troops. The *Leviathan* was almost twice her length and would have nearly nine thousand soldiers aboard when she made her next crossing, maybe more. Additional bunks had been jammed belowdecks while the ship was tied up in Liverpool.

Bryan was not immune to the pressures of his unique command. Shortly after the ship was safely moored at Hoboken on the afternoon of April 17, he let his feelings slip out as he dined in the Ritz-Carlton with the young bride of one of his wife's brothers. Earlier that day the U-boat crewmen had been loaded aboard a navy tug on their way to a POW camp at Fort McPherson, Georgia. Many of the German sailors had waved to the crew and shouted their farewells as they were led down the gangplank under marine guard. Bryan understood as well as they did how incredibly lucky they were to have been rescued, and in a moment of candor, he touched on one of his anxieties with his visitor.

What should he do, she asked, if they spotted a small boat loaded with the desperate survivors of a torpedoed ship? Could he stop to rescue them?

He let the question sink in before giving his answer.

He wouldn't stop.

"I must always think of the thousands aboard my ship," he said. "Who knows, that small boat may be a decoy to draw us to a mined area." He'd keep going, increasing the ship's speed to get away from the lifeboats. The thought of the *Leviathan* taking a torpedo hit while carrying ten thousand soldiers was too ghastly to imagine.

A few hours later, Bryan left the ship to catch a late train for Washington, DC, where the details of the next voyage—the first to Brest—were spelled out, and where he received the latest report on how many soldiers the *Leviathan* would be carrying. All concerns about the potential risks had been tossed overboard, underscored by a recent remark by General March: "I propose to get the men to France if they have to swim."

Bryan also received the most recent assessment of the fighting on the western front and the back-to-back German offensives that threatened to achieve a war-ending breakthrough. While his ship was still heading for New York, the Germans had unleashed their second attack of the spring. The Allies were desperate for American troops, and it had become obvious to everyone that the navy's transport service had to get them to France in increasingly larger numbers or the war was lost. *Leviathan* was needed more than ever.

With that imperative weighing on him, Bryan understandably may not have given much thought to a short note recorded in the ship's log on April 18. At 9:30 a.m., seaman second class Carl Frank Johnson died aboard the *Leviathan* of lobar pneumonia. A day earlier he'd been placed in the sick bay suffering from chills, coughing, and rapid, shallow breathing. His sputum had a frightening rust color. The infection laid waste to his lungs in a matter of hours, killing him less than one day after he fell ill.

Lessons in Trench Warfare

WHEN A MAGNIFICENT rainbow broke through the gray skies on April 8, 1918, Corporal Freddie Stowers and other members of the 371st Regiment were getting their first good look at the Atlantic Ocean. After a run of bad luck, they might have taken the colorful spectacle in the eastern sky as a good omen. For two days, their ship, the SS *President Grant*, had been stuck in the mud off Virginia Beach at the entrance to the Chesapeake Bay. The ship had run aground barely an hour after shoving off from Newport News, and it had taken an armada of seagoing tugs to pull her free in the rain. When the sun finally came out, so did the regiment's fine band. The men began to sing along to the brassy jazz tunes and enjoyed the sweeping views as their ship finally headed out to sea. The golden interlude lasted barely two hours. When they glimpsed the last misty outlines of Cape Henry, rain was falling heavily again.

On this trip, the ship was loaded to capacity with nearly 5,500 troops, half of them white, half African American. The two groups were kept apart, and the white officers of the South Carolina regiment were charged with guarding the ladders and entrances to the mess hall, where the men ate at 8:00 a.m. and 4:00 p.m. The 371st bunked in the forward decks, the white troops in the aft compartments. In the heavily segregated military, the two groups slept and ate apart, took part in separate abandon-ship drills, and were assigned separate lifeboats. Navy and army guards were posted throughout the ship to make sure there were no unpleasant encounters. The men ate, did calisthenics, and took showers at different times, but everyone hit the rack right after sunset when the lights were turned off and learned to sleep with a life preserver tied around his neck.

When shouting erupted on the morning of Tuesday, April 23,

Stowers made his way up on deck with the rest of C Company to see what was going on. Six American destroyers fanned out around their ship, sometimes darting ahead or dropping back as they patrolled for enemy submarines. A French dirigible was also shadowing them. The men enjoyed the show as they were escorted into the harbor at Brest, which was jammed with Allied shipping. It was a fine spring afternoon, the weather cool and clear. The fields and hills overlooking the city and harbor were a deep emerald green, and the water glittered in the sunlight.

The men of the 371st were in high spirits, especially at the sight of so many ships flying the American flag. Finally in France, they were eager to get started. The regiment's band was booming out marching tunes as Stowers and his men lined up with their packs strapped to the shoulders and began to disembark, each man carrying his newly issued Springfield rifle. Coming off the pier, they marched through Brest to the Pontanezen Barracks several miles to the south and were hustled to a section reserved for African American troops. There was no time for much gawking at the quaint streets and picturesque shops as the soldiers hiked through the town, many of them still unsteady on their feet after nearly two weeks at sea.

The men were warned in advance about the slurs and insults that were guaranteed to come their way and urged not to take the bait, and they were repeatedly told that their entire race would be judged on their performance and to conduct themselves with pride and dignity. There'd already been trouble.

Less than a week earlier at the port city of Saint-Nazaire 120 miles down the coast, members of another African American regiment, the 372nd, came close to assaulting a white officer who'd kicked one of their men for allegedly talking back when he was accused of feigning illness. Tension had been building there because the African American regiment, unlike the white units arriving at the camp, had been ordered to help unload trains and ships at the railroad yards and docks. Trained to fight, the men had borne this insult in silence for a few days, but they weren't about to remain quiet when one of their men was assaulted. Several white noncommissioned officers ran up with their automatic pistols drawn as African American troops crowded around, ready to settle the score.

A black officer pushed through the crowd and demanded an explanation from the white NCOs, a gutsy move that calmed the situation down enough for his men to cool off and march back to their quarters. Unwilling to let the matter drop, the African American officer reported it to the camp commandant, who promised an investigation. "This incident restrained, for the time being, the intimidating impulses that existed with the white officers and noncommissioned officers," a member of the regiment wrote later. Another infuriating insult quickly followed when the regiment's white officers strung a curtain between their side of the barracks and the much smaller side occupied by the African Americans. "A feeling of disdain and disgust was justly aroused both in the Negro officers and the men, and shouldered day after day, only to be aggravated by some other disagreeable event. Thus it was that the first ten days in France were spent."

The 372nd was composed of National Guard troops from the District of Columbia, Ohio, Massachusetts, Connecticut, and Maryland and, unlike the 371st, had a mix of white and African American officers. The 371st had white officers only, Southerners who seemed to get along better with the African American men in the ranks, most of them draftees from South Carolina. Raised in the South and accustomed to entrenched discrimination, the soldiers of the 371st may have been more willing to let racial slights pass and not complain. That's how they'd learned to survive in a part of the country where lynchings were still a common occurrence.

TWO DAYS AFTER arriving at Brest, the 371st boarded the cramped, toy-size French railway cars that produced laughs until the men realized they actually had to squeeze into them and make do for a long trip. Each car was painted with the words 40 HOMMES, 8 CHEVAUX, meaning that forty men or eight horses could fit inside. There were no seats, bathrooms, or windows. The occupants had to sit on soiled straw and relax as best they could until the train stopped and they were allowed to climb out for a hurried break to relieve themselves. Their freight train rolled along at twenty to thirty miles an hour through a long, rainy day and night until they arrived at Vaubecourt, a small town nearly four hundred miles from Brest.

It was 1:00 a.m. and still pouring when Stowers and the others pried themselves out of the cramped boxcars. The regiment was greeted by a cadre of French officers who were shocked to see all the baggage and wondering where to put it, since the new arrivals would soon be getting French equipment. The regiment's commanders, surprised there were no American officers in the welcoming party, learned the truth at a nearby rail station where there was a telephone. A quick call to AEF headquarters at Chaumont confirmed it. Their unit "had been turned over to the French Command." Until that moment they had no idea that General Pershing had agreed to loan the French four African American infantry regiments, including the 371st and 372nd. Pershing insisted that the regiments would be returned to American command after the crisis ended, but that never happened. "Unfortunately, they soon became identified with the French and there was no opportunity to assemble them as an American Division," the US commander wrote in his memoirs. "Very much to my regret these regiments never served with us."

Stowers's first order of business was to line up his company for a nearly four-mile hike in the darkness and rain to the village of Marat-la-Grand, a centuries-old farming community where they were quartered in stables, barns, sheds—wherever they could find enough space to lie down. The rest of the regiment was sent to another village and to Rembercourt a few miles away, where the headquarters command post was set up.

The men were startled in the morning when they got a look at their new surroundings. The villages where they were bivouacked had been heavily shelled during the first German drive in 1914, and the scars of the fighting were visible everywhere. Each of these small towns had a church, a public square, and a cluster of homes and shops. Many roofs were missing; jagged holes were punched through the stone walls and timbered ceilings; and all the churches were in ruins. The sound of hundreds of guns arrayed on the Verdun front less than fifteen miles away brought it home.

Over the next few days, Stowers was the main conduit of information for his company and often had plenty of surprising news to pass along. For starters, they were getting new equipment, all of it French. The Springfield rifles recently issued at Camp Jackson and the source of much soldierly pride were being replaced with the French Lebel. A poor substitute for the American rifle, the Lebel wasn't accurate at long range and carried only three rounds in its magazine instead of the Springfield's five. At the same time, the broad-bladed American bayonet was being replaced with the longer, rapier-like French model. Considered crucial for tactics that stressed artillery bombardment followed by a frontal assault, the bayonet had long been the French army's principal offensive weapon. The men weren't happy about either option, and many of them armed themselves with long, curve-bladed "bolo knives" to augment their new bayonets.

Stowers and his men wore the American army's khaki uniform, but their helmets were French. The Adrian helmet, named for the general who designed it, was made of steel painted horizon blue with a raised crown, a short visor, and a medallion embossed on the front of an exploding bomb. It was lighter and had more style than the wide-brimmed British "Tommy" helmet worn by the

Americans. The 371st also wore French leggings, strips of leather wrapped around the legs from the top of the boots to midcalf, that were considerably more durable than the cotton leggings worn by the British and Americans.

The regiment began intensive training with French instructors, who explained the essentials of trench warfare, what to expect, and how to improve the odds of staying alive. The Americans were taught how to use mortars and the light, jam-prone Chauchat machine gun nicknamed the "cho-cho," an awkward weapon with a pistol grip that could be fired from the hip and was considered indispensable for attacking trenches. Working with translators, the men learned how to recognize the distinctive sounds of incoming and outgoing shells and their calibers and how to gauge how much time they had after a bombardment ended to scramble out of their dugouts and get into firing position to meet an attack.

Of crucial importance was learning how to tell when shells were carrying gas—they made a low-impact plopping sound when they hit the ground—and how to slip their masks over their faces and control their breathing. They were taught not to run away in panic during a gas attack, when a soldier was most likely to gulp for air and suck the deadly vapors into his lungs. They found out they could recognize gas by its smell and that mustard gas, the most deadly of all, smelled like garlic or onions, clung to low places, and could burn the skin at the slightest contact even days later. They were repeatedly reminded that a soldier who got his gas mask on in time and kept his cool could fight and survive. "The practical lessons in trench warfare were priceless," their commanding officer wrote, "far more valuable than the close-order drill and rifle-range lessons of their too-brief training in the United States."

The tutorials included the basics in trying to keep free of lice, an impossibility, and protecting food supplies from rats. Less important, but probably the source of the most complaints and grumbling to noncoms like Stowers, was the French food ration. Their new meal plan was like nothing else these Americans from the Deep South had experienced, emphasizing *la soupe*, a poor substitute for the hearty stews and cornbread they preferred. The French wine ration also meant trouble, an incredible two quarts of red wine per day per man. Fearing the consequences, American officers made sure wine was never issued to the 371st; instead, the men were given more sugar for their coffee.

Lessons were held on how to handle French money, and C Company had a "finance school" to explain how it was valued and changed and that a franc was the equivalent of a quarter. The colorful five-, ten-, and twenty-franc notes looked like play money to the men, who were paid in French currency. Their pay rate—a dollar a day plus an extra bonus for overseas duty—astounded the French soldiers, who received less and marveled at the lively dice games that broke out after every payday. "The first time the French saw our men sit down, roll the bones and pick up anywhere from twenty to five hundred francs at one cast of the dice, they nearly died."

THE 371ST RECEIVED something else from their French instructors and from the residents of the villages and farms were they were bivouacked, something they had never experienced in the United States: expressions of gratitude. They were thanked repeatedly for their service by men and women who didn't hesitate to invite them into their shops and homes. A white officer with the regiment, Lieutenant John Smith of Greenville, South Carolina, described what he witnessed at places like Rembercourt and Marat-la-Grande. "The colored men were given different treatment by the French people from what they had been accustomed to receiving at home. The French people couldn't grasp the idea of discrimination on account of race.

"They said the colored men were soldiers, wearing the American uniform, and fighting in the common cause, and they could not see why they should be discriminated against socially. They received the men in their churches and homes and places of entertainment. The men accepted this, and it did not seem to appear strange to them. They seemed to understand that the customs over there were different from ours in the South, and let it go at that."

German planes were already flying over their lines, scouting out how many new troops were moving up to the front. The German aircraft had a distinctive low-pitched whine, and the men usually picked up the sound of the engine first, then seconds later spotted a German Albatross or Fokker, a black cross painted on the fuselage and wings, buzzing over the camp at several hundred feet as white puffs of antiaircraft fire burst around it. The pilots flew daringly low, so low their faces could be seen behind the cockpit windshields.

As the days passed, rumors spread that the Germans were nearing a breakthrough in the north around Verdun and that spies had been captured wearing French uniforms. Their French instructors repeatedly reminded the Americans that the Germans were formidable fighters. The message: expect no mercy.

CHAPTER 10

Lost in the Fog

CAPTAIN BRYAN STARED into the murky gloom from the *Leviathan's* bridge, hoping for a break in the heavy fog that had suddenly rolled in, the kind the Brittany coast was notorious for in early May. They were nearly one hundred miles off the French coast, and other ships were somewhere out there in the white mist, including four American destroyers that had been shadowing them ever since they entered the submarine danger zone. With visibility choked off to less than fifty yards, the destroyers were impossible to see, and a radio call in these submarine-infested waters was out of the question. Bryan gave the order he'd dreaded: All engines slow!

The forty-six hand-fired coal boilers that had been pushing the *Leviathan* through the Atlantic at nearly nineteen knots cut the ship's speed to a crawl. They were now almost dead in the water with nearly twelve thousand men and women aboard, including the crew. As with every one of her wartime cruises, no ship in history had ever carried as many passengers. If she took a torpedo, it would be catastrophic.

Every time Bryan put to sea, he was setting another record, transporting nine thousand soldiers on this voyage, most of them members of the Eleventh Infantry and Fifteenth Machine Gun Battalion. The ship also carried aboard over four hundred nurses from two base hospitals; the young ladies loved to dance and play cards late into the night in the Navy Officers' Lounge on C deck. There'd been plenty of beefing from army officers, who weren't allowed inside the ornately paneled navy lounge, formerly the *Vaterland*'s beer garden, but for the most part the mood aboard ship had been upbeat. Other than the oppressive overcrowding belowdecks and their running into this fog, there hadn't been any trouble on the *Leviathan*'s third voyage of the war and her first to France.

The seas had been remarkably calm, especially in the Gulf Stream, where the water temperature sometimes hit 73 degrees. The warm weather attracted schools of porpoises and large migratory dolphins known as blackfish, a big, sleek fish with a sharklike dorsal fin that had an unsettling way of resembling a submarine periscope as it cut through the water. A day earlier, the ship's starboard batteries had mistakenly opened fire on one.

The run of fine weather started almost from the moment the *Leviathan* pulled out of New York Harbor on April 24 and had held until May 1, when thick sheets of fog rolled in from the east. Bryan ordered all lookouts to keep a sharp watch for ships and for the telltale wake of a torpedo. If an enemy submarine had been shadowing them before the fog swept in and had stuck close these last few hours, her captain might be rewarded with the shot of a lifetime.

Bryan had another problem. They were lost.

It was hard to get his bearings in the fog, and the charts weren't much help.

The near whiteout lasted for two hours. No one could see a thing off the bow or stern, until a lookout gave a shout. He'd spotted a ship off the starboard beam!

Bryan turned to see the dark outline of a ship slowly emerging through an opening in the fog bank, a sleek-looking vessel with a stubby smokestack. It was one of the destroyers that had steamed from Queenstown, Ireland, to rendezvous with them off the coast of France. The skipper of the smaller ship skillfully maneuvered alongside.

An ensign stepped onto the *Leviathan*'s flying bridge and shouted through a megaphone, "We don't know where we are. Do you?"

The answer was prompt and short.

"No!"

It was like a punch in the stomach. They were a perfect target.

Earlier that morning Bryan had received a secret "movement order," which provided the latest information on the location of enemy mines and submarines. U-boats were known to be patrolling the northwestern approaches to Brest, and at least fifteen ships had been sunk there over the last two months. They were definitely in a bad place.

Bryan weighed his options. They could get under way again and possibly risk a collision, or they could hold their position and hope for the best. Before he could make a decision, there was a shout from the destroyer.

"Black and white buoy on starboard beam!"

Good news! The buoy meant they were right where they were supposed to be, in one of the main channels that led straight into Brest's guarded harbor.

Bryan gave his order: All ahead slow.

As long as they knew their position, it was better to get under way again, fog or no fog.

With the *Leviathan* steaming slowly toward Brest, the twice-daily abandon-ship drills continued, and Elizabeth Weaver happily discovered that as soon as the bugler sounded the alarm, she was able to get to her lifeboat—each held twenty-nine passengers—as quickly and easily as it took to walk to her place in the dining saloon, table number five, seat number two. Elizabeth had soon mastered all the other shipboard bugle calls—those for dinner, taps, and reveille. Her appetite was excellent, as it almost always was, and she enjoyed the oranges, oatmeal, bacon, scrambled eggs, and fresh bread served at breakfast.

She was having the adventure of her life. On one of her first nights at sea, she spotted Captain Bryan in the dining saloon. He usually ate his meals alone in his cabin, but on this evening he stopped at some of the tables, chatting politely with the army officers. Elizabeth found him a "very fine looking man [with] snow white hair. Stunning looking."

The nurses shared tables in the dining saloon with hundreds of army officers but had little chance to interact with the enlisted men except when everyone poured out on deck during the abandonship drills. Elizabeth and the other nurses from the University of Pennsylvania's Base Hospital 20 and from Base Hospital 33 in Albany, New York, had cabins on C and D decks, whereas most of the doughboys bunked on the lower decks. She and two other nurses shared a cabin in which signs of the ship's former Germanic elegance were hard to miss. The spacious room had four beds, two marble washstands with water taps marked KALT, HEISSE, and AUF, two full-length mirrors, electric fans, and a plush carpet. Elizabeth once got a peek at the Kaiser's Suite, with its wide picture window offering a breathtaking ocean view, rosewood furnishings, piano, private bath, and a sumptuous dining room decorated with Sèvres china and a gold tea set. Many of the signs posted throughout the ship were still in German.

During their last days at sea, the nurses slept in their clothes and kept their life jackets within arm's reach. "The jackets," Elizabeth wrote, "have a wide Elizabethan ruff around the neck and are tied all the way down the front and make the thinnest person look as if she weighed 200 pounds." Before the fog settled in, Elizabeth and her friends took walks around the upper decks, and in good weather it was fun to flop down on a bed of life jackets near the bow, where they could watch the ship's wake churn out far behind them as they wrote letters home.

Elizabeth also loved standing at the railing on C deck and letting the spray splash her face, marveling at how the color of the water seemed to change with the sky, turning gray when the clouds were low and then, as if a switch had been thrown, becoming deep blue when the weather was fine, as it had been for most of the voyage.

She could tell the *Leviathan* was steering a zigzag course, noticing one afternoon that the "sun [was] on one side of the vessel and shortly afterward it was on the other side." With the ocean unusually calm, Elizabeth didn't have any trouble with seasickness, and at night she liked the sensation of being rocked to sleep. She never took off the charm bracelet her mother had given her.

Elizabeth worked a shift in the sick bay with nine other nurses from Base Hospital 20. There were about one hundred patients there, most of them with minor illnesses and sprains, but a few had broken bones. Elizabeth spent most of her time on duty making bandages, rolling the pieces of linen into long strips, and checking temperatures. She liked talking to these young men, inquiring where they were from and offering to write letters home for them.

Dances were held almost every night in the Navy Officers' Lounge—formerly the social hall. On the *Leviathan*'s last evening at sea, a jazz band played and the talk was about their arrival in Brest.

Then the fog swept in. Elizabeth went to bed that evening wearing her life jacket and praying that a submarine wouldn't find them. She'd been warned that this was the most dangerous moment of the voyage and that the U-boats would do anything possible to sink them. It was a long time before she fell asleep.

What a relief it was then to wake up in the morning and see that the sky was clearing and that the ship was moving along at a brisk clip. When she and her cabinmates saw four US destroyers flanking the *Leviathan*, two on each side, she thought, Let a U-boat come now. Let them dare!

As they approached the coast of France, the fog gave way to bright sun and a metallic blue sky. A rainbow as broad and bright as any Elizabeth had ever seen suddenly arced across the horizon in front of them—"a good omen."

"Vive la France!" she wrote in her diary. "We've Come! We heard you calling us! Viva la France! La belle France!"

Standing at the railing, she watched as the ship came through the Goulet, the narrow strait barely a mile and a half wide that connected the Atlantic with the Brest roadstead. Two French airplanes flew overhead patrolling for submarines as the *Leviathan* was escorted into the bay by one of the American destroyers—the others had peeled off—and four French patrol boats. Even anchored two miles out in the crowded harbor, where it tied up to the large floating buoy brought over from New York, the ship looked like Gulliver among the Lilliputians.

Troops immediately started unloading, the soldiers filing down five gangways into barges that had pulled alongside. Each man carried his full equipment, including a blanket roll and rifle. From her vantage topside, Elizabeth noticed that tomahawks hung from some of their belts. When the barges started to move away, packed to the brim with soldiers sitting on long benches, the army bands broke out in marching tunes while thousands of men still waiting their turn on board shouted out good luck to those who were departing. The unloading continued through the night and into the following morning.

Elizabeth wound up spending two more days on the ship because there was no place for all the nurses to stay in Brest, and army officials weren't about to send them to the raw encampment rapidly expanding just south of the city. They finally left the ship on Sunday, May 5, boarding a British lighter for the two-mile trip ashore. The nurses, Elizabeth thought, looked chic in their long blue military overcoats buttoned to the neck, dark blue velour hats, and tan shoes and gloves. Their send-off was boisterous, as most of the ship's two thousand crewmen lined the railings two and three rows deep to cheer them on their way. Elizabeth and the other nurses shouted their thanks to these "sailor boys" as their ferry shoved off.

"I wonder where we go from here?" she later jotted in her diary.

The answer came soon enough. She was sent to a fashionable vacation resort in the Auvergne Mountains, where an army of workers was transforming posh hotels with names like the Continental, Du Parc, Excelsior, and Hermitage into hospitals. A railroad line that connected the village with Paris two hundred miles away soon became one of the main corridors for troop trains carrying the American wounded, who were starting to arrive from the battlefields.

Hand Grenades and Brownings

THE SIX ARMY instructors lined up on the main firing range at Camp Meade, where the silhouette targets were six hundred yards out. Wearing the army's distinctive Montana Peak campaign hat, each was armed with one of the new Browning light machine guns that were just starting to come off the production lines. They stood with their legs slightly apart in the classic standing firing position as they made the final sight adjustments and checked the magazines on the long-barreled weapons.

Then the order was shouted: Begin firing!

Sergeant Royal Johnson and the other noncommissioned officers in the 313th Infantry flinched as the first shots boomed out in a demonstration of raw firepower such as they'd never seen from a handheld weapon. The .30–06 rounds tore the targets to shreds, ripping up clouds of dirt behind them as the instructors opened up with fully automatic fire. During some of the earlier training sessions, the noncoms had watched in awe as belt-fed machine guns that fired at a rate of 450 rounds a minute tore into oil drums, making them jump like tin cans.

The new Browning Automatic Rifle, or BAR, was meant to provide "walking fire" for soldiers attacking German trenches, forcing the enemy to keep their heads down. The weapon was just coming into service, and Johnson's regiment was one of the first to receive them. The young congressman, already a fine marksman from his many deer and grouse hunts in South Dakota, was skilled with the army's main infantry weapon, the Springfield rifle, but it was nothing like the Browning, which fired a twenty-round clip. As a sergeant, he wasn't likely to carry a BAR, but every soldier was expected to have some familiarity with the weapon, and he was sure to have paid attention as the instructors demonstrated how quickly the new weapons could be field-stripped and cleaned.

It was early May, and Johnson was finishing two weeks of intensive training at the "Big Range," the live-fire range where the men lived in white dome-shaped canvas tents on the edge of Camp Meade. The new military base was located on eight thousand acres of what had once been orchards and farm fields in Anne Arundel County, Maryland, about midway between Baltimore and Washington.

After enlisting as a private on January 6 with the 313th, which drew heavily from the Baltimore and Washington, DC, area, Johnson had recently been promoted to sergeant. One of at least four members of the House of Representatives who were in uniform—the New York congressman Fiorello La Guardia was among them—he'd made a comment that was picked up by some of the Washington papers when he boarded a train for the trip to Camp Meade: "I'm going to be the lamest private in camp."

The congressman slowly worked himself back into the physical condition he'd enjoyed as a catcher for the Yankton College baseball team in South Dakota. He was thirty-five years old, and the training was rougher than he might have expected. By April his regiment was pulling twenty-mile round-trip hikes to the outskirts of Baltimore and back. On an outing where each man carried a sixty-five-pound pack, not one member of the 313th had fallen by the wayside, whereas dozens of exhausted soldiers from other regiments of the 79th Division dropped out and were pinned with red tags to be picked up by the ambulances that followed behind the long column.

There had also been savage practice sessions with the bayonet. Squaring off with an instructor and using rifles equipped with wooden bayonets, soldiers found out quickly about feints, speed, and how to pick the best angle of attack. Of critical importance was developing the tough mental attitude that convinced a soldier that no matter how hopeless or desperate it seemed, he'd survive if he fought hard and smart. Trained to be aggressive, infantrymen were encouraged to growl, scream, and grunt as they closed with an enemy during bayonet encounters, where a moment's hesitation could mean death. Johnson also learned how to use the bayonet as a knife. When stealth and silence were critical, especially at night, the American bayonet with its seventeen-inch blade was the weapon of choice, and the instructors—some of them French infantry officers—emphasized repeatedly that at such moments a soldier had to kill his man. To delay for even a second was to risk death. Encounters in the trenches were explosive, bloody, and fast, and the Germans were exceptionally good.

Johnson also learned that the hand grenade was often a game changer in trench battles, and that British and French soldiers frequently went on night patrols armed only with pistols and grenades, leaving behind all other weapons that could rattle or clank and give them away. Along with training in gas warfare—they wouldn't be issued masks until they got to France—artillery tactics and how best to neutralize machine guns were subjects barely touched on at all. Some of the men were given the chance to toss a few disarmed grenades, but most didn't pick up a live grenade until they reached Europe. It wasn't until he arrived on the battlefield that Johnson found out how much their training had neglected to cover and how unprepared they were for what was coming.

The regiment's commander, a fifty-year-old colonel named

Claude Sweezey, was a career soldier and West Point graduate from Indiana who'd been in the cavalry and had the horse soldier's compact, wiry physique. Sweezey spoke with a slight stammer, wasn't afraid of arguing with superiors, and seemed more interested at times in hosting dances and teas than in training. The camp was about twenty-five miles southwest of Baltimore, and the colonel frequently invited many of the city's most prominent citizens to these social gatherings. So many of the men and officers, quite a few of them lawyers like Johnson, came from the Baltimore area that the regiment was soon nicknamed "Baltimore's Own."

By late spring, few of these men could have had any illusions about what was at stake as they were hurried through their final days of training at the sprawling camp, where two-story frame barracks were being thrown up and occupied as fast as the carpenters could finish them. A recent comment by the French premier, Georges Clemenceau, to an American reporter had been widely circulated: "Tell your Americans to come quickly."

The German offensive, which had started in March and was renewed in April, had overrun 1,250 square miles of France, allowing the enemy's long-range guns to shell Paris, and showed no signs of slowing. General Erich von Ludendorff, the German High Command's chief strategist, was preparing yet another assault, this one aimed at the French.

With the war's outcome in doubt, Johnson made a rare trip to the Capitol on May 14 to vote in favor of legislation that gave President Wilson the wide-ranging authority to regulate government agencies and organize the nation's sputtering economy. The move was taken after a Senate investigative committee determined that the war effort had almost ground to a halt because of mismanagement at almost every stage of the military's supply chain. Using his emergency war powers, Wilson had already taken over the railroads by executive order in December 1917, and now he wanted to establish price guidelines and industrial priorities.

Johnson would have needed authorization to make the trip into Washington from Camp Meade, as preparations were moving full speed ahead to get the 313th ready to sail. As a sergeant he was sure to be noticed in his absence, but amid concerns that the so-called Overman Act might not pass Congress—the measure was named after its sponsor, the Democratic senator Lee Slater Overman of North Carolina—he was encouraged to get to the Capitol and vote.

Soon after Johnson, in uniform, took his seat, a page stopped at his desk and told him that the House Speaker, Champ Clark, wanted a word with him. He made his way to the Speaker's rostrum at the front of the chamber. James Beauchamp "Champ" Clark of Missouri—tall, heavyset, his snow-white hair parted down the middle—had managed to hang on to his office despite opposing America's entry into the war. He'd been a near miss as a presidential candidate in 1914, losing to Wilson after thirty votes at the Democratic convention. Johnson might have expected the sixty-seven-year-old Clark to discuss the politics of the vote.

Instead, the Speaker leaned over the edge of his desk and shook his hand.

"Royal," he said, smiling, "do you realize that you are the first enlisted man who ever [voted] in the history of the United States? I don't know what some others may think of that," the Speaker said. "But I'm with you no matter who objects."

As the 313th continued getting ready to ship out, its commanding officers could be grateful the men were healthy despite weeks of intense training and bivouacking in tents during one of the coldest winters on record on the eastern seaboard. In the spring of 1918, as one historian put it, "few paid attention to how many were coming down with the sniffles in America."

CHAPTER 11

"Blitzkatarrh," or "Flanders Fever"

I F ANYONE HAD been paying attention, and very few were, the flu outbreak at the Ford Motor Company plant in Detroit in the spring of 1918 might have triggered warning bells. During the month of March, 1,066 employees were sent home, most of them for a minimum of four days. A more virulent outbreak came in April, when five hundred of the 1,900 inmates at the prison in San Quentin, California, fell sick with the flu and at least three men died. Three more deaths were reported in the small town of Haskell, Kansas, where eighteen severe cases of flu occurred suddenly after an unusually cold winter.

Nothing appeared unduly remarkable about these seemingly random events. It was well known that influenza frequently occurred during the winter or early spring. No one was keeping track—a national health service didn't exist yet—so a link wasn't established between these outbreaks and others that were starting to flare up in cities and towns all over the country. Flu wasn't a reportable disease in 1918, which explains why few records were kept even in cases that resulted in death.

The military more closely monitored its members, keeping detailed records that might have provided a more comprehensive picture of the first wave of the great flu pandemic of 1918, but even after a troubling outbreak at Camp Funston, an army training base at Fort Riley, Kansas, the dots hadn't been connected. On the morning of March 11, a company cook there reported sick to the hospital and was soon followed by nearly one hundred other men in various stages of collapse. Within a few days, five hundred soldiers were so ill they couldn't pull themselves out of bed, and by the end of the month, thousands were sick. It got worse: "the flu epidemic was ominously trailed by a pneumonia epidemic—233 cases that month, of which 48 ended in death."

The navy also experienced a number of seemingly random flu outbreaks, which in hindsight strongly suggested an epidemic in its early stages. In January, "a suspicious outbreak" of twenty-one cases occurred on board the USS *Minneapolis*, an aging cruiser with a crew of 370 anchored at the navy yard in Philadelphia. A month later, four other ships had similar outbreaks, including vessels moored in Boston and New York. The worst outbreak by far that month roared through the newly opened Naval Radio School on the campus of Harvard University in Boston, a brand-new high-tech facility where as many as four hundred of the five thousand students were laid low, including at least eleven men who developed pneumonia. No deaths were reported.

In all these cases, especially those resulting in death, the flu victims didn't fit the usual profile: middle aged to elderly or very young, in poor physical shape and offering little resistance to serious illness. Those who tended to die that spring were males between twenty-one and twenty-nine years of age, often in peak physical condition and with no history of significant illnesses. That alone should have raised some concerns, but except for the Army Medical Corps, no state or national agencies had been set up to investigate such outbreaks. Also missing was any kind of death analysis from the many American cities where short-lived spikes in flu cases were reported that spring, cases sometimes followed by fatal pneumonia, a nasty complication that initially escaped notice. In earlier flu epidemics, victims hadn't been nearly as likely to develop pneumonia.

New York City, Chicago, and San Francisco, to name a few far-flung examples, all reported higher-than-usual numbers of flu cases that spring. And in Chicago at least one pathologist noticed something that later came back to haunt him: during autopsies performed on flu and pneumonia victims, the lungs were often churned almost to pulp by virulent hemorrhaging. Army pathologists were starting to make the same rarely seen observations— lungs that were "so abnormal that pieces of them, which should have been as buoyant as a child's balloon, sank when placed in water. Their most conspicuous feature was the enormous quantity of thin, bloody fluid."

SOMETHING THAT SOUNDS a lot like the modern flu was first described by the Greek doctor Hippocrates in 412 BC. The illness popped up with distressing regularity in Europe over the centuries, and by 1699 Cotton Mather was writing that the Massachusetts Colony had been ravaged by what was most likely flu, especially in Boston, where many deaths were reported. Pandemics cropped up in the United States in 1847 and 1889, and a flu epidemic had occurred as recently as 1915, but none of them compared with the 1918 event.

The outbreak that spring was more advanced in Europe, spreading first among the hundreds of thousands of troops on both sides of the lines and from there to the cities. At least 10 percent of the sailors who manned the British Grand Fleet were laid low that May. The virus raced through both the British and French armies. Among the Germans, it hit hardest on the western front, where ailing French and English soldiers probably sent the illness across no-man's land. The Germans called it *"Blitzkatarrh,"* or "Flanders Fever." To the Americans, English, and French, it was usually referred to as flu, grippe, *la grippe*, Three-Day-Fever, or its punchier derivative, Knock-Me-Down-Fever.

On May 9, the US Twenty-Sixth Infantry Division had the twin misfortune of enduring both a German gas attack and a flu outbreak. On April 20, the "Yankee Division" had been bloodied during the German spring offensive when it was hit with high-explosive shells, gas, and a storm trooper raid along a normally quiet sector on the Marne. Over five hundred men were killed, gassed, or wounded—casualties that were rivaled by the flu attack in May that sent hundreds more to hospitals. The Forty-Second Division, the famous "Rainbow Division" that got its nickname because it included units from twenty-six states and was said to spread across the country like a rainbow, was likewise battered by flu during that same difficult month, and once again some nasty complications started appearing. "For most [victims] it was mild, but some developed a secondary pneumonia of a most virulent and deadly type."

The increase in flu cases that spring wasn't widely reported in the United States or in Europe. According to a Navy medical document, "At that time the disease was more or less mild in character and there were not enough fatalities to excite real apprehension." One exception was in Spain, where an estimated eight million people fell ill in May and June. Spain wasn't a belligerent nation, so wartime censorship didn't conceal the extent of the epidemic in that country, and it was soon called "Spanish influenza." Some doctors there thought the outbreak would have been even more severe if the snow-capped Pyrenees hadn't served as a barrier to block or at least impede the spread of the disease from France and Italy.

Soldiers and sailors on their way to and from Europe aboard troop transports that spring were also coming down with the flu, sometimes accompanied by pneumonia. A few weeks after a sailor died aboard the *Leviathan* in April, thirty-six soldiers from the Fifteenth US Calvary were infected and six died while on their way to France on another ship. A second sailor died from pneumonia on the *Leviathan* on May 15, 1918, while the ship was undergoing yet another frantic refitting in Hoboken aimed at adding more bunks and increasing the number of troops she could carry.

The demand for troops was simply too great, the need too compelling. When the time came, the world's largest troop carrier would sail for France no matter how many desperately sick soldiers barely made it up the gangplanks.

An Even Better Target

EARLY ON THE afternoon of May 2, 1918, a U-boat attacked an armed troop transport on her way to New York about one thousand miles west of Brest. Captain Bryan learned about the encounter as soon as the *Leviathan* returned from France on May 12. Surfacing about seven thousand yards behind the USS *Pocahontas*, the submarine had opened fire with two cannons. The gun crews on the American ship returned fire but their weapons were outranged by the Germans', so the only thing to do was make a run for it. The ship's engines squeezed out just over sixteen knots, and the captain was shocked to discover that the sub could almost go that fast on the surface, a disturbing performance considering that the maximum speed for a transport was typically thirteen to fourteen knots. The implications were grave; it meant a submarine like this could overtake most merchant ships or transports.

For fifteen minutes, high-explosive shells bracketed the zigzagging ship and showered the bridge with shrapnel fragments. The submarine swung her broadside and commenced rapidly firing both guns, lacing the transport with more steel fragments, but not scoring any direct hits. As the *Pocahontas* pulled out of range, the German gun crew took one last shot, which fell just short. Surprised that he'd been ambushed so far out at sea, the captain sent an urgent radio alert that a newer, faster, and more long-ranged German submarine was on the prowl.

U-boat activity west of the Azores had been a rarity, but in the late spring of 1918, as America was increasing the number of troops sent to Europe, U-boats of a radically new design were ranging over a far wider area. The fear was that these larger, faster German subs could attack at any time or place they wished in the Atlantic, including the coastal waters of the United States. The submarine that chased the *Pocahontas* "in all probability was one of the first headed for our Eastern seaboard." The boat's presence so far beyond the western boundary of the North Atlantic danger zone meant that destroyers that previously rendezvoused with troop ships three hundred miles from shore would have to push these critical linkups even farther out to sea.

On May 20 Bryan received secret orders that gave him an update on the most recent submarine information available. As with earlier U-boat alerts, the "greatest activity" was in the English and Irish Channels, and he now also had to consider an encounter in the mid-Atlantic. The attack on the *Pocahontas* by a long-range submarine meant there were no comparatively safe waters anymore. His orders directed that he leave Hoboken on May 22, clear the Ambrose Lightship at the entrance to New York Bay, and proceed for five days at 18.5 knots until he rendezvoused with his destroyer escort on May 28. They'd steam for Belle Isle, a small, crescent-shaped island off the coast of Brittany, then head straight to Brest, where he was expected to arrive on May 31.

During the ship's nearly two-week refitting in Hoboken, Bryan had to oversee yet another expansion of the *Leviathan*'s troop capacity, which added space for 700 extra soldiers by cramming even more of the tiered bunks into the few open spaces that remained on the lower decks. This would increase the total passenger count to 11,450, including 10,700 troops—most of them from the 131st and 318th Infantry—and 750 navy personnel on their way to France.

Counting crew members, the *Leviathan* would carry 14,000 soldiers and sailors.

Such astronomical numbers aboard a single ship likely made the navy's senior command gasp, but there were no plausible alternatives. American and British transport ships were maxed out, and the Germans' big offensive push was gathering momentum. Soldiers would have to share bunks, a practice known then as "turn in and out," or today as "hot racking," meaning they'd take turns sleeping. After navy transports carried eighty thousand soldiers over in March and twice that in April, the number would explode to a quarter-million men in May. From July until the Armistice in November, ten thousand American soldiers arrived in France every day.

On Monday, May 20, the same day Bryan received his report on enemy submarine activity, soldiers began boarding the *Leviathan* at 11:35 a.m. and continued coming aboard in long lines until 7:50 a.m. the following day. By the twenty-second, the last of the baggage was loaded, and at 4:03 p.m., the lines were cast off and the ship backed away from her slip into the Hudson River. After the tugs got her turned around, Bryan gave a terse order to get under way: One-third ahead, both engines.

With the pilot standing next to him and conning the ship from the bridge, they passed Battery Park at 4:42 p.m. Six minutes later, the ship sailed by the Statue of Liberty on the starboard beam, and within an hour it entered Ambrose Channel. Bryan ordered the engines stopped to drop off the pilot, who had been trained to handle the tricky maneuvering of big ships in and out of port and now boarded a small cutter sent out to meet him. The *Leviathan* continued at one-third speed for a few minutes until the captain gave another order to the engine room.

Standard speed, seventeen knots.

By 6:45 p.m., as the ship turned into the Atlantic with the sun setting behind her, Bryan and other officers on the bridge had their last fleeting contact with the mainland, the flashing white light from the powerful Ambrose Lightship stationed nine miles to the east.

AT ABOUT THE same time, a German submarine, Unterseeboot-90, was sailing to her cruising station three hundred miles west of the French coast. It was the fifth war patrol for Kapitanleutnant Walter Remy, one of Germany's most aggressive and skilled submarine commanders. His boat was based at Kiel, where over a decade earlier he'd attended the prestigious German Naval Academy. His mission was to sink as many Allied ships as possible. The task had become more difficult ever since the British and Americans started sending their ships across the North Atlantic in convoys, making it harder to pick off loners. Even then, a U-boat skipper had to be careful. Those solitary vessels often looked too good to be true and could turn out to be a "Q-ship," a heavily armed raider decked out to look like a merchantman. Their disguises sometimes included sheets draped on the masts to resemble sails. "Get too close to one of those," wrote one naval historian, "and a U-boat could find itself in real trouble."

On May 24, two days after the *Leviathan* pulled away from her pier in Hoboken, Remy decided to take a chance on a small convoy he'd spotted off the western coast of Ireland, six steamers and their escorts. Unfortunately, his boat was leaking oil, and when he maneuvered the U-90 into position for a torpedo attack, the destroyer escorts spotted the long slick and moved in for the kill, pelting the sea with depth charges. The submarine took a hammering but escaped damage, yet another example of the exceptional strength and design of the steel hulls of German U-boats. It was one of the major technological surprises of the war to discover that these seemingly fragile-looking vessels could dive to unexpected depths, nearly two hundred feet, while taking a ferocious pounding. They could also disappear beneath the surface within thirty seconds, which didn't give a pursuing destroyer much time to drop depth charges. The U-90, one of Germany's new long-range submarines, carried sixteen torpedoes and could reach nearly seventeen knots on the surface and just over eight knots submerged; the cruising range was an impressive 7,600 miles. Her twin diesels generated 2,400 horsepower, and she was armed with a 105-millimeter gun, a machine gun, and four torpedo tubes—two on the bow and two in the stern. Remy's submarine was a formidable weapon.

His crew consisted of thirty-two enlisted men and four officers, and since going into operation nine months earlier, the U-90 had logged 28,000 nautical miles during four patrols. Besides the leaky oil tank that had nearly sunk him, the starboard engine was balky, but Remy wasn't about to turn back, not when he still carried all of his torpedoes, the larger 50-centimeter models. He wasn't heading back to his base on the Baltic Sea until he'd fired as many of them as possible at Allied targets.

The U-boat skipper—a picture shows a dark-haired officer in a peacoat standing on the U-90's deck with the rest of the crew—wasn't happy with missing a shot at the convoy. Remy perhaps wasn't in a league with Korvettenkapitan Lothan von Arnauld de la Periere, the ace of aces of U-boat commanders, who sank fifty-four ships during one twenty-four-day cruise in 1916, but he was an exceptionally audacious commander, and if he'd failed with the convoy, maybe he could get a shot at an even better target. Perhaps a troopship would come his way.

CHAPTER 12

U-Boat Attack

THE DAYTIME WEATHER was beautiful for late May—blue skies, temperatures in the upper sixties, and that rarest of all conditions for the North Atlantic, glassy-smooth seas. It was equally delightful in the evening, but Captain Bryan of the *Leviathan* and Kapitanleutnant Walter Remy, the skipper of the U-90, weren't paying close attention to the fine late-spring weather. They were more concerned about the bright full moon that made their vessels stand out in black silhouette against the sky. Both captains were taking precautions—Remy limiting his cruising time on the surface and keeping lookouts posted; Bryan making sure the no-smoking rule was vigorously enforced. A soldier who'd been caught lighting up a cigar when they were one day out of New York had been thrown in the brig.

Plagued by mechanical problems, Remy's cruise had been far more challenging than Bryan's. Ever since he'd reached his patrol station, several hundred miles off the French coast, the German captain had been struggling with a misfiring diesel and had had trouble raising and lowering his main periscope. At one point it came crashing down, narrowly missing him.

The *Leviathan*, by comparison, hadn't had any significant trouble, but Bryan had had to deal with a serious medical emergency. The transport was two days at sea when an army officer trying to familiarize himself with the vast ship nearly had his leg severed during a routine test of the watertight doors. Somehow he'd turned the wrong way and stumbled, pinning his leg as the steel door came down. A navy doctor stitched him up, but the medical staff was worried he'd lose it.

On Wednesday, May 29, Remy was nearing the end of what had been a long, largely unsuccessful cruise that had started nearly four weeks earlier—but the U-boat captain's luck was about to change.

At 5:04 p.m., the *Leviathan* received an SOS message from the SS *Carlton*, a British tanker that had just been torpedoed and was sinking fast. The ship's position, 47 degrees north latitude and 20 west longitude, was less than one hundred miles away and right in the *Leviathan*'s path. Bryan ordered a change in course, dropping farther to the south; he didn't want to go anywhere near the stricken ship. Leaving the crew of forty men in open boats upset him greatly, but with a German submarine still out there, he had no choice. His orders were clear in such cases: He wasn't to respond to any SOS calls in the danger zone. There were absolutely no exceptions. German submarine commanders were notorious for sending out false distress calls, luring an unsuspecting ship their way and then sinking it with gunfire or a torpedo.

Earlier that morning, the *Leviathan* had rendezvoused with four American destroyers that were now flanking the big transport as she raced toward the French coast. As twilight darkened the horizon and the moon climbed, Bryan remained worried about the fate of the crewmen who'd abandoned the *Carlton*. At 7:34 p.m., over two hours after they received the first SOS, he flashed a message to the lead destroyer, the USS *O'Brien*.

"Recommend sending after dark vessel of escort to position where *Carlton* was reported torpedoed."

The commander of the destroyer escort may have been sympathetic, but this wasn't going to happen. His orders were equally clear and unequivocal. "No," he flashed back. "Our duty is with you."

A few hours earlier, Remy had had the good luck to intercept another outward-bound convoy far larger than the one he'd been unable to attack five days earlier off the Irish coast. Reaching the western limit of the danger zone, the convoy's destroyer escort had cut them loose and the ships had scattered. Moving in fast for the kill, the U-90 sank the SS *Begum*, a British freighter, then torpedoed the *Carlton*, scoring almost back-to-back hits. The submarine surfaced and shelled the burning tanker with its 105-millimeter gun to speed her on her way to the bottom. The ship was still in flames and barely hanging on when another tanker pulled into view, a sitting duck that realized the danger and quickly fled. Just as the U-90 started to give chase, her port diesel broke down. The captain was furious. "Unable to catch the tanker on just one engine," wrote historian Dwight R. Messimer, "Remy watched angrily as the tanker disappeared over the horizon."

Despite the success with the *Begum* and the *Carlton*, three times now in less than a week Remy had been forced to break off an attack on a convoy or on a straggler because of last-minute mechanical problems or because destroyers had spotted his leaking oil and had driven him down with depth charges. He'd been running the U-90 hard for weeks and was paying the price, but his engineers got the balky diesel back on line.

About that same time, Bryan increased the *Leviathan*'s speed to twenty-two knots as he changed course and started making a hard run for the French coast. "Moonlight held no charms for us," the ship's history recounts. "The rays reflecting upon the water lighted up the huge ship and made her a fine target for a lurking U-boat." Bryan made sure the lifeboat crews stayed at their posts and after a long, tense night was relieved to learn that another ship had picked up the *Carlton*'s survivors.

As dawn broke, more reports came in, including a radio transmission that a British dirigible had spotted oil slicks in the area of the *Leviathan*. Bryan also exchanged messages with the naval base at Brest, arranging a rendezvous with the small boat that carried the French pilot who would guide them into the harbor. The meeting never occurred.

AT 12:25 P.M. on May 30, with the green hills of Brest rising in the distance, an officer standing next to Bryan on the bridge noticed a sudden break in the water about two thousand yards off the *Leviathan*'s port bow. Lieutenant (Junior Grade) John Beebe, the ship's young assistant navigator, called out the location to the captain.

He reported that it looked like the wake of a submarine and that it was chasing them.

Bryan ordered them to hold their course, then sounded the general alarm.

He raised his glasses in the direction the lieutenant was pointing. Black smoke from a destroyer on that side obscured his vision, but soon he focused on a curling wave running along with the ship. "I saw the break [in the water]," he wrote afterward. "It was clearly the bow wave of a submarine not entirely submerged, moving at considerable speed."

Four minutes had elapsed since Beebe's first sighting, and now he could easily make out the conning tower. Hugging the *Leviathan*'s port side, the submarine was 750 yards out and running on a parallel course at about twelve to fourteen knots.

Bryan ordered the green-and-white flag raised, which signaled a submarine attack, and increased the *Leviathan*'s speed. He also directed the helmsman to stop zigzagging. If the ship continued weaving back and forth, the submarine would soon have an excellent shot at her fully exposed side. He kept the commands coming, ordering guns six and eight to open fire. Located on the ship's port side, they were the only cannons that could be brought to bear on the target. Their crews fired three flat-nosed rounds, the explosive shells sending up twenty-foot-high geysers of water near where the conning tower had last been spotted.

The submarine dived, disappearing beneath the surface only to reappear again thirty minutes later in roughly the same position. The same guns fired, seven shots booming out, followed a few minutes later by nine more rounds. For the next fifteen minutes the U-boat ran along with the *Leviathan* at a distance of about one thousand yards, playing a cat-and-mouse game, diving and resurfacing at short intervals—textbook tactics for German submarines trying to maneuver into position for a shot. It was common practice for a sub to make four or five quick periscope sightings, some for as short as five or ten seconds, as it moved within the preferred firing distance of under one thousand yards.

Each time the submarine appeared, Bryan ordered the same batteries to commence firing. At 1:19 p.m., the two guns fired seven more shots.

As the chase continued, the *Leviathan*'s decks filled with soldiers in khaki and dozens of blue-cloaked army nurses who'd quickly hurried topside from their lunch to watch the show. Taking positions along the railings, they greeted every shot with cheers and shouts of encouragement. It was almost like a ball game, the crowd going wild with each home run or touchdown. One of the destroyers, the *Cummings*, tried to reach the spot where the *Leviathan*'s shells were landing, then pulled back when they started falling short. Fearing they'd hit the ship, Bryan quickly ordered a cease-fire.

Throughout the nearly forty-minute encounter, the *Leviathan*'s officers, especially those on the bridge, consistently reported seeing a German submarine. The officer of the deck, another young lieutenant (junior grade), wrote on the following day that when the submarine surfaced for the last time at 1:19 p.m.—he had no doubt it was a U-boat—it was about 1,700 yards from the *Leviathan*. The gunners were just starting to find the range when Bryan called another cease-fire. He had no choice. A small French fishing boat suddenly veered between the *Leviathan* and the submarine, narrowly avoiding getting hit by one of the 105-pound shells. Taken aboard the *Leviathan* a short time later, the shaken captain knew how close he'd come to being blown out of the water.

The *Leviathan* didn't slow down until she reached the harbor entrance at 1:45 p.m. There was no question in Bryan's mind that they'd been stalked by a sub, and many of his officers believed more than one U-boat was involved and that the Germans had laid a careful trap, springing it at the exact moment the ship was slowing down to take the pilot on board. "The exact number of submarines encountered," according to the ship's history, "is not known, but it is believed there were at least three, and very probably more." American newspapers were soon reporting the *Leviathan* had been attacked by as many as twenty submarines and evaded multiple torpedoes. There were also reports that spies had tipped the Germans to the ship's rendezvous with the pilot boat, not an unlikely assumption considering how numerous spies were in Brest. One headline reported: "Spies Put U-Boats on *Leviathan* Trail." Another: "Flotilla of Submarines Lay in Wait for Her Near a French Port."

Bryan insisted that he'd seen only one submarine. In a letter written the following day to Admiral Sims, his commander in England, the captain backed his navigator's account that a submarine surfaced about seven hundred yards off the *Leviathan*'s port side and followed the ship at varying distances over the next forty-plus minutes toward Brest, diving then resurfacing several times. Dwight Messimer also believes that only one submarine was involved, most likely the U-90.

It was the only German submarine operating in those waters at that time.

Shortly after reaching Brest, the *Leviathan* tied up to her mooring buoy and began unloading over eleven thousand troops into the square-ended barges that were quickly filled with soldiers who packed the long, bench-like seats. The ship also started to recoal, the crew's "black gang" loading 4,500 tons in a matter of hours as

Bryan pushed hard for a quick turnaround. He planned to sail for New York no later than June 1.

"Don't Lose Hope—I Beg You"

O N THURSDAY MAY 30, the same day the *Leviathan* dodged a submarine attack and began unloading a record number of soldiers in France, General John Pershing was in Paris, where the odds appeared excellent that the city would soon fall into German hands. It was a lovely spring day, warmer than usual and with none of the drizzling rain that had been falling off and on for nearly a week, but the city was on the brink of panic. Once again, thousands of frightened men and women struggling with bags and suitcases had poured into the streets, trying to get out any way they could. The French government was doing the same at the Hôtel de Ville, packing official papers into crates as the various department ministers got ready to catch a fast train to Bordeaux. So were American embassy officials, who brought in trucks to haul records to US supply bases near Brest and Boulogne, areas "outside of the zone of the British armies and south of Paris, and hence comparatively safe."

Pershing figured nearly one million people had fled the city since April, trying to find safe havens from the air raids, the sporadic shelling by Big Bertha, Germany's massive long-range gun, and the lingering prospect of an imminent invasion. The evacuees included his lover Micheline Resco, who was still in Bordeaux with her mother.

Earlier that morning, General Philippe Pétain had begged Pershing to send American soldiers to Château-Thierry, a town about thirty miles northeast of Paris, to blunt the German juggernaut.

Without his help, Pétain told him, Paris would surely fall.

The most dramatic German breakthrough of the war was still

unfolding, and the retreating French army was in near collapse. The surprise attack had been launched at 1:00 a.m. three days earlier along a twenty-four-mile front, thirty German divisions spearheaded by elite *Sturmtruppe* smashing into four French and three British divisions. The French didn't even have time to blow up the bridges over the Aisne and Vesle Rivers. With the door wide open, the Germans had advanced thirty miles and captured Soissons. By May 30, the fourth day of the attack, they had reached the Marne and Château-Thierry, taken sixty thousand prisoners, and driven the demoralized French army in confusion toward Paris.

Pershing knew it wouldn't help to remind his friend that American intelligence officers had anticipated the attack before it was launched along the Chemin des Dames, or "Ladies Path" (so named for the two young daughters of Louis XV who used it to visit a favorite château), a strategic fifteen-mile highway along a ridge running east of Soissons. Fifteen German divisions had recently taken position behind the ridge. Officials at the French army headquarters had been notified of American suspicions the day before the attack but brushed off the warning, insisting that "everything was quiet and that they did not expect an offensive there."

The German offensive had compromised America's first significant engagement of the war, an attack made May 28 at Cantigny seventy miles north of Paris. From his residence in the city at 73 rue de Varenne, Pershing had been in almost constant telephone contact with his headquarters at Chaumont, receiving updates on the fighting. His men were being pounded by artillery, and some were starting to crack under the pressure, with one report of a hysterical officer who started firing an automatic pistol at his own soldiers until a German shell killed him.

Located on high ground long occupied by German troops and artillery, Cantigny had no strategic significance, and when compared with the major collision among the French, British, and Germans under way at Soissons, the Marne, and Château-Thierry, it was a small-bore engagement at best. But it was the American army's first major offensive, and the pressure to succeed was intense.

At the beginning of May 1918, the United States had 618,642 enlisted men in France and 32,642 officers, and after being at war for almost fourteen months had little to show for it by way of victories. Cantigny was meant to change that reality.

Determined to win this one, Pershing dropped by the First Division's headquarters before the battle, exhorting his officers to hold the town at all costs. The Twenty-Eighth Infantry Regiment took the village easily on May 28, but the situation soon deteriorated because of the German offensive. The French were forced to shift much of their artillery and air support to the disaster unfolding at Soissons, a move that gave the Germans an opportunity to bring artillery to bear at Cantigny, where their planes were also soon strafing and bombing the American lines. After four days of intense shelling and beating back six or seven German counterattacks, the Americans still held the village at a cost of over one thousand dead, compared with the fifty killed taking it the first day.

Even with the outcome at Cantigny still in doubt, Pershing responded immediately to Pétain's plea for help. The two men shared a mutual trust. Pétain, the hero of the 1916 Battle of Verdun, was also probably the best tactician in the French army and was considered as ambitious and driven as Pershing.

The American commander knew that if Pétain was this desperate, the need was grave. The US Second and Third Divisions were within distance of Château-Thierry and were ordered to head there immediately, the soldiers piling into large open-backed trucks and taking off with little more than their rifles and gas masks. Others marched overland along with the supply trains. The first element of the lead group, the Seventh Machine Gun Battalion, was expected to reach Château-Thierry the next morning on May 31.

That afternoon, Pershing climbed into one of his new Cadillac staff cars and drove to Sarcus, a town seventy miles northeast of Paris that served as the headquarters of Marshal Foch. He had a gloomy dinner with the marshal and his staff in their ornate nineteenth-century château. "It would be difficult to imagine a more depressed group of officers," Pershing wrote later. "They sat through the meal scarcely speaking a word as they contemplated what was probably the most serious situation of the war."

After dinner, Pershing waited for a chance to catch Foch by himself. He told him he had some additional troops available, soldiers who weren't engaged elsewhere and could be thrown into the effort to stop the German offensive. Foch jumped at the offer, and Pershing made some quick telephone calls. Two battalions were cobbled together from noncombatants with the First Division, which was still at Cantigny. A collection of typists, clerks, cooks, and fresh recruits was quickly assembled, given weapons and ammunition, and sent toward Château-Thierry. Their orders: "You are to die east of the railroad," the men were told. "That is all the order you need."

ON SATURDAY, JUNE 1, Pershing was attending an emotionally charged meeting of the Allied Supreme War Council in Versailles while the Second Division moved up along the main Paris highway and dug in at Château-Thierry. A day earlier, the Third Division had spread out along the Marne for ten miles, blown up the main bridge, and fought off every German attempt to cross. The heaviest action was just west of Château-Thierry, and Pershing received regular reports as the meeting continued in a crowded, smoky room in the most glittering palace in Europe.

Thousands of fleeing French troops were pouring through the American lines, many shouting *"La guerre finie!"* They frequently came in groups of three or four men, the disorganized remnants of "a beaten, routed Army." The Germans, who'd been charging forward since May 27, arrived in force at Château-Thierry and also poured into neighboring Bouresches, Vaux, and the forest of Belleau Wood. Their artillery started pounding the Americans, who fired back with their borrowed French 75s and 155s, which were soon spitting out shells so fast the barrels glowed at night.

The fight was on. To a French general's message that they dig trenches behind their lines "just in case," the American commander responded: "We will dig no trenches to fall back to. The Marines will hold where they stand." They not only held, they moved forward.

The effect was electrifying. The German advance was halted. Paris, at least for the moment, was out of danger, and Marshal Foch later said that the Second Division had virtually saved the city. Pershing felt the same way. The last-minute arrival of his men "effectively stopped the German advance on Paris," he wrote in his memoirs. "It must have been with a decided feeling of relief that the worn and tired French soldiers, retreating before vastly superior numbers, caught sight of Americans arriving in trucks . . . eagerly hurrying forward to battle." The French, he said, had been defeated.

Before the outcome of the fight at Château-Thierry became clearer, Pershing found the heated meeting at Versailles as depressing as his last encounter with Foch. Once again he was verbally assaulted by Britain's Lloyd George and France's Georges Clemenceau. Both men repeated earlier demands that the United States send only infantry and machine gun units to France instead of the support troops and equipment Pershing argued were needed to build up an American army that he increasingly believed might have to carry on the battle virtually alone. Pushing back, he asserted that the use of the American troops was a matter for him to decide and not the Supreme War Council. And there was a limit to how many men America could send. In no way, he told them, was it possible to ship what they were requesting—250,000 trained soldiers for each month of June and July.

General Foch became increasingly agitated. He kept waving h[is] hands and repeating, "The battle, the battle, nothing else coun[ts]

When the meeting resumed after a recess to cool tempers, the tension in the room was still palpable. Supported by Clemenceau and Lloyd George, Foch kept pressing his demand for "exclusive shipments" of infantry and machine gunners in June and July. When Pershing objected, Foch hit him with the question he'd often raised before.

"You are willing to risk our being driven back to the Loire?"

"Yes," Pershing said. "I am willing to take the risk."

"Well, we will refer this to your President," Lloyd George said.

"Refer it to the President and be damned," Pershing said. "I know what the President will do."

"The whole discussion was very erratic, as one of the Allies would take exception to nearly every statement made by the other," Pershing wrote. The British and French couldn't even agree among themselves on how many troops they had available. Foch said 150 divisions; the British, 169.

Pershing understood that the Allies were exasperated and had little confidence in either him or his staff, though they were certainly pleased with the stiff fight the Americans were putting up just down the road at Château-Thierry. The Allied leaders kept hitting him with demands for American troops "to build up the armies of the British and French, and each [demand] was greater and more pressing than the one before." Summarizing the mood in a confidential memo for the army chief of staff and the secretary of war, Pershing wrote that he considered the military situation "very grave" and that the attitude of the Supreme War Council was "one of depression."

The American commander later worked out a private agreement at Versailles among Foch, the British representative, and himself that called for sending 170,000 American combat troops to France on a priority basis in June and 140,000 in July, for a total of 310,000. Another 190,000 support troops also would be sent during these months as transport space allowed. Some of these troops would be poorly prepared, but the present emergency justified "a temporary and exceptional departure by the United States from sound principles of training especially as a similar course is being followed by France and Great Britain."

It was a victory for Pershing, but everything depended on what the German armies did in the field.

Driving back to Chaumont from Versailles on Tuesday, June 4, Pershing took a detour to visit with the commanders of the Second and Third Divisions for an update on the fighting around Château-Thierry and Belleau Wood. On the way, he ran into long, ragged columns of French refugees "fleeing from their homes, many on foot, men and women with bundles on their backs, leading the smaller children," driving their sheep, goats, and cows before them and hauling all their worldly possessions in carts of every imaginable size and shape. He found the scenes "almost indescribable" in their poignancy and heartbreak.

On Thursday, June 6, the marines moved into Belleau Wood in a fight to the bloody finish that lasted for twenty days. The Germans occupied a natural strongpoint of dense forests strewn with boulders and underbrush—a wilderness they skillfully laced with machine gun nests. Like Cantigny, the woods and two adjoining villages held no strategic value. They weren't on the road to Paris and led virtually nowhere, but were of extreme psychological importance. Knowing they were facing Americans in force, the Germans put some of their best soldiers in the woods in what was known from the outset as a test of wills—nearly three weeks of attack and counterattack, continuous shelling and hand-to-hand combat punctuated by the use of gas and flamethrowers. "Men with a hand or foot shot off continued to fight until they were ordered to the rear or collapsed from shock and loss of blood. Men stepped on grenades to shield their comrades, losing a foot. Others drove ammunition trucks in broad daylight down a highway where high explosive shells were dropping like rain."

The *Chicago Tribune* reporter Floyd Gibbons was hit twice by machine gun fire and lost an eye as he rescued a badly wounded marine officer. On that same day, 1,087 marines were killed, among the heaviest single-day casualties in USMC history, the men moving to the attack behind a sergeant who yelled, "Come on, you sons-o-bitches. Do you want to live forever?" Finally driven from the woods, the Germans were impressed with the Second Division, grudgingly considering them almost as tough as their own assault troops. "The individual soldiers are very good," a German intelligence officer wrote. The troops "are fresh and full of straightforward confidence. A remark of one of the prisoners is indicative of their spirit: 'We kill or get killed.'"

PERSHING WAS BACK at his headquarters at Chaumont. After catching up on paperwork at his austere office in building B, he returned to his garishly furnished château and wrote a note to Micheline. "I have time for nothing but work," he wrote. "These days are very hard, but it's necessary that we will be victorious. It is the will of God."

The previous two weeks had been exceptionally difficult for him, and he looked forward to seeing Micheline again. Since she'd left Paris he'd hoped that he could arrange an inspection tour to the army's supply base at Bordeaux, where they might be able to meet, but with fighting raging on several fronts, he wasn't sure he could make such a trip.

On June 13, with the outcome of the fight in Belleau Wood still in doubt, he reminded her that exactly one year had passed since he'd arrived in Paris and that it was the anniversary of their first meeting. "I recall it as yesterday, but many things have happened" he told her. The war was at a turning point and the carnage at the front was almost impossible to put into words, but he was certain the Allies and the American army would win out.

"I don't know when I will see you again," he wrote, "but don't lose hope—I beg you."

CHAPTER 13

Submarines and the Sky Pilot

A PALL HUNG OVER Captain Bryan and his officers and crew as the *Leviathan* cast off from Brest after a two-day stay early on the evening of June 1 for the return trip to New York. They were still trying to digest appalling news. One day earlier, a German submarine had torpedoed the *President Lincoln* about five hundred miles off the French coast. The *Lincoln* was the fifth-largest troop transport in the American fleet and had just delivered five thousand doughboys to Brest.

After discharging her passengers, the ship had left for New York on May 29, the day before the *Leviathan* arrived in the French port. According to early reports, most of the 715 persons on board had survived the sinking, but at least 26 men had drowned, including 16 clinging to a raft that was sucked beneath the waves as the ship went down stern-first. The other victims were trapped belowdecks or killed in the explosions. Two torpedoes hit the ship—one in the bow, the other in the stern—sinking her in twenty-five minutes. The gunners kept firing as the *Lincoln* went down, pumping out shells at the submarine until the sea washed over the main deck and they had to abandon ship.

Bryan also learned that one half hour after the *Lincoln* disappeared, a large German submarine, the U-90, had surfaced and approached the wreckage and lifeboats. After taking a young lieutenant prisoner—they were looking for the captain or a senior officer—the sub headed to the northwest at five knots and was soon

out of sight. At about eleven o'clock that morning, two US destroyers spotted the submarine running on the surface and attacked her
about sixty miles northeast of where the *Lincoln* had gone down.
After the U-90 dived she left a hard-to-miss oil slick, and, following it like a trail, one of the destroyers dropped a tight pattern of
depth charges, each crammed with three to six hundred pounds
of TNT. The American ships were running low on fuel, and when
they finally headed back to their base, they did so having found no
wreckage or evidence to indicate they'd sunk the submarine. The
presumption was that the boat was still out there.

Kapitanleutnant Remy, the U-boat's captain, later reported in
his log that the submarine did a "fast dive" to two hundred feet
and was tossed around by the powerful underwater blasts. "Eleven
medium depth charges and screw sounds heard above and on both
sides of U-boat." After such a long cruise and so many close calls,
this could have been the end for the U-90, but the submarine rode
out the explosions. When Remy ordered the ship back to periscope
depth an hour later and took a 360-degree sweep of the horizon, he
was relieved to find the sea empty of ships.

Bryan passed along to his officers all the details that were known
about the *Lincoln*'s sinking and emphasized the importance of having
the *Leviathan*'s lookouts keep close watch, especially the gun crews.
It was almost impossible to pick up a low-riding submarine in choppy
water or when the sea was sunlit. They couldn't afford to be surprised. The lookouts aboard the *Lincoln* had failed to spot the submarine that sank them and hadn't realized they were under attack until
they'd seen the white trails of torpedoes heading in their direction.

Bryan wondered whether the attacker could have been the same
submarine that had given them a bad scare when the *Leviathan* had
approached the harbor two days earlier. He wanted all his crew
members on their toes as they cast off at 6:12 p.m. and slowly moved
away from their mooring buoy. Less than an hour later, after the
Leviathan cleared the harbor and its approaches, Bryan ordered the

engine room to increase speed to 20.5 knots. As she headed into the open sea, the ship was shadowed by two destroyers, the *Nicholson* and the *Wadsworth*. They were to accompany her until she reached the western edge of the submarine danger zone. The officers on board must have realized they were following the same route as the *President Lincoln* and would pass near the spot where she'd sunk.

At about 7:20 p.m., the cry went out from multiple voices on the *Leviathan*: "Submarine on starboard quarter!"

The officer of the deck sounded general quarters, and within moments Bryan spotted the submarine tailing them at a distance of about two thousand yards. He ordered full speed ahead and the engine room increased the revolutions to 162, nearly the maximum, generating about twenty-four knots.

The ship's gunnery officer saw the bow wave of a submarine through his binoculars about 1,500 yards to the stern and turning to the right. The only guns that had a clear shot were on the stern, numbers five and seven.

The gunnery officer barked out the orders:

"Range 3,000, numbers five and seven commence firing!"

Their salvo fell about two hundred yards short, so the officer quickly made an adjustment:

"Range 1,800. Shift to long-pointed projectile. Commence firing."

This time their aim was only forty yards short and right on target. They followed with another salvo similarly placed, close enough that the officer thought they'd scored a direct hit.

Turning so sharply her decks were awash, the *Nicholson* raced toward the location where the shells had fallen. The destroyer dropped sixteen depth charges in a long curving arc, the concussions rocking the *Leviathan* and almost lifting her out of the water. Men were thrown off their feet and tableware was shattered in the galleys. The gun crews abruptly stopped firing when the *Nicholson* moved between them and the submarine.

The destroyer's blinker light flashed a message to Bryan, who was watching from the bridge.

"We saw periscope of submarine and laid barrage of depth charges around the spot."

Within ten minutes it was all over. The *Leviathan* dropped back to a standard speed of just over twenty knots and resumed her course to the west. At 7:30 p.m., the destroyers heeled around and caught up with her, retaking their positions on both sides.

That evening the crew and passengers, which included a sprinkling of American women and their children who'd been trapped in France when the war broke out, gathered on the main deck for a prayer service. The sun was low, casting long shadows on the water, a beautiful hour at sea when it was the custom for the ship's chaplain—known in the navy as the "sky pilot"—to say a daily prayer for the safety of all on board. On this particular evening, there was a special urgency for the gathering. After the recent submarine encounter, nearly every passenger and crew member was there as the chaplain stepped out on the bridge and began to recite the Memorare, an ancient Catholic prayer.

Even Captain Bryan, who usually wasn't interested in organized religion, was moved as the chaplain recited: "Remember most gracious Virgin Mother, Star of the Sea, that never was it known that anyone who fled to thy protection, implored thy aid and sought thy intercession was left unaided."

THE NEXT MORNING broke clear and fine as the *Leviathan* sailed west. During the night the destroyer escort had peeled off to accompany a convoy of troopships heading back for France. Relying as always on her speed, the *Leviathan* kept up a steady 20.5 knots.

But after back-to-back encounters with submarines, Bryan wanted to sharpen the performance of his gun crews, and he ordered a practice round, following up two days later, on June 6, with a marksmanship contest. Two floating targets were dropped into the ocean, one on each side of the ship. When they were about 2,500 yards away, the firing started. Each of the *Leviathan*'s eight guns fired five rounds, and any shot that landed within fifty yards of the target was considered a hit. "The drill went off well, and a high percentage of hits were scored," wrote one historian. "The Leviathan's gunners were good."

At the same time, the lookouts were trained to focus on the slice of horizon and ocean that was their area of responsibility, looking for anything that appeared suspicious. Bryan had received reports that German submarines prowling America's eastern seaboard were sinking ships in the area the *Leviathan* would soon be passing through. "There was alarm," the secretary of the navy later remembered, "along the coast, from Cape Cod to Key West." The British had warned the US Navy in early May that a new, larger type of German submarine was headed for the American coast, prompting alerts to every naval base along the eastern seaboard.

The German raider soon made her presence known. On May 25, three small schooners were sunk, the *Hattie Dunn*, the *Hauppauge*, and the three-masted *Edna*, all of them attacked by the U-151, which took their crews on board as prisoners to keep her presence a secret. On June 2, the U-boat had sunk or disabled three more schooners, a small steamer, and two steamships off the New Jersey shoreline. Ranging along the Atlantic seaboard over the next week, the submarine sank six more steamships before releasing her prisoners and sailing back to Germany.

Unsure if he was heading into a maritime turkey shoot, Bryan kept the *Leviathan*'s speed up all the way to New York. By then one of the U-151's prisoners from the *Edna* had a story to tell: the submarine and others that would follow her were all hunting the big troop transport. Fluent in German, the sailor had overhead the crew talking about the ship. Their mission, the sailor told American naval authorities, was to lie in wait for the *Leviathan*, and sink her.

It's not known whether the U-151 ever had the ship in her periscope sights, though the submarine was certainly hanging off the East Coast in early June and aggressively attacking ships at the very time the *Leviathan* was returning to New York. Was the submarine the *Leviathan* encountered shortly after leaving Brest Remy's U-90? His boat was probably the only German submarine operating in those waters, but it's a stretch to think the *Leviathan* had two run-ins with the U-90, according to the naval historian Dwight Messimer, who doesn't believe Remy would have stuck around after he sank the *Lincoln* on May 31 and was depth-charged the following day. Remy's battered submarine was low on fuel, food, and water, and he'd been at sea for weeks. On the other hand, "He was a ballsy bastard," Messimer said, "so maybe he did."

"Another Way of Spelling the Word 'American'"

I RVIN COBB HAD arrived in Brest nearly four months earlier, in February 1918, for another extended stay in France. He considered himself a humorist first and foremost, and that element shows up consistently in his war dispatches published in the *Saturday Evening Post* and later assembled into a book. His chatty, keep-them-smiling style can be tiresome when read today, but it may have been the only way that Cobb was able to handle the danger that he lived with for weeks during the spring of 1918, when he was frequently within shelling distance of the German guns. He was based in Paris when Big Bertha—it was also called the Paris Gun—began bombarding the city on a daily basis. From March through August, about twenty rounds a day—each weighing 264 pounds—were fired at roughly twenty-minute intervals, some of them from as far away as seventy-five miles. The Germans, Cobb recalled, followed a fairly exact schedule with their mayhem, starting at seven in the morning and concluding at 6:20 p.m.

Life went on in Paris despite Big Bertha and German air raids. Fashionable women still shopped along the rue de la Paix, students crowded the sidewalks on the Left Bank, artists and writers gathered at the Café le Dôme in Montparnasse, barely raising their heads from their espresso and croissants unless one of the shells landed a little too close.

Cobb found himself in the line of fire one afternoon while he was in his room at the Hotel Lotti, a deluxe hotel on the rue de Castiglione near Notre-Dame Cathedral. Wearing his brand-new American war correspondent's uniform, complete with a stylish Sam Browne belt, he tried to calm down a frightened maid after a few shells exploded in the distance. He'd just finished telling her the attack was probably over when a tremendous blast about 150 yards away shook the walls. Shrieking, the maid fell to her knees. Cobb stepped out on the room's small balcony and saw clouds of dust rising over the nearby roofs. He couldn't tell what had been hit. The maid practically pulled him back into the room by the strap of his belt, then fled into the hallway. "I heard her falling down the stairs to the floor below," he wrote later. "The next day I had a new chambermaid."

Cobb wasn't in the city on March 29, when the Paris Gun scored its most deadly hit of the war. A shell fell on the roof of one of the oldest churches in Paris, Saint Gervais and Saint Protais, while it was filled with worshippers for the afternoon Good Friday service. Rescuers pulled ninety dead and sixty-eight wounded from the rubble. During six months of intermittent terror, the gun's tally was 250 killed and 640 wounded.

As the German spring offensive kept rolling forward in one slashing attack after another, Cobb spent weeks visiting British and American troops at the front. In late March, he and two other journalists talked an American Red Cross driver, a kid from Texas, into taking them to the French and British lines around Compiègne, which were starting to give way to a strong German attack. They reported later how the British put up a determined fight before being forced to retreat. Cobb quoted a young surgeon he met in Soissons, who described the attack: "I saw them caught by our machine-gun fire and piled up, heap on heap until there was a windrow of them before the British trenches that must have been six feet high. . . . I myself watched them scrambling up among the bodies—and they slid down on the other side and ran right into the wire entanglements, where those of them that were killed hung in the wires like garments drying on a line. They died there in such numbers that they fairly clogged the wires. And still they kept on coming."

Cobb was with the US Forty-Second Division in May, visiting a forward observation post on the edge of the Argonne Forest. He was walking with another journalist and a young lieutenant, an intelligence officer, on a miserably hot day after a rain when the steaming mud was ankle deep in the trenches. He spent a few hours with soldiers who'd been trading shots with German snipers barely two hundred feet away and expertly concealed; they showed Cobb where the bullets had clipped the branches off the stump of a willow tree near their parapet. The men were crouched down, some of them casually reading newspapers and talking about rumors that Ty Cobb was going to be traded from the Detroit Tigers to the New York Yankees. This deadly scene was the new normal for these young men, as they kept an eye on the reporter to make sure he didn't do anything that might get him or themselves killed.

On the way back to their car, Cobb suggested getting out of the trench and the mud and crossing an open meadow to save time. Guns were firing in the distance, but they were protected by a hillside, and Cobb figured the Germans were at least half a mile away. No one was shooting in their direction, so they started walking.

The first shell fell in front of them when they were halfway across the field, which now suddenly seemed much wider. A minute later another shell crashed to their left, then one slammed down to their right, neatly bracketing them. Cobb was carrying his jacket and wore a vest with a red flannel back. He quickly slipped his coat on and tossed away the cigar he'd just lit up.

"I wonder," he asked, "if those Germans are getting the range on the rear elevation of my vest?"

Four more shells fell near them in quick succession, kicking up thick clods of dirt as Cobb and the others ran for their lives back to the trench.

A WEEK BEFORE he left for New York aboard the *Leviathan*, Irvin Cobb made his most remarkable journey of the war, if not of his life, a trip that started with a visit to Freddie Stowers's regiment on May 25 as it trained near Rembercourt.

Cobb arrived at the base for the 371st Regiment in a staff car reserved for prominent journalists after seven hard hours on the road. His first observation was that Rembercourt had been badly shot up. His driver parked by a shattered, shell-scarred garden wall, where Cobb heard men singing. Behind the wall, twenty or more young soldiers were lying on a patch of grass in the sunshine, singing a spiritual that Cobb recognized, "My Soul Bears Witness to the Lord." From the tone and pitch of their southern accents, he correctly identified them as natives of South Carolina or Georgia. The soldiers, he wrote later in a typical Cobb description, were all fine physical specimens. "Almost without exception they were big men with broad shoulders and necks like bullocks and their muscles bulged their sleeves almost to bursting. Nine out of ten were 'coal-black.'"

His narrative opens with a joke, in this case an anecdote recounted by one of the officers, a white soldier from Tennessee, about the alleged unwillingness of black troops to stand guard near a cemetery the Germans had shelled. Most of the graves had been ripped open and the caskets and their contents ghoulishly scattered. In Cobb's retelling in the dripping racial dialect that was his specialty, a black NCO begs a colonel to spare them guard detail at the cemetery: "Kernul, suh, we don't none of us wanter be shot fur runnin' way, but dat's perzactly whut's gwine happen ef ary noe of us has to march back and fo'th by dat place w'en de darkness of de night gets in." That same officer also told Cobb that the men would soon prove themselves excellent fighters and that he'd stake his life on them. "I'd take a chance on going anywhere with these black soldiers at my back," he said. "So would any of the rest of the officers."

Shortly before Cobb's arrival, Freddie Stowers and his company had been practicing with a new type of French hand grenade. American soldiers hadn't received much training with grenades of any kind, but with help from French instructors, the 371st was trying to make up for lost time before moving into the line and facing German troops, a moment everyone knew was coming soon. They knew the enemy had crossed the Marne, creating a bulging salient between Reims and Soissons. Officers from the regiment and some of the NCOs had already hiked up to an observation point atop "Dead Man's Hill," from which they could examine the enemy positions through high-powered telescopes. They also got their first look at the heights of Montfaucon rising in the distance like a craggy tabletop, a German strongpoint.

For soldiers sent to attack machine gun–laced positions, the grenade had become one of the go-to weapons, especially for raiding parties that infiltrated enemy trenches.

Cobb described the instruction, how the men lined up three or four in a row, each gripping a live grenade. "At the call of 'One' from the squad commander the men strike the cap ends against a stone or something [hard]. At 'Two' they draw back the thing full arm length, and at 'Three' they toss it with a stiff overhead swing."

The fuses were timed to explode five seconds after the grenade was struck on a rock. Soldiers like Stowers worked hard at getting the three-count timing down cold. "If you fling your grenade too soon a Heinie is liable to pick it up and throw it back at you before it goes off," the instructors told them. "If you hold it too long, you're apt to lose an arm or your life."

Many African American enlisted men "were familiar with Cobb's work and regarded it as damaging to their race," observed one historian. Other African Americans and progressive whites who considered Cobb a supporter hoped that through exposure and experience, he'd eventually abandon his ingrained racial prejudices, which many Americans shared at the time.

After another long drive down a dusty white road that ran through a forest of poplars, Cobb arrived at the encampment of an African American unit from New York City, the 369th. German and French batteries five miles apart were exchanging fire—shrapnel, high explosives, gas—the outgoing shells passing directly overhead, but no one appeared to pay much attention. Cobb soon noticed that the soldiers from this unit were different physically from the big men from South Carolina. "They were apt to be mulattoes or to have light-brown complexions instead of clear black; they were sophisticated and town wise in their bearing . . . almost without exception they were city dwellers and many of them had been born North."

Shortly before his arrival, the regiment learned that the French were going to award the Croix de Guerre with a golden palm for valor to two of its soldiers, Henry Johnson and Needham Roberts. A few weeks earlier, on the night of May 13–14, the two young soldiers and three other men were trapped in a forward position when a German raiding party numbering at least a dozen attacked their trench with shotguns and stick-grenades. Three of the Americans were cut off when the explosions shattered the support timbers in their dugout. Wounded by gunfire and grenade fragments, Johnson and Roberts fought back, emptying their rifles and throwing grenades as they held their ground. When Roberts, who was bleeding heavily, could barely move, Johnson attacked with his empty rifle, swinging it like a club, and finally pulling out his bolo knife when the raiders tried to carry off the other soldier. Shot by a German with a Luger, Johnson killed at least two of the men with his double-edged weapon. The Germans had enough, and pulled back through the American wire, carrying their wounded and at least five dead. Roberts and Johnson both survived their many wounds.

The details of their heroism had spread among the troops of the 369th, who were eager for a similar encounter with the Germans. Almost all the men, Cobb observed, were quietly cleaning and oiling their weapons, waiting for the orders to move forward. He admitted the experience forced him to reexamine some of his longest-held prejudices. His transformation wasn't immediate and never total, but his change of heart was still remarkable, considering that same summer a prancing Eddie Cantor sang in blackface "When the Boys from Dixie Eat the Melon on the Rhine" and the best-loved song about black troops was "Mammy's Chocolate Soldier."

Cobb, who considered himself "a Southerner with all of the Southerner's inherited and acquired prejudices touching on the race question," wrote that the two soldiers demonstrated that the "color of a man's skin has nothing to do with the color of his soul." The time had come, he realized, to reexamine a word used all too commonly. "As a result of what our black soldiers are going to do in this war, a word that has been uttered billions of times in our country, sometimes in derision, sometimes in hate, sometimes in all kindliness—but which I am sure never fell on black ears but it left behind a sting for the heart—is going to have a new meaning for all of us, South and North too, and that hereafter n-i-g-g-e-r will merely be another way of spelling the word American."

*   *   *

ON HIS TRIP home aboard the *Leviathan* in early June, Cobb was leaning against a railing on the main deck enjoying the spectacular orange-streaked sunset when the U-boat suddenly surfaced off the starboard side and the ship's guns began firing. Cobb tried to get closer to the starboard-side cannons as they pumped shell after shell at the submarine that was trailing them 1,500 yards off their stern. He was convinced that at least two subs were chasing them, one acting as a decoy while the other fired a pair of torpedoes at the ship. Other passengers who were watching the action from the decks didn't see the torpedoes, because they were distracted by the U-boat that had surfaced and by the excitement of the gunfire, Cobb recalled later. "One torpedo passed just back of our . . . stern and the other missed our nose by forty yards or so. Only a few on the *Leviathan* were cognizant of the attack and few still betrayed a jittery feeling."

Cobb wasn't alone in reporting that he'd seen a torpedo boring through the water. An army lieutenant on B deck spotted what looked like "a straight white line on the surface . . . about 100 meters in length and bearing from astern at about a 60 degree angle to the ship." A navy enlisted man who was also on B deck saw "the wake of a torpedo which appeared to have crossed from port to starboard, almost 100 feet to 150 feet astern of the ship."

Still shaken, Cobb phoned his wife, Laura, from the dock shortly after the *Leviathan* reached New York on the morning of June 8.

"Hello," he said. "Hello, Loll."

"Hello," she said. "Who is this?"

"Why, it's me," he said. "It's Irvin."

"Irvin who?" Laura said.

"Your husband."

"I'm sorry," Laura said. "I'm afraid I don't understand who you are."

"Look here, woman," he said. "Just how many Irvins are you married to, anyhow?"

CHAPTER 14

40 Hommes/8 Chevaux

CARRYING HIS SIXTY-POUND pack and Springfield rifle, Sergeant Royal Johnson and other members of D Company of the 313th Infantry slowly approached the inspection station in a long line that snaked up the gangway and disappeared into the side of the largest, most queerly painted ship he'd ever seen. The congressman turned soldier had just gotten off the ferry he'd boarded at Jersey City earlier that morning for the short trip down the North River to the *Leviathan's* pier at Hoboken. There didn't seem any way to cram on board all the towering mounds of baggage, equipment, and ammunition stacked haphazardly on the wharf, but navy and army crews were methodically carting it up gangways as cranes hoisted trucks and field pieces high over their heads and onto the deck.

Johnson had left Camp Meade before dawn that July 8 and marched to the railhead for the train ride to Jersey City. After a short stop at the inspection table, where the soldiers' names were checked off a master list, a smiling middle-aged woman wearing a Red Cross armband handed him a sandwich and two sweet rolls and he started up the gangway.

It was a sweltering July afternoon, and after stowing their bags and gear, Johnson and the rest of his unit were allowed on the main deck, where they watched the ship cast off. An army band was playing out on the fantail, their instruments glinting in the sun. From his vantage it looked to Johnson as if many of the city's residents were going out of their way to see them off. The sidewalks and piers were lined with waving spectators all the way down the Manhattan shoreline past Riverside Drive and Battery Park. Ferries packed with commuters blasted their whistles as passengers on their way home from work waved to them and shouted good luck.

The men were allowed to stay on the upper decks until later that evening, when the ship was joined by a camouflaged destroyer, the USS *Walke*. With twilight starting to fall, Johnson and an entire boatload of soldiers—another record for sheer numbers at 10,534— were ushered through the fast but efficient meal lines, where a typical dinner included roast beef or turkey, creamed potatoes, asparagus, fresh bread, and apple pie.

Up on the bridge, Captain Bryan was happy to be under way on what would be his sixth trip to Brest. He was concerned about the increased risk of submarines operating off the coast, so it was reassuring to see the destroyer hugging the *Leviathan*'s starboard bow as they headed into the open sea. Just before they'd shoved off, he'd received more information about the latest sinking, and it wasn't good. The USS *Covington*, another of the confiscated German liners, had been torpedoed one day out of Brest on July 1. That seemed to be the preferred German tactic—try to pick off the transports as they left the French port, when the convoy of destroyer escorts was usually smaller. Six sailors had been lost on the *Covington* and, almost miraculously, over seven hundred on board had been saved. It wasn't one of the larger transports like the *President Lincoln*, but the ship had dropped off 3,500 soldiers on her last voyage.

Bryan was hoping for an easier trip than the last one. Two days after they'd left New York on June 15, the ship's steering gear had broken down shortly after he'd ordered a change in course. By the time they made repairs and got under way again, they'd steamed in a complete circle. Fortunately, the breakdown hadn't occurred inside the danger zone, but it was bad enough to be drifting out there unable to steer at a time when German U-boats were expanding their cruising range. During the return trip, they'd had another submarine scare. It followed the typical scenario—the day after they'd left Brest, a lookout spotted a suspicious object three thousand yards behind them. A conning tower? It was hard to tell. The ship's stern batteries fired nine shots, and whatever it was disappeared. Bryan doubted it was a submarine but couldn't afford to take any chances.

As the sky started to brighten the morning after leaving New York, Bryan was called to the bridge. They were nearing an expansive field of floating debris, the wreckage of a freighter that either had been hit by a torpedo or struck a mine—pieces of plywood and timbering, crates, even chunks of metal, but no sign of any lifeboats or bodies. So many ships had been sunk over the previous few weeks up and down the Atlantic seaboard that it was impossible to say what ship this may have been or when it had been torpedoed. From the quantity of debris, Bryan figured it was probably a good-size freighter. There was no way of knowing how many had been on board or whether there were any survivors.

Soldiers trying to get some fresh air after a tough night in the stifling heat below deck stood at the railing, most of them staring silently at the wreckage that spread out for hundreds of yards as the ship slowed down to steer through it. Bryan was relieved when the debris was finally far behind them. From that moment on, they had a safe run all the way to Brest, the only problem the lingering heat. A score of soldiers passed out nearly every night and had to be carried up on deck.

THE REGIMENT STARTED slogging through ankle-deep mud shortly after the men disembarked, marching through Brest and then two miles into the hills to the American military base spread out around Pontanezen Barracks. Over thirty thousand soldiers were encamped there in primitive plank barracks and tents, so many men that Johnson and the rest of the 313th Infantry had to hike another mile to an open plot of ground where they could pitch camp on what looked like a shallow lake of mud. The tents and supplies, tons of matériel, had to be carried and pulled through the muck. Johnson and the others would soon start calling the place a "rest camp," because they figured they'd remember it for the rest of their lives.

Fortunately their stay there was short. Two days after arriving in Brest on July 15, they took down their tents and packed up again. At dawn the next morning, thousands of men started squeezing into the dilapidated 40 HOMMES, 8 CHEVAUX freight cars for a meandering three-day trip through the misting rain and the beautiful French countryside to Laignes, a village about ninety miles southeast of Paris. Johnson and the rest of D Company were assigned to a nearby village, where they set up housekeeping in a couple of barns. A luckier group of two hundred men were billeted in a medieval château complete with a moat and owned by an elderly French woman who spoke flawless English and couldn't do enough for the Americans.

Johnson barely had time to look around. After the brief stop near Laignes, the regiment climbed into a convoy of French military trucks for another long ride through a succession of quaint villages and towns, arriving at 3:00 a.m. at an American encampment near Champlitte. Dating to Roman times, the village was perched on a hill above a charming valley about sixty miles southeast of Laignes. Johnson and his men spent the few hours that remained of the night sleeping in the trucks or under them, or sprawled out in the mess shacks.

Almost all the soldiers with the 313th Regiment had arrived at their new base by Monday, July 29, and soon began the backbreaking routine of setting up camp. Some were assigned places to pitch tents; others moved into barns or livestock sheds, cleaning out the dung with shovels and buckets. Within a few days, improvised rifle ranges were set up in fields, and the men started wearing their hot, cumbersome gas masks throughout their increasingly long training periods. Steel helmets were also worn during every drill and long march.

The first weeks in Champlitte were difficult because the men were out of shape after the long trip from the States. Also complicating their training at nearly every level was the sudden infusion of green troops. In the weeks before shipping out to France, the 79th Division had sustained an incredible 66 percent turnover rate. As the army struggled to create new divisions to meet the increasing need in France, existing divisions were stripped of experienced officers. New recruits—many of those from Camp Meade had had fewer than six weeks of training—were grafted on to divisions and regiments. With so many men unskilled in even the basics of handling a rifle, Johnson and other NCOs were on their own trying to organize even limited time on the firing ranges. Much of the training focused on drilling, long six-hour marches out into the country and back, or on bayonet exercises, in which the men attacked straw dummies fashioned to look like German troops.

French officers were assigned to help with the instruction, focusing on how to fight from trenches. Pershing, on the other hand, wanted to stress open warfare training aimed at breaking the stalemate on the ground. In what was becoming an all-too-obvious vicious circle, this style of fighting depended on skill with the rifle and hand grenade, which many soldiers in the 79th Division hadn't acquired. Worse, the men had no idea what to do when confronted with skillfully concealed machine gun nests.

Tactical training also suffered. During the few short weeks they spent in camp, Johnson's infantry regiment, along with three others and the two machine gun battalions and three field artillery regiments that formed the nucleus of the 79th Division, trained only sporadically at the divisional level, in which exercises were conducted over miles of open ground. The officers who directed these drills were often inadequately trained in this crucial skill set, a major shortcoming for what was to come. Another failure proved even worse—the lack of coordinated training with the key weapon of the Great War, massed artillery. All these skills would have to be learned the hard way: under fire.

During these early weeks in France, Royal Johnson and a number of other NCOs were promoted to second lieutenant to try to fill a critical need for line officers. The new officers joined the nightly tactical sessions held by lantern light in the often uncomfortably warm mess shelters. The men gathered on Saturday evenings outside Champlitte's beautiful old city hall, where the regimental bands played for soldiers and village residents gathered in the square. Almost all the locals were women and children or elderly men. All the other men, those between ages twenty and sixty, were either in the army, dead, or wounded.

WHEN THE *LEVIATHAN* headed back to New York on July 18, a convoy of four destroyers picked her up as soon as she steamed out of the harbor. It was another sultry day, and she was carrying a remarkable group of passengers that included 160 wounded American soldiers as well as the skipper of the *Covington* and many of his surviving officers. Captain Bryan was eager to talk to Captain R. D. Hasbrouck about what had happened to the *Covington*, a 608-foot two-stacker that could do over sixteen knots and was one of America's largest troop transports. Her loss was a blow.

Hasbrouck reported that he'd sailed from Brest on June 30 in a convoy that included seven other transports, of which the *Covington* was easily the largest and most recognizable. They were escorted by seven destroyers, which had ranged out on the sides and brought up the rear. Late on the evening of July 1, the ships were sailing in two lines at fifteen knots when the *Covington*'s lookouts spotted the wake of a torpedo two hundred yards out and heading straight at them.

The executive officer immediately ordered the rudder shifted to hard right.

The German luxury liner SS *Vaterland* arriving at New York Harbor on July 29, 1914, a few days before the start of World War I. The ship was later seized by the US Navy as a troop transport and renamed the USS *Leviathan*. (*Courtesy of the Naval Historical Foundation, Collection of Capt. Cyrus R. Miller, USN, U.S. Naval History and Heritage Command Photograph*)

Captain Henry Bryan on the bridge of the *Leviathan* around mid-1918. *(Naval History and Heritage Command Photograph)*

Assistant Secretary of the Navy Franklin D. Roosevelt visiting a US naval battery on the western front in 1918. *(Naval History and Heritage Command Photograph)*

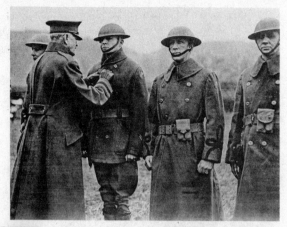

Right: General John Pershing decorating Brigadier General Douglas MacArthur with the Distinguished Service Medal. *(MacArthur Memorial Photograph)*

Left: Royal Johnson shortly after returning to Congress in late 1918 a few months after he was wounded in combat in France. *(Library of Congress Photograph)*

Below: Returning doughboys jam the decks as the *Leviathan* steams into New York Harbor. *(Naval History and Heritage Command Photograph)*

US sailor Humphrey Bogart around the time he served on the USS *Leviathan*. *(National Archives and Records Administration Photograph)*

General John Pershing inspecting troops in Coblenz, Germany, after the armistice. *(Photo courtesy of U.S. Army Heritage and Education Center)*

Fireboats welcome the *Leviathan* to New York. *(Naval History and Heritage Command Photograph)*

Nurse Elizabeth Weaver celebrating the Fourth of July in New Holland, Pennsylvania, probably in 1919, after her return to the United States. *(Photo by Edna P. Groff, courtesy of Charlie Miller)*

The cigar-loving Irvin S. Cobb wearing one of his favorite writing smocks. *(John Springer Collection/Getty Images Photograph)*

Damon Runyon shown at an unidentified port sometime after his return from France during World War I. *(Bettmann/Getty Images Photograph)*

Micheline Resco (left) and a friend during one of Micheline's trips to the United States to visit General John J. Pershing. *(Bettmann/Getty Images Photograph)*

The statue of Corporal Freddie Stowers on the campus of Anderson University in Anderson, South Carolina. *(Photo by Janice C. Hernon)*

The *Leviathan* in her war paint, with tugs in attendance, in 1918. *(Naval History and Heritage Command Photograph)*

Ten seconds later, the torpedo slammed into the ship at the forward engine compartment, throwing a geyser of water higher than the smokestacks. The *Covington* listed heavily to port and within fifteen minutes was stopped dead. Hasbrouck, who was on the bridge when the torpedo struck, ordered the crew to abandon ship and the bugler sounded "silence," the signal for everyone to head to the lifeboats without speaking or saying a word. Twenty-one boats were lowered and the survivors were soon picked up by the escorting destroyers. For the next seventeen hours, Hasbrouck and a volunteer party of thirty officers and enlisted men tried to save the ship, but it was a lost cause. Three tugs had her in tow and were trying to get her back to Brest 150 miles away when she started listing sharply again. With the *Covington* leaning at a 45-degree angle and in imminent danger of sinking, Hasbrouck and the rescue party abandoned ship and the tow lines were released. The *Covington* sank stern-first at 2:30 p.m. with her flag flying.

Both the *Lincoln* and *Covington* had been sailing in the middle of their convoys and were attacked by U-boat skippers who'd apparently shadowed them for some time. Because the vessels were traveling with slower ships, it gave the faster submarines a chance to make an end run around the convoy and line up the perfect shot.

More than ever Bryan was convinced the *Leviathan's* main defensive advantage was her twenty-two-knot speed, higher if she needed to pour it on. And it was far safer to travel alone rather than slow down so that other ships could keep up with her.

For now, as they knifed through calm seas at a steady 22.5 knots, the captain and his crew couldn't help being cheered by the contagiously upbeat attitude of the wounded soldiers they were taking home. Almost all of them looked happy despite their wounds. One soldier in particular, a man identified only as McGonigle in the ship's history, made an impression on everyone. The soldier had traveled to France aboard the *Leviathan* on her first trip of the war. During a trench fight, he'd lost both hands and a piece of his left foot when the grenade he was getting ready to throw exploded, a blast that killed his sergeant and three other men.

Despite his injuries, McGonigle and some of the other wounded men volunteered to help move coal in the fire room. During a musical show put on for the wounded, the soldier stood up and wisecracked that he wanted to make a short "stump speech," telling the captain and crew how happy he was to be returning home on the best ship in the world.

The King of Gasses

THE STEAM KETTLES were throwing out streams of warm mist in the narrow, barracks-style room where the patients lay in beds arrayed under sheets that were pitched like tents. Working in one of the wards at Base Hospital 18 where the victims of gas attacks were treated, Elizabeth Weaver quickly learned that mustard gas deserved its reputation as the king of gasses—worse than chlorine or phosgene, which attacked the lungs and respiratory system and were plenty bad enough. It was devastating to witness the racked breathing and choking of phosgene victims, who coughed up as much as four pints of yellow-colored fluid an hour.

Mustard gas destroyed the lungs and had the added cruelty of attacking the skin, raising large, mustard-colored blisters that were raw, sticky, and hard to treat. The wounds had to be washed as soon after exposure as possible, especially the eyes. Temporary blindness was common, and if left untreated permanent blindness was likely. Soldiers who could still walk when they reached the hospital had to strip out of their clothing and take hot showers immediately; those who couldn't stand were washed in their stretchers. The gas easily penetrated uniforms, and the burns where the soaked cloth touched the skin were the worst of all.

Elizabeth arrived on June 1 after an agonizingly slow train ride from the Base Hospital 20 compound at Châtel-Guyon. The highlight of her journey was the two days she spent in Paris, which was under attack from German air raids and Big Bertha. During the eerie citywide blackouts, the only illumination in the streets came from dim blue lights placed at the intersections, and she quickly learned to find in the dark the air raid shelter in the basement of her hotel.

Base Hospital 18 was in Bazoilles-sur-Meuse, a town on the banks of the Meuse in the Lorraine region close to the Belgian border and fifteen miles from the front. Wounded soldiers were starting to arrive by the hundreds after the recent battle at Cantigny and other flash points. The Americans ran hospitals on both sides of the Meuse at Bazoilles, large, hastily constructed encampments that consisted mostly of plywood barracks, huts, and tents. The wounded came by ambulance convoy or in trains, and as the Germans pressed their offensive, increasing numbers of them arrived gassed.

Working twelve-hour shifts, Elizabeth made sure the steam kettles kept putting out the warm vapors thought to help gas victims breathe more easily. Patients, many wearing eyeshades, were given steam inhalations several times a day. Elizabeth bathed the wounds of some mustard gas patients three times daily with sodium bicarbonate and repeatedly irrigated affected eyes with an antiseptic solution. She applied wet dressings to severe burns, covered the wounds with sterile gauze, and fastened them with bandages and adhesive straps. Severe gas burns were treated with alkaline compresses that were freshly reapplied throughout the day. The soldiers rarely complained or cried out in pain; the exceptions were usually mustard gas patients, who lay thrashing in their beds fighting for every breath, barely able to speak above a whisper. They often begged Elizabeth and other nurses to do something to help them breathe, telling them it felt as if their throats were closing.

One of the patients was a private from Tulsa, Oklahoma, who'd been gassed in late April. Helping him with his inhalations, Elizabeth learned that he'd been awarded the Distinguished Service Cross for volunteering to drive an ambulance while under fire from German batteries during a skirmish on the Saint Mihiel front. He'd made several runs in broad daylight, carrying the wounded to a dressing station as shells fell on both sides of the twisting road. His luck finally ran out when his Ford ambulance took a direct hit. Thrown clear of the wreckage, he landed hard, giving him a concussion and wrenching his back. Coming to, he limped to the American trenches and begged for another ambulance. At first the medical officers refused to let him go, because he could barely walk, but after taking time to let his head clear, he climbed into another vehicle and was back at it. He'd also been gassed.

At night, Elizabeth and the half-dozen nurses from Guyton who'd volunteered with her always made sure their gas masks were attached to their beds and within easy reach when they went to sleep. Their main fear was that they'd be gassed or bombed by a German plane. When the wind was from the northeast, they could hear the sound of the guns. "Very often," she remembered, "the lights had to be put out on short notice when expected air raids were likely to occur."

Elizabeth got used to getting by on little sleep and spending long hours on her feet, moving from patient to patient or to the operating rooms, where teams of doctors worked round the clock on wounds that often left their victims horribly disfigured. During her two weeks at the hospital, she received training in treating wounds with the Carrel-Dakin antiseptic solution, probably the most life-saving medical breakthrough of the war. What passed for surgery in 1914 often resembled the ghastly treatment found on US Civil War battlefields fifty years earlier—overworked doctors quickly sawing off arms and legs because of infection and the spread of gangrene. Men often fell on muddy ground and their wounds quickly became infected. The breakthrough came when a brilliant French physician, Alexis Carrel, who'd worked at the Rockefeller Institute for Medical Research in New York with the chemist Henry Dakin, realized that an antiseptic solution Dakin had concocted using diluted household bleach (sodium hypochlorite) cleaned wounds without damaging living cells. The trick was coming up with a drip-bag irrigation system, which Carrel devised and began using at a hospital near the front.

The results were dramatic even with the worst wounds, the kind often caused by shrapnel then exposed to mud and infection. Elizabeth had to be careful to make sure the solution was mixed and administered with precision, or it would only irritate the skin or not work at all. Tubes were often inserted into holes cut above and below the wound to make sure the infected area was adequately irrigated.

Battlefield wounds weren't the only concern. Elizabeth learned that the nurses who'd spent the previous winter at the hospital had had a hard time coping with various illnesses, and there were already worries that the approaching flu season would be a bad one.

CHAPTER 15

Two Men Overboard

THE *LEVIATHAN* WAS five days out of New York on August 8 when a powerful summer storm broke unexpectedly, kicking up rogue waves that crashed as high as the base of her smokestacks. The weather had been blissfully fair ever since the ship had started for France, and she was cruising in the Gulf Stream at a time of year when big storms were unusual. Nonetheless, this was one of the worst blows Captain Bryan had ever experienced. The *Leviathan* was taking a pounding as he tried to maintain her course and speed, but it was nothing compared with what the two smaller ships sailing with him were going through.

Bryan asked for status checks on the *Great Northern* and *Northern Pacific*. Following in his wake, both were struggling to keep up in the high seas, their bows lifting at a sharp pitch then slowly climbing over the crest of the next wave before crashing down into the trough as they fought to stay close to the *Leviathan*. Bryan wondered how much longer they could keep going like that before he'd have to reduce speed. It was the last thing he wanted to do as they neared the submarine danger zone, but with the two ships taking such punishment, he was concerned he didn't have a choice.

For the first time, the *Leviathan* was sailing in a convoy with two other ships, the only vessels in the entire transport fleet capable of keeping up with her. Appropriated by the War Department from a private operator at the beginning of the war, the *Great Northern* and *Northern Pacific* were sleek, beautifully appointed racers with raked funnels. They had been part of a lucrative passenger route between Seattle and San Francisco. Half the size of the *Leviathan*, each carried about 1,500 soldiers. Making her seventh crossing of the war, the *Leviathan* was hauling another record number of troops—10,893, including the Fifty-Fifth Infantry and the Twentieth Machine Gun Battalion.

At 10:48 a.m., a signal blinked from the *Northern Pacific*.

"Man overboard!"

Bryan gave a series of quick orders that were flashed to the two other ships. They'd start circling to see if they could find the man. For nearly an hour as green waves crashed over the decks, the ships crossed through the approximate location where he was last seen. Other messages indicated it was a soldier, an apparent suicide who'd left a letter. Bryan was under orders not to stop, but decided to keep searching as long as possible. He ordered life buoys dropped over the side.

Another jolting alert came from the *Northern Pacific*. Incredibly, she had a second man in the water, a soldier who had slipped and fallen overboard.

The three ships slammed back and forth for nearly two hours. Bryan knew it was hopeless, as did everyone else on the bridge. No one could live in that ocean, and it was beyond anyone's faculties to try to imagine the horror of someone out there alone, riding up and down in the big waves, maybe catching a glimpse of the ship pulling away. The *Great Northern* and *Northern Pacific*, both struggling, kept at it until Bryan decided they'd had enough.

Moments after he ordered the ships to resume their northeasterly course, one of the aft gun batteries frantically reported that they'd spotted a man floating in the ship's wake.

Bryan asked for a bearing. The *Leviathan* was already swinging around to her regular course. There was a long pause, then word came to the bridge that they couldn't get a bearing. The man had disappeared from sight as the ship started turning, and now the gunners couldn't see him with their glasses or with the powerful sighting telescope attached to their weapon.

The officers on the bridge were watching the captain, waiting for his order. Bryan had little choice. They had no more time to spare.

He called down to the engine room to reduce speed one quarter and continue on course.

The *Leviathan* had to slow down so the two ships trailing her could keep up. It was crucial for them to be close together when they reached their rendezvous point and met their destroyer escort. Getting there on time after riding through the storm would be a challenge. After the wind and rain slackened the following day, Bryan ordered a return to standard speed, 20.5 knots. With over a thousand seasick soldiers groaning in their bunks, he couldn't get to Brest soon enough.

THE CONTROVERSIAL DECISION for the *Leviathan* to travel in a convoy had been argued for months at the navy's highest command levels, ever since the ship first started carrying troops back in November 1917. It pitted the commander of naval operations in Europe, Rear Admiral William Sims, against Rear Admiral Albert Gleaves, who was in charge of transport operations. Sims thought it would be too dangerous for the three ships to sail together and would increase the risk of collision. Gleaves argued that that would be a virtual impossibility, as the ships could easily get out of each other's way. It would be safer, he said, for the *Leviathan* to have the two smaller vessels along as company because both were heavily armed and could function as "large destroyers" capable of rushing in to help the bigger ship if she came under U-boat attack.

His view ultimately prevailed, and the three ships made the next two crossings together, creating a spectacle when they arrived at Brest in tight convoy for the first time on August 11, sailing between the narrow cliffs that marked the entrance to the city's sheltered harbor.

Except in the roughest weather, the smaller and more graceful transports from the Pacific Coast could keep up with the bigger ship, and it was impressive to see them racing across the North Atlantic, traveling faster than anything else afloat. Combined, the ships delivered fourteen thousand soldiers to Brest on that August day.

It was precisely the kind of strength the Germans noticed and feared, and which explained their exuberance a few weeks earlier, on July 22, when a wire service in Berlin reported, "The American Troop Transport Steamer *Leviathan* (formerly the steamer . . . *Vaterland*) had been sunk on the 20th." The dispatch, which quickly spread across Europe, was an understandable mistake. On that same day, a British troop transport, the SS *Justica*, was torpedoed and went down twenty miles off the Irish coast in 230 feet of water, killing sixteen sailors. Two German submarines had gone after the big three-stacker, firing a total of six torpedoes into her hull over the course of two days. The ship was on her way from Belfast to New York to pick up troops and supplies when she was attacked twice during a running battle in which one of the German submarines was also sent to the bottom.

It took a while for these details to get sorted out, and in the confusion the German press ran wild. The chief of the German Admiralty Staff issued a glowing report on the value of the victory, a document that underscored how important the *Leviathan* was to them. The destruction of the famous transport, according to the report, "must have the greatest possible effect in the whole world," demonstrating the prowess of the German submarine fleet. "There can be no more expressive evidence of their capabilities than the fact that they have succeeded in sinking at their first opportunity, the gigantic ship the robbery of which was celebrated by the Americans like a great victory." The enemy was hoping the big ship would deliver tens of thousands of troops to the battlefields of France, but now "our opponents have suffered a very heavy blow which is nearly equal to the loss of a battle."

The Germans eventually had to retract the story, but the takeaway for Bryan and other top navy officials was that the hunt for the ship would only intensify. It also explains the angry reaction of Admiral Sims when he learned that American newspapers had published a recent photograph showing the *Leviathan* moored at Brest. Bryan had just arrived there when he found out about the admiral's displeasure. The recent U-boat attack on the *Justica*, coupled with the German announcement that they'd sunk the *Leviathan*, showed how much the enemy was "laboring under the impression that the ship [was] using Liverpool" as her main European anchorage. The photograph of the *Leviathan* in the French port would likely clue the Germans in to the truth. As a result, Sims urged "rigid censorship" over all photographs of ships that might identify their ports of call.

After only two days, the *Leviathan* left Brest for New York on August 13, accompanied by her speedy new sailing partners. They were one day out when a submarine suddenly popped up between the *Leviathan* and the *Northern Pacific* and briefly traveled along with them before disappearing beneath the waves. No one had time to do much more than shout a warning. It was possible the sub was French or English, so Bryan was grateful no one opened fire. The brief encounter was the only highlight of a quick, uneventful trip home. Certainly no one thought anything of the notation in the ship's log for August 8: at 6:55 a.m. an army private named Edgar Rubin died of lobar pneumonia, most likely following a sudden attack of the flu.

Visiting the Front with FDR

GENERAL PERSHING HAD a short visit with Assistant Secretary of the Navy Roosevelt on August 24 when the AEF commander was in Paris to meet with Marshal Foch. In the midst of planning what would become the Saint Mihiel offensive and fighting off more demands from the French and English for American troops, Pershing had little time or inclination to play host to Roosevelt, who was in Europe conducting a frenetic series of inspections, tours, and frat-boy partying. The general often found such visitors a nuisance, even when they were VIPs who showed up "with his party eager for a tour of the front. 'Like everybody else," commented an observer, "'they wanted to get shot at with a guarantee against a hit and smell dead men and horses.'"

Primed for action, Roosevelt had arrived in England one month earlier aboard the USS *Dyer*, a brand-new destroyer. He'd occupied the captain's cabin during an exceptionally smooth crossing and even enjoyed a submarine scare when the skittish gun crew opened up on what turned out to be a floating barrel. He'd adopted his own naval wardrobe consisting of "khaki riding trousers, golf stockings, flannel shirt & leather coat." By the time Roosevelt visited Pershing he'd already talked the French into letting him tour the battlefield at Belleau Wood, where he hiked around shell holes filled with water and took in a scene littered with "rusty bayonets, broken guns, emergency ration tins, hand grenades, discarded overcoats. . . . and many little mounds, some wholly unmarked, some with a rifle stuck, bayonet-down, in the earth, some with a helmet, and some too, with a whittled cross with a tag of wood or wrapping paper hung over it and in a pencil scrawl an American name." Visiting a succession of shattered villages in three gray touring cars, his party stopped at Mareuil-en-Dôle, another demolished village about twelve miles northeast of Château-Thierry, where the Germans had retreated barely a day earlier. Roosevelt saw dead Germans in the field and in one place "a little pile" that lay unburied.

Lusting, as one historian put it, for "danger and glory," Roosevelt soon got his wish. Moments after he climbed out of his car for a closer look at the battlefield, a German shell exploded a short distance away. An American gun crew allowed him to fire "toward the German lines one of a battery of 155's (did he kill a man?)." At another stop, this one close to Verdun, Roosevelt was wearing a French steel helmet and carrying a gas mask when he got out of the car to take photographs of a village left in ruins. He had to be hurried along when German observers started calling in artillery fire and a shell dropped on the exact spot where his party had just stopped.

Roosevelt was having the time of his life—meeting King George at Buckingham Palace; inspecting Anglo-American naval operations at Queenstown, Ireland, where the American destroyers that escorted ships like the *Leviathan* were based; swimming on a deserted beach in France; and enjoying a weekend with old friends the Waldorf Astors. He stayed at their regal English country estate at Cliveden, where, he noted: "Within a five-minute walk is the big hospital which they started in the tennis courts building but which the Government took over and enlarged to 1,100 beds." He and a friend also found time "for a good deal of shopping, using an Admiralty car with a uniformed chauffeur to do the driving and guard their packages," which included three pairs of silk pajamas.

While in Paris, Roosevelt stayed at the Hotel Carillon and enjoyed "a lively tour of Parisian nightclubs, beginning at the Folies Bergère, but soon moving on from there in the wake of a knowing midget hired as a guide" and arriving back at their hotel around four in the morning. During his meeting with Premier Georges Clemenceau, the Frenchman described a scene he'd just witnessed returning from the front—a Boche and Poilu, both dead and standing partially buried in a trench in a locked embrace, each trying to bite the other. "As he told me this," Roosevelt recalled, "he grabbed me by both shoulders and shook me with a grip of steel to illustrate his words, thrusting his teeth forward toward my neck."

Touring northern Scotland, he visited the US Navy's Battleship Division Nine, which operated with the British Grand Fleet, and inspected the Northern Mine Barrage, an idea he'd advocated back in Washington to lay mines from the Orkney Islands to Norway to try to seal off the North Sea from German submarines. He also found time to go fishing in the pouring rain and drink some fine single-malt scotch "like undergraduates."

By then Roosevelt had been going nonstop for nearly five weeks, sleeping less than five hours a night and pushing his small staff to the point of disintegration. On his way to Brest, he stopped to inspect a naval battery of fourteen-inch guns that were moving slowly toward the front mounted on railway cars, each marked U.S.N. The guns could fire a shell weighing 1,400 pounds nearly twenty-five miles. Roosevelt, dapper in a tweed jacket and leggings and carrying a cane, decided to have some fun with the commanding officer, Rear Admiral Charles Plunkett. Trim and gray haired with a long, drooping mustache, Plunkett was wearing an army uniform complete with Sam Browne belt. Roosevelt joked that the admiral was out of uniform and enjoyed his flustered explanation that navy whites would get too dirty and dress blues were too warm for what he and his men were doing.

Roosevelt asked Plunkett if he could sign up and was delighted when he was told, sure, just as long as he could curse enough in French to keep the French trains out of their way. Roosevelt quickly demonstrated his prowess, hurling "a line of French swear words, real and imaginary, which impressed [Plunkett] greatly." Plunkett offered to take him on at a rank of lieutenant commander. This would have been perfect for Roosevelt, giving him a chance to join the navy and still get near the front—but not too close.

He resolved to resign as assistant secretary of the navy as soon as he got back to Washington. He wrote his wife, Eleanor: "Somehow I don't believe I shall long be in Washington. The more I think of it, the more I feel that being only 36 my place is not at a Washington desk, even a Navy desk. I know you will understand."

After making a short run into Belgium to meet King Albert and visiting Rome, where he unsuccessfully tried to talk the Italians into getting more involved in the naval war, Roosevelt finally arrived at Brest on September 8 for the trip home. The *Leviathan* was waiting for him out in the harbor, a gray monster with black coal smoke trailing from her tall stacks. By the time Roosevelt boarded her, he could barely stand.

He'd been showing signs of illness for days. A week earlier, he'd run a 102-degree fever during a hair-raising all-night drive to Paris without headlights over crowded roads. He ignored the symptoms and refused to rest, pushing himself without letup. According to Roosevelt biographer Kenneth Davis, "For weeks on end he had been driving his body beyond its capacity for self-renewal, using up every reserve of its strength in reckless disregard of the protests it made." He was knotted up in pain when he was piped aboard the *Leviathan* and met Captain Bryan.

After a few tight-lipped pleasantries with the captain—Bryan would have naturally been solicitous of the assistant secretary—Roosevelt barely made it to his cabin, where he collapsed in bed. The ship's log makes no reference to his illness or to the congestion and spiking fever that would soon get much worse.

CHAPTER 16

A Near-Death Experience

THE BARGE WITH thirty-seven navy-issue steel caskets, each covered with an American flag, pulled alongside the *Leviathan* at 3:00 p.m. on September 12. The ship's ensign had been lowered to half mast, and as the caskets were carried up the gangway, an honor guard snapped to attention as other sailors in dress blues, white caps, and white leggings helped move the bodies to a storage area below deck. The men had been killed seven days earlier when the *Mount Vernon*, another former German luxury liner converted to a troop carrier, was torpedoed after leaving Brest on her return trip to New York.

When the caskets were secured and the remaining supplies hoisted aboard, Captain Bryan went over the final preparations for the departure. It was more complicated than usual, thanks to all the VIPs sailing back to the United States. In addition to Assistant Secretary of the Navy Roosevelt, who was confined to his stateroom running a dangerous fever, four congressmen were on board, as was Prince Axel of Denmark and three of his military aides, who were heading to Washington for a naval conference.

Bryan had received a message from Admiral Sims, reminding him to notify Roosevelt's family of the ship's approximate arrival date, which was set for September 19. The initial medical reports were that the assistant secretary had the flu, and Bryan had begun paying more attention to such cases. Over just the last day, four crew members had been hospitalized, and there was no telling how many others on board also might be infected.

The *Leviathan* cast off her lines right on schedule at 5:00 p.m. and backed away from her buoy. Over at the dry dock, the *Mount Vernon* was already undergoing repairs. A hole about ten feet wide gaped in her bow, and the sparks from blowtorches were cascading down the side of the ship where a torpedo had slammed into her, flooding a boiler room. Like the *Leviathan*, the former German luxury liner *Kronprinzessin Cecilie* was immediately recognizable by her size, tall funnels, and war paint. Bryan was reminded again how lucky they'd been on their last trip to Brest.

The best guess was that the German commander was probably hunting for the *Leviathan* when he targeted the other ship, at 706 feet one of the largest troop transports afloat.

A lookout on the *Mount Vernon* had spotted the torpedo when it was six hundred yards off her starboard bow. The helm was immediately thrown over, and the ship started to turn, but not in time to avoid the torpedo, which was moving at twenty-five knots when it hit, lifting the bow of the ship completely out of the water. One cannon was torn from its mounts, but another gun crew managed to fire several rounds at the U-boat, forcing it to dive as six destroyers that were shadowing the American ship and another transport in the convoy charged in that direction. The badly damaged *Mount Vernon* was saved only because her watertight doors were closed in time to limit the flooding to one of the large fire rooms. The men who died were either killed by the explosion or were trapped far belowdecks and drowned when seawater poured into the compartment. One man escaped by squeezing his slim, 155-pound frame through a rectangular air vent that measured a meager eight by fifteen inches.

Almost all the dead were firemen who stoked the ship's boilers. They had to know they were doomed as soon as the watertight doors slammed shut, sealing them in a compartment that rapidly filled with water. Even after the flooding was under control, the ship was still at risk of another U-boat attack until she could get under way again. Despite the real threat of sinking, the engine room crew stayed at their posts and got enough steam pressure back so that some of the boilers could be restarted. During the fight to save the ship, a special "collision mat" was lowered down the side to plug the hole. With two destroyers laying down smoke screens to conceal the stricken ship from submarines, the *Mount Vernon* struggled back to Brest at fifteen knots.

One day out of Brest, the *Great Northern* reported she spotted a periscope two miles astern of the *Leviathan*. With nerves already taut—this was the time and place when U-boats often attacked—all those on the bridge swung their glasses in that direction as the captain ordered maximum speed and put the crew on full alert. They saw nothing. The periscope had vanished as quickly as it had appeared, but a destroyer steamed over to check the area. When there was no sign of the sub after ten minutes, Bryan brought the *Leviathan*'s speed back down.

By now he may have been hoping that this would be his last U-boat scare, and he had good reason to be optimistic. A few days earlier he'd learned that he would be relieved of command of the *Leviathan* when the ship reached New York. It appeared that he was going to be assigned to Brazil as head of a naval training mission to that country. He would have preferred another sea command in a war zone and had made his feelings known, but he was told to consider the reassignment a promotion and that his linguistic skills played an important role in his selection. He'd have a short home leave before he sailed for Rio, and the truth was he could use some rest. For weeks he'd slept only a few hours a day and was worn out.

The ship's doctor apprised him of Roosevelt's condition when they were near the midway point in the North Atlantic. "Within the iron walls of *Leviathan*," wrote biographer Kenneth Davis, "he lay helpless and miserable . . . suffering from a combination of double pneumonia and influenza." It was the kind of flu that most worried doctors. Roosevelt, flat on his back, continued to run a high fever, shivering in bed and fighting bronchial congestion. Bryan was worried. So were the ship's doctors. "Roosevelt, in mid-Atlantic, came near to death."

FDR WAS STILL dangerously ill when the *Leviathan* arrived in Hoboken at 10:10 a.m. on September 19. His wife, Eleanor, and his mother were waiting at the pier with a doctor and an ambulance when the ship tied up. Captain Bryan would have made sure to personally welcome the assistant secretary's wife when she came on board to see her husband and to arrange for orderlies to carry Roosevelt off the ship on a stretcher. Eleanor briefly visited with several other passengers who also were laid up with the flu.

Roosevelt was driven to his mother's five-story townhouse on East Sixty-Fifth Street and carried up the short flight of front steps. It would be weeks before he recovered his strength, and by then his marriage would be in shambles. While going through Franklin's baggage from the *Leviathan*, Eleanor discovered a stack of love letters written to him by her social secretary, Lucy Mercer. It was a life-altering moment as she realized her husband had been having an affair.

Bryan must have been relieved to see FDR and all the other VIPs leave the ship. More attention was paid to them, it seemed, than to the departure of some real heroes—the thirty-seven sailors who'd died on the *Mount Vernon*. Bryan was on deck and standing at attention when their bodies were carried off the ship on their way to the New York naval yard.

On September 21, a Saturday, he left the *Leviathan* for the last time after giving his successor a tour. Captain William Phelps had been skipper of the *Northern Pacific*, and Bryan had known him for years and was happy he was taking over. His departure was mentioned, typically, in a few brief lines in the logbook. At 11:30 a.m.

"Capt. H. F. Bryan left ship having been detached from command to report for temporary duty to Chief of Naval Operations; completion to duty as Senior Member of Naval Commission to Brazil." His bags were waiting for him on the pier.

Moving Up to the Front

EVENING SHADOWS WERE spilling across the ground as Lieutenant Royal Johnson and other soldiers from D Company climbed into the back of one of the big blue French military trucks. They'd just spent nine hours in the cramped, straw-filled boxcars of a slow-moving troop train, then pried themselves out and marched toward Bar-le-Duc. By 8:00 p.m. on September 11, a mile-long convoy of over 250 trucks was waiting for them. The tired soldiers, all carrying large packs, slumped into the bench seats, fifteen men to a truck, and tried to settle in for what everyone knew was likely to be a long, bumpy ride.

Recently promoted to lieutenant, Johnson was pleased to find out that the rumors sweeping through their camp near Champlitte had been correct for once—they were finally heading toward the front. The truck drivers were from French Indochina, small men in thin, baggy trousers who sat behind the oversize steering wheels of the bulky French trucks smiling nonstop at the Americans and falling stone-cold asleep within seconds whenever the convoy halted. A light rain was falling as the convoy slowly started moving on the muddy roads. A few hours later, sometime after midnight, Johnson noticed flashes on the horizon that looked like lightning. When the road swung north—the sky was black now—he heard the guns. It kept going like that for four hours, hundreds of trucks packed with American soldiers watching the flashes and listening to the thunder of a battle unfolding twenty miles to the east.

The spectacular bombardment marked the opening of the battle to eliminate the Saint Mihiel bulge, what Foch liked to call a
"hernia" that extended into the Allied lines to a depth of sixteen
miles. The apex of the triangle was at the village of Saint Mihiel,
with the base running between Haudiomont and Pont-à-Mousson.
It was the first major offensive for the newly constituted American
army, consisting of 550,000 doughboys and 110,000 French troops.
Pershing had rounded up additional soldiers wherever he could
find them, even bringing men in from Château-Thierry. He'd been
planning this offensive since August and had assembled an American air force totaling 1,400 planes, not one of them built in the
United States.

Finally, at 1:00 a.m. on September 12, over three thousand cannons opened up at once, the muzzle flashes exploding in a continuous line of dazzling light along the twenty-five-mile front. The
spectacular bombardment went on for four hours, up to eight
hours in some places. "The sky over the battlefield, both before and
after dawn, aflame with exploding shells, star signals, burning supply dumps and villages, presented a scene at once picturesque and
terrible," Pershing wrote later, exultant that after eighteen months
an American army was finally fighting under its own flag.

From his seat in the back of one of the French camions, Johnson watched the eerie flashes in the distance. The rain—sometimes
a soft mist—was whipped along by a cold wind, and when the
dawn finally arrived, the scene was hellish as they passed through
a succession of shattered villages and fields pockmarked by four
years of shelling. As they got closer to the front, the destruction
became more widespread—entire forests turned to kindling, the
trees sheared off by shelling, the splintered trunks scorched and
blackened. Their destination remained a mystery, but Johnson and
everyone else in the convoy recognized that they were about to
make their debut in combat.

They'd received as much training as they were likely to get and were mercifully unaware that they were on their way to attack an exceptionally well-defended position, probably the most difficult objective of the war. The newly assembled regiment had bonded since its arrival in France, and the men were eager to show what they could do in a real fight. The drivers were racing along bumper-to-bumper with their headlights off.

They reached their drop-off at 7:00 a.m. on Friday, September 13. Piling out of the trucks with stiff backs and legs, they marched to two encampments hidden in the woods, where they were concealed from German airplanes. They tried to catch some sleep, and in the afternoon Johnson and other line officers were briefed on their mission, at least in its preliminary details. They'd be taking over positions that had been held for nearly two months by the 371st Infantry, the African American regiment from South Carolina attached to the French army. Johnson got his first look at the men they were going to replace, and it seemed strange to see all these battle-hardened African American troops wearing French helmets and carrying French-made gas masks and rifles. The men didn't look happy to be leaving their positions. Their regiment had two black-and-white rat terriers that went with them, and it wasn't long before the new arrivals discovered why such dogs were considered so valuable.

That evening, Johnson's unit was assigned to the new American sector along a front that covered over a mile. Moving out single file and cautioned to avoid jangling their rifles and bayonets, they slipped into shallow trenches that ran parallel with the German lines, which were concealed behind a row of skeletal trees. The men were on edge, their adrenaline pumping as they tried to take it all in. Johnson couldn't see the enemy, but later that night the Germans set off some red flares by way of introduction and fired a few artillery rounds their way.

The soldiers soon settled into a routine of manning an outpost for two hours, then resting in dugouts behind the front lines for four hours. The first night, everyone was jumpy, especially those in the forward positions, who had to get used to the unnerving sensation of facing an enemy in the dark, knowing his skill for raids and expecting to get hit at any moment. Several gas alarms turned out to be false, and it would take time before the men learned how to spot the important German rocket signals. The signal for an artillery barrage was a yellow rocket; white meant a "fire of destruction," a bombardment designed to level any defenses; a green rocket meant gas.

During the morning briefing, Johnson and the other officers were cheered by the latest reports from the Saint Mihiel offensive. Launched at 5:00 a.m. in wet, miserable conditions, it caught the Germans unprepared. Expecting a major attack elsewhere, they were already pulling back when the Americans fell on them. Within the first day, hundreds of prisoners were taken, more than three hundred emerging from a single dugout with their hands up. Even in retreat the Germans fought stiffly enough to prevent the US First Army from cutting off their escape route, which allowed most of them to get away. Still, it was good news to hear that all the American objectives had been taken quickly and that Pershing reportedly was in an atypically jaunty mood. For the more cautious, there were concerns that the speed of the victory may have produced a dangerous sense of overconfidence. "American success," wrote one historian, "came a bit too easily at St. Mihiel, engendering perhaps an unwarranted optimism and confidence similar to that which afflicted the South after winning the battle of Bull Run."

As they waited for their turn, Royal Johnson and D Company settled down to their new life on the front lines. It didn't take long for the Germans to test the regiment's mettle. Less than a week after their arrival, an American outpost was shot up by German raiders who struck at 1:00 a.m., then came back an hour later for more of the same before they were driven off by rifle fire. At dawn the body of a German second lieutenant was found lying just outside the trench. His papers identified him as the son of a major general, and a member of the First Division Prussian Guards, a troubling discovery that meant one of the German army's elite regiments was facing them.

Continuing the pressure, the enemy hit the regiment again two days later on September 22 with a barrage that lasted an hour and a half and pulverized some of the trenches. The Germans followed up with a strong raid on a platoon defending Avocourt, a woebe-gone ruin that anchored part of the defensive line. The Americans were starting to take casualties by now, including their first deaths; one company lost three men and suffered seven wounded. Several more men were captured.

Johnson had to get used to the chronic lack of sleep, especially at night, when staying awake was a matter of life and death for any-one on duty. This was true even in the rear shelters, which regu-larly came under shell fire. The trenches and dugouts were infested with rats, the big black variety the soldiers had to club to death, and no matter how much the men tried to stay clean and keep their hair cut short, the lice, or "cooties," were always with them, burrowing into their uniforms and blankets until they were scratching or pick-ing nits nearly every waking moment. In the morning, tormented soldiers angrily ripped off their shirts, looking for the vermin that abounded in the collars and sleeves.

Soon after his arrival, Johnson got his first look at what they al-ready knew would be their objective—Montfaucon. Rising almost four miles in front of them and cresting a steep hill, the village had been in German hands since shortly after the war started. Johnson could easily make out the smashed homes and buildings up there, and if he looked through binoculars, he saw soldiers walking along the rubble-littered streets. A ruined forest covered the open ground that spread out in front of the hill, and a cemetery lay just to the east. A shattered church dominated the heights, which were heav-ily fortified. About one hundred yards beyond the church was an

observatory cunningly concealed in the ruins of an abandoned château. The word was that Crown Prince Wilhelm had used a powerful telescope from that vantage to watch how his armies were
doing in their futile attacks against the French nearly nine miles
away at Verdun in 1916. The Argonne Forest lay to the west.

The Germans had held Montfaucon, with its unparalleled view
of the most strategic ground on the western front, almost from
the beginning of the war, and they had spent four years skillfully
improving the trenches, machine gun pillboxes, underground
tunnels, crossfire zones, and observation posts to the point that it
was nicknamed "Little Gibraltar." It contained one of the most advanced precision telescopes in existence, a device mounted atop a
periscope within a thirty-five-foot-tall tower of reinforced concrete
and projecting through the roof, where it was camouflaged with
air vents. The telescope allowed the Germans to aim their superb
artillery with incredible accuracy. According to the historian William Walker, "The crown prince's observatory was one of Germany's most closely held secrets. Before the dominance of airpower,
Montfaucon's telescopic periscope was the equivalent of today's spy
satellites, providing timely, precise information that could help destroy any target within a twenty-mile radius."

After a week in the trenches, the 313th was relieved by other
infantry units and pulled back to a staging area concealed in deep
woods behind the American lines. The drizzly weather remained,
but there was plenty of warm food, the best they'd had since arriving at the front.

Their pullback meant something big was coming. Artillery
pieces of different calibers, mainly the long-barreled French 75s,
were being hauled into the woods, where gun emplacements were
dug deep. Ammunition trucks, tractors, and ambulances were too
numerous to count, and there were reports that an American tank
battalion was on its way. All this traffic stayed off the roads in the
daylight to try to conceal the buildup from the Germans, who were

becoming increasingly aware of the growing American presence in front of them.

It didn't take long for Johnson to recognize the unique sound of German aircraft engines, which had a lower, louder pitch than those of French planes and were often heard making regular sorties over the American lines as their pilots tried to get a better picture of what was happening on the ground. The men were ordered to draw bandoliers and extra clips of ammunition and sort out their excess baggage. As they sat under shelters in steady rain, smoking unfiltered American cigarettes and enjoying double rations, Johnson and other soldiers were pretty sure what they were going to attack. The only question was when.

ABOUT THE SAME time the 313th Regiment was moving into the trenches facing the fortress of Montfaucon, Corporal Freddie Stowers and the 371st Regiment were in a slow-moving truck convoy driven by the same diminutive men from French Indochina. Loaded down with their packs, rifles, and ammunition, the soldiers of the 371st were heading about forty miles west to the village of Heiltz l'Évêque in the Champagne region. They weren't happy to leave a sector where they'd become familiar with the ground and with the enemy, but they were now part of the French 157th Division, which was heading to a new position near the Argonne Forest. Stowers and his men couldn't have been happy with the stares and stupid grins they likely received from some of the white soldiers who relieved them. There was no excuse for that, especially given the sharp differences in experience. These newbies were going to have to learn quickly on the job or get killed. None of them had spent any time in the trenches facing battle-tested German veterans who were guaranteed to give them an education. The 371st had been squared off against the enemy since late June and had taken casualties as its men had learned how to fight, hold their ground, and stay alive. They had good reason to consider their combat skills as far superior to those of the soldiers who'd just replaced them, so some of them were probably in a sour mood as the trucks started down the road in a long caravan heading west.

Their commander was General Mariano Goybet, the fifty-five-year-old officer in charge of the 157th "Red Hand" Division of the French Fourth Army. With a thin, ascetic-looking face and fierce mustache, Goybet was known for aggressiveness, so if he had anything to do with the change of scenery, it probably meant the 371st was heading into a fight. A man of no pretensions, the Saint-Cyr graduate dressed in a simple field uniform and liked to mingle with the troops, usually traveling close to the front with only two aides and wearing a holstered pistol. Stowers and his men respected the general, who'd lost two sons in the fighting and had earned a reputation before the war as a daring climber and skier who commanded the Chasseurs Alpins, an elite mountain corps. He'd also helped design the division's eye-catching flag, which depicted the Stars and Stripes and the French tricolor with a bloodred hand between them.

Goybet was known for his talent for spotting mistakes. A short time after the Americans arrived, the general ordered that all sentries in the front lines should double up, a decision prompted by the death of a sentry who was cut down at his post a few days earlier. The soldier had done his duty, managing to shout out a warning before he was killed, but Goybet figured his life might have been saved if another man had been out there with him. He also was a stickler for making sure soldiers always carried their rifles wherever they went.

"A man," he said frequently, "must never be without his rifle."

Orders from the general were required reading for Stowers, whose job was to make sure they were understood and passed down the line. They covered the gamut. Many men, Goybet said, had fallen into "the bad habit" of stacking their rifles while off duty. He'd personally found soldiers asleep on the front lines and warned company commanders that they'd be held responsible for such incidents. Machine gunners were told to make sure they had a fixed reference point if they had to fire at night, and everyone was reminded repeatedly about the importance of discipline. "The exterior marks of respect are not given at once," he admonished them. "There is hesitation . . . men saluting with cigarettes in their mouths and so on." Almost worse, some soldiers didn't know his name. "After a month everybody ought to know that he belongs to the Division Goybet," he said. That's how he wanted it, no numbers, just his name. A number could tip off the enemy about which division he faced.

The previous few months had been an unforgiving school for Stowers and the soldiers of C Company. Men had been killed and many others wounded. Some of the worst losses had occurred during a night raid in July. Two corporals were killed, men Stowers knew, and another thirty badly injured when American trench mortar shells fell short of their target and landed on them as they hunkered down in front of the German trenches. The artillery fire had already cut through two lines of barbed wire, allowing them to move forward, but they'd run up against a third line and were kneeling there in the darkness trying to figure out what to do next as German flares illuminated the sky.

An officer was searching desperately for an opening through the wire when three shells crashed nearby, terrific explosions that partially buried them in the mud. Carrying as many wounded as they could, the survivors were forced to retreat under machine gun fire and an artillery bombardment that killed another four men and wounded fifteen others. They sought protection from the shelling wherever they could find it, rolling into water-filled shell holes or hugging the ground until the firing stopped, then crawling forward again. When they got back to their lines, the survivors couldn't understand what had gone wrong. They didn't buy that they'd arrived at the wire too early and had gotten ahead of the barrage, or that the rain had somehow made the mortars fall short. The experience left them embittered.

Going out on night raids and patrols was a regular part of life for the 371st, and Stowers certainly had his share. In one raid on July 29, which included three NCOs like himself from C Company as well as an officer and thirteen privates, they crawled from their trenches at 11:30 p.m. Their objective was to set up an ambush in front of an enemy listening post and try to capture some prisoners. Each man carried six hand grenades and two pairs of wire cutters along with rifles and pistols. They didn't succeed in snatching a prisoner— only one German was ever captured during their long stay in the trenches—but safely returned to their lines at 3:30 a.m., providing a detailed sketch of the ground they'd covered. On other patrols into no-man's land, the men carried only grenades, pistols, and bolos, leaving behind their tin hats, bayonet scabbards, and any other equipment that might rattle. If they carried rifles, they blackened the barrels to make sure they wouldn't reflect light from flares.

Much of the responsibility for making sure all this was done properly fell on NCOs like Stowers, and when mistakes occurred, the news traveled quickly. Soon after the 371st arrived at the sector, a corporal manning a forward position at twilight spotted a German patrol within easy range of American artillery. Instead of grabbing the field telephone right next to him and calling in the coordinates, he sent in a written report, which took over an hour to reach a commanding officer, and by then the Germans were long gone. The corporal thought he was following standing orders about not using telephones for fear the Germans could listen in. The regiment's very angry commander fired off a memo "to all concerned," excoriating the man's poor judgment and urging everyone to use the telephone under similar circumstances. It wasn't long before every soldier in the 371st knew the corporal's name and that he'd been relieved of all duties as an observer.

The NCOs were expected to remind their men about the important things such as always carrying their gas masks, which were contained in a canister slung around the neck. They were using French masks, which were more effective and better made than the British models. They'd been lucky so far and hadn't experienced any gas attacks, but everyone knew that wouldn't last, so the NCOs made sure everyone understood how the canister opened and how the mask was placed around the head and neck, and that the face piece had to fit tightly to be effective. As with their rifles, they were expected to carry the masks wherever they went. No exceptions.

They also had to learn how to recognize the smell of gas. At the first alert or the appearance of a smoky, ground-hugging cloud, it was crucial to get the mask on and tightened quickly. A delay of even a few seconds could be fatal. Soldiers were reminded that if they dozed off, their masks always needed to be within arm's reach. Corporals like Stowers were key to delivering the message that gas attacks could be survived if a soldier didn't panic and, above all, didn't run. The dugouts were kept largely gas free by making sure the thick curtains at the entrances fit snugly and were sprayed down with a chemical solution if there was an attack.

Stowers was frequently reminded to keep a close watch over his men to cut down on "accidental woundings"—often the result of carelessness but sometimes done deliberately. Soldiers in forward positions were frequently shot accidentally by men in the trenches behind them, but others considered a self-inflicted wound a one-way ticket home. The problem was epidemic in the British army, and Robert Graves, in his classic on the war, *Good-Bye to All That*, recounts stories of soldiers who exposed themselves to sniper fire hoping to get a "cushy," a clean gunshot wound through the hand or foot that would get them out of the war. Sometimes their plans backfired. Graves mentions a soldier who waved his hands, then his arms over the top of the trench for a couple of minutes, trying to draw a shot from the German lines. When nothing happened, he did a handstand in his trench and waved his legs. Again nothing happened, so figuring no Germans were out there, he peeked over the top and was promptly drilled through the head.

Stowers was expected to know his men and their varying moods and watch for any signs of mental breakdown or cowardice. A widely distributed memo from General Goybet stated the prevailing attitude: "Men who are accidentally wounded through their own carelessness. . . . are guilty of desertion in face of the enemy."

WHEN THE 371ST Regiment finally reached Heiltz l'Évêque, the men were first told they'd be there at least two weeks for training, but four days later, on the evening of September 20, they were ordered to pack up and start marching north toward Champagne and the Argonne Forest. They marched through the night and before the sun rose moved into the small villages along the road where billets were found in the usual barns, sheds, and assorted outbuildings. The artillery—more than Stowers had ever seen—was concealed in the woods. By day, when German aircraft were prowling the skies, no one moved and the roads looked white and empty for miles. By nightfall they were jammed with hundreds of trucks, batteries of French 75s, 155 Howitzers, and 155 Longs, machine gun carts, short-barreled French tanks, ambulances, and thousands of infantry marching in column, often stumbling into ditches as the heavier traffic pushed them off the road.

The corporal and every man in the regiment knew that they were heading to the big show. The march went on for four nights. By September 24, they reached the Champagne plateau and were about nine miles behind the frontline trenches occupied by the French Fourth Army to the west. The American First Army was to the east near Montfaucon, where the 371st had just come from.

The men settled down on a ridge overlooking the wide valley of Champagne to the north and the Argonne Forest to the east. The NCOs passed the word: strip down to battle gear. Everyone was issued extra ammunition and canteens of water. No one had been told when the drive would start, but as they lay in their blankets that night they received a strong clue. At eleven o'clock the biggest artillery display any of them ever witnessed opened with a roar. The gut-churning thunder of the guns shook the ground, and the men quickly rolled out to watch the entire horizon light up. The French guns were behind them. "The flashes from the batteries made an almost continuous line of fire along the front," according to the regiment's history. "Shells from the rear sounded like freight trains over us." The firing went on for hours, and at five in the morning, the 75s started a rolling barrage.

As dawn broke, the sky was filled with French and American planes and French observation, or "sausage," balloons. Word arrived that French and Moroccan divisions had attacked, driving the Germans back to their secondary positions, where they were resisting fiercely. The guns were still pounding. One of the regiment's French instructors later said, "It was wondrous—it was insanity and the fever of it gripped us all."

The next day, September 26, Freddie Stowers and his company got their orders to move forward.

CHAPTER 17

"Everyone Attack"

A FORTRESS IN ROMAN times, Verdun had successfully resisted an attack by Attila the Hun in the fifth century, and when General John Pershing arrived there on Saturday, September 21, his first stop was the famous citadel. During his motor trip to what had already become a monument to the unspeakable, the effects of the battle that had been fought there two years earlier were readily visible in the shattered buildings and countryside, where overlapping shell craters pockmarked an area of roughly one hundred square miles. The German drive to push the French from their stronghold on the river Meuse had broken against a wall of fierce resistance—and at a monstrous cost.

Pershing made a casual inspection of the underground fortress and a network of tunnels hollowed out beneath fifty feet of rock, where the first shells of the German bombardment had fallen. Entering the subterranean officers' club, he stopped in his tracks. Painted in bold black letters on the wall in front of him were General Robert Nivelle's words: ON NE PASSE PAS ("They will not pass") The slogan seemed to galvanize Pershing and those with him. For several minutes no one spoke.

On that same day he met with General Pétain, who had also uttered words of defiance that resonated with the American commander: *On les aura!* ("We'll get them")—a rallying cry borrowed from Joan of Arc.

Pétain, a friend of Pershing's, had taken over the Verdun defense soon after the massive German assault began on February 21, 1916, which threatened to overrun the French defenses along an eight-mile front. The French held on heroically. A single road that was often under fire and that brought supplies to the front from fifty miles away was later called the Voie Sacrée, or "the Sacred Way." After a six-month battle of bombardment, attack, and counterattack, the Germans ultimately didn't pass. An estimated twenty million shells were fired, forever altering the landscape and leaving the ground ripped apart for miles. Villages, some of the oldest and most historic in France, simply vanished. "Worse by far was the destruction of human life," one historian wrote. "By the end of June over 200,000 men had been killed and wounded on each side."

Verdun was soon to be part of Pershing's command. He'd recently moved his command post for the American First Army to Ligny-en-Barrois, a village about twenty-five miles southeast of Saint Mihiel, in preparation for the attack that would start five days later on the Meuse-Argonne front.

During his meeting with Pétain, he discussed some of the final details for the offensive, especially how best to coordinate with the French Fourth Army, which would fight on his left and immediately to the west of the Argonne Forest. The grand offensive was charted by Marshal Foch as an "arpeggio" of four major attacks against the German lines: Pershing and his new First Army held the extreme right of the Allied line; the French occupied the center; the British were on the left; and the Belgians were positioned on the sea. Foch's idea was remarkably simple—keep slugging until the enemy couldn't continue to fight. As the marshal put it: "Everyone attack as soon as they can, as strong as they can, for as long as they can."

Pershing had been given the most difficult and strategically important part of the battle plan, a front twenty-four miles wide and thirteen miles deep that was located between the fortified heights of the river Meuse on the east and the all-but-impenetrable Argonne

Forest to the west, "a wild Hans Christian Andersen land of giant trees cunningly interwoven with the nests of machine guns" and lines of barbed wire too numerous to count. A thick ridgeline ran up the center, fortified with strongholds at Montfaucon, Romagne, Cunel, and Barricourt. At the US headquarters in Ligny-en-Barrois, Pershing's map laid out the German defense lines, or *stellungen*, that cut across the area and were named after three Wagnerian witches—Giselher Stellung, Kriemhilde Stellung, and Freya Stellung. Montfaucon was the key to the Giselher Stellung. The last of the defensive positions, the Kriemhilde Stellung, the most important and heavily defended, was also called the Hindenburg Line.

The Germans had had four years to add a devilish array of defenses to the already challenging landscape of hills, ravines, and woods—seemingly countless numbers of machine gun pillboxes, a network of trenches, and barbed wire in lines four and five deep and concealed over the years with lush vines and brush. Artillery was positioned to provide flanking fire on infantry trying to move between the Meuse and the Argonne. This masterpiece of interlocking, mutually supportive firepower was designed to defend a critical railroad in the rear, the Sedan-Mezieres line, the only escape route to Germany. If it were broken, the German army would be trapped, unable to be resupplied or reinforced. The war would end.

The hope of wading through this defensive nightmare with any chance of success with largely green, inexperienced troops constituted a long shot at best. Everything would depend on surprise and speed. Pershing's intelligence officers told him that the enemy could reinforce their lines with up to 15 divisions within three days. The only possibility of victory depended on hitting the Germans with overwhelming force before they could bring up all those support troops. Pershing's battle plan called for sending a quarter-million men over the top in a crushing, lightning advance on the first day that would cover ten miles, drive the Germans from the Argonne Forest, and allow the Americans to link up with the French at Grandpré. This would be followed by another ten-mile leap to Stenay-Le Chesne to outflank the enemy fighting the French Fourth Army north of the Aisne River. The third step was an attack against the east bank of the Meuse to eliminate the German artillery along the river. All this would be followed by a drive on the Sedan-Mezieres railroad. The initial attack was to break through the enemy line by capturing the heights of Romagne, the key to the Kriemhilde Stellung, with its two fortified knolls—Hill 288 and the Côte-de-Châtillon.

Events soon showed that Pershing had been hopelessly optimistic in his assessment of what his troops could accomplish on the power of élan, a favorite word in the French war lexicon that meant smashing through obstacles on the battlefield with style and unrelenting drive. Pershing preferred the word "push," but no American division had ever made a ten-mile attack on the first day of a battle in the war, or even come close. Nine American divisions would face five understrength German divisions, but four of those US divisions lacked their own artillery, and some were rife with untrained troops with only six weeks' experience in the army, and most of that spent traveling to France. "Incredibly," according to historian Donald Smythe, "some had never handled a rifle."

Pershing worried about sending so many untrained soldiers into battle, yet he believed the desperate circumstances required it. He thought it was reasonable to count on the "aggressive spirit of our troops to make up in a measure for their inexperience, but at the same time the fact was not overlooked that lack of technical skill might considerably reduce the chances of complete success against well organized resistance of experienced defenders." Pétain had already told him that he didn't think American forces could get beyond the strongpoint of Montfaucon before winter.

If all that wasn't daunting enough, a few days before the battle was to begin the staffs of the five most inexperienced divisions were robbed of key officers to provide students and instructors for an upcoming General Staff College session, a move that proved disastrous. "The amount of confusion and mismanagement resulting from this was tremendous," George C. Marshall Jr. said later. Marshall, then a staff officer at the US General Headquarters (GHQ), was largely responsible for the often tangled but successful movement of men and equipment to the Meuse-Argonne front—many of the troops coming from the Saint Mihiel sector—all done under cover of darkness. Both Royal Johnson and Freddie Stowers were caught up in massive traffic tie-ups as their regiments moved to the front along three designated roads already jammed with artillery and supply trains. A single AEF division required one thousand trucks—a line that extended four miles.

On Wednesday, September 25, the day before the attack, Pershing visited the headquarters of his corps and division commanders strung out around Verdun to give them a final pep talk. "They were all alert and confident," he said later, "and I returned feeling that all would go as planned."

He couldn't have been more mistaken.

The artillery barrage that started shortly before midnight prefigured the chaos, confusion, and horror that was about to erupt across a wide front. The intensity shocked veterans as well as the new arrivals—nearly four thousand guns of varying calibers raining fire on German positions—frontline trenches, barbed wire entanglements, and supply bunkers far in the rear. Taking off before dawn in his French fighter, Eddie Rickenbacker saw the horizon lighting up below him in a stream of jagged flashes, a fireworks display on steroids with rolling light, bright flashes, and jets of flame. Another pilot found it "the most gorgeous thing imaginable," then realized countless numbers of men were dying below him. "Have all men gone mad?" he asked himself.

Fear of a "Flu Trip"

DURING THE TEN days before the *Leviathan* set sail again for France on her ninth crossing of the war, William Phelps, her new captain, and other senior naval officers were worried about the likelihood of a "flu trip." Ever since the ship had returned from Brest with the dangerously ill assistant secretary of the navy aboard, the prospect of an epidemic exploding aboard American troopships bound for France appeared more and more likely. The illness spread fast, and within the tight confines of a ship at sea it could explode like a bomb.

Phelps, who took command of the *Leviathan* on September 21, quickly initiated a series of steps that he hoped would curtail the outbreak. Guards would double down at the gangways to keep anyone who looked sick from boarding the ship, but Phelps was concerned that large numbers of recently infected soldiers wouldn't be spotted and would come aboard. Trying to take whatever initiative he could, he made sure additional quarantine space was set aside belowdecks and that the ship's infirmary was ready for a crisis. He insisted on strictly enforcing regulations that required spraying the noses and throats of crew members twice a day and wearing gauze flu masks except while eating. Phelps figured he wouldn't be able to stop the spread of the illness among the doughboys, but he would do whatever he could to protect his sailors. He also ordered that the soldiers be kept on deck in the open air as much as possible.

Meanwhile, the outbreaks of influenza kept increasing. On the same day that Phelps took command, the USS *Yacona* steamed out of New London, Connecticut, bound for Nova Scotia but got only as far as Boston, dropping anchor there when eighty of her crew of ninety-six came down with the flu. In Philadelphia, six hundred sailors from the naval yard were in the hospital, and in Camp Lewis, Washington, 173 cases had been reported.

Congress finally took notice and appropriated $1 million to fight an illness that many medical authorities were predicting would hit epidemic levels, but even the grimmest estimates were nowhere close to what happened in the United States. In Philadelphia, the hardest-hit city in the nation, nearly eleven thousand would die during the month of October.

By early September, with the flu starting to hit troopships, the acting surgeon general, Charles Richards, warned Chief of Staff Peyton March about the prospect of even worse outbreaks on vessels bound for France, "which under present conditions of overcrowding may be expected to result in thousands of cases of disease, with many deaths." Richards recommended not sending any military unit until it was free of flu. No one objected, but it didn't stop what would soon happen aboard the *Leviathan*.

Captain Phelps remained uneasy about the next trip, in which they expected to sail with 9,500 troops, about a thousand fewer than on the last voyage. As lean and trim as Bryan was full faced and broad, the forty-eight-year-old Baltimore-born Phelps traveled with an English manservant and, as the captain told a reporter, a white-haired fox terrier named Lord Nelson, who was "the greatest seaman I have ever met." As much a stickler for discipline as Bryan, he probably had a better sense of humor. A reporter with permission from the Navy Department to come aboard was stopped at the gangway by a guard who refused to let him proceed. When an officer arrived and asked what was wrong, the frustrated reporter said, "The blanked old captain of this ship won't let his men admit me to the decks." The officer smiled and told the reporter to follow him and strode up the gangway to the main deck, where the grateful newsman asked for his name. "Oh, that's all right," the officer said. "I'm Phelps, the blanked captain of the ship."

Phelps had just one black mark on his record. He had been reprimanded during a court-martial in 1917 that found him guilty "through inattention and negligence" when the ship he was commanding, the USS *Louisiana*, an aging battleship used for training, ran aground on a submerged wreck in the York River in Virginia. Phelps lost a few pay grade points that were later restored, and except for that one incident, his record had been impeccable since he graduated from Annapolis in 1889.

His wife, Susie, often came on board to hand out boxes of candy, cigarettes, and books. The crew also got used to seeing the couple's son, a student at a nearby military academy, touring the *Leviathan* with his father. The sailors soon discovered that their new skipper had a peculiar habit of sending anyone punished during a captain's mast to see the ship's chaplain, a Catholic priest who'd been with the *Leviathan* since her first trip to Europe. And if the evening prayer at dusk wasn't mandatory, it was close. Maybe Phelps figured he needed all the help he could get on the next trip to France.

The *Leviathan* would sail on Sunday, September 29. The soldiers would start showing up at the pier on Saturday, thousands of them with their mountains of baggage, trucks, and equipment. As the day to shove off approached, Phelps couldn't help wondering how many of them would become sick.

CHAPTER 18

A Bad Wound

A T 2:30 A.M. on Thursday, September 26, Lieutenant Royal Johnson and the other members of the 313th Regiment huddled in the "jumping-off" trenches grew stunned as the bombardment that had lit the sky for three hours dramatically intensified. Batteries hidden miles behind them—big-bored artillery pieces of different calibers, including 340-millimeter French naval cannons—opened up in one of the greatest artillery barrages in history, nearly four thousand guns building to a climax through the night, so many it was later calculated that there was an average of one cannon for every nine yards across a twenty-mile front. As described by a participant: "To the men waiting in the trenches, the rush of shells through the air sounded like a succession of express trains passing overhead. From far in the German lines came dull thuds as the projectiles landed and bashed in the dug-outs, trenches, [and] shelters. The noise along the entire front was terrific."

Adding to this otherworldly uproar, German batteries were soon pounding the American lines to return the favor.

Part of the reserves, Johnson and the men of D Company were scheduled to move out immediately after the first wave opened the Meuse-Argonne battle. At 5:30 a.m. troops would start going over the top into no-man's land, and as "H hour" neared, the lieutenant ordered his men to fix bayonets and check their watches. It was also his responsibility to tell the NCOs to try to keep an interval of ten to fifteen yards between each man.

A thin, steady rain had given way to mist and fog. As the sky started turning a milky gray in the east, Johnson could make out the dim outlines of the steep hill that was their objective about two and a half miles dead ahead—Montfaucon. The shattered remains of a church stood near the summit, with the ruined town and a cemetery spread out on the nearby slopes, concealing Lord knows how many machine guns. Johnson's map showed a forest to the left, the Bois de Malancourt, followed by a patch of open ground, then more woods, the Bois de Cuisy. The worst part of the advance would come when the men moved out of the woods and into the open ground that dipped in a shallow ravine then gently climbed for at least a mile to Montfaucon, the first day's objective. They would be exposed to machine gun and artillery fire every step of the way.

When the whistles were blown, the troops immediately climbed out of the trenches and started forward, holding their rifles at the ready. Others carried BARs. Johnson made a quick check to make sure his men had their gas masks in canvas sacks looped around their necks. When it was D Company's turn to go over the top, the men advanced through clouds of murky black smoke released as camouflage. The smell of high explosives was thick, and the German lines couldn't be seen. There was enough daylight now to notice something disturbing: they'd barely gotten started and were already hopelessly separated from their artillery barrage. The infantry was supposed to follow the barrage by about one hundred yards, and they'd been trained to advance by that distance every five minutes, but the German shells and difficult terrain had slowed everyone to a crawl, and within an hour the protective line of artillery fire had moved over a mile ahead of them.

Johnson found it tough going in no-man's land, slogging over muddy ground torn up by crater holes fifteen feet deep and often laced with tangled bands of barbed wire. The bombardment was supposed to cut holes in the German wire, but it hadn't come close to doing that. The woods had been chewed down by the shelling, and the stumps of trees still offered limited cover. Incoming fire increased as they passed over the most advanced German lines, which had been abandoned.

As the men moved on, German soldiers who had been hiding in the trenches—so-called suicide troops—emerged from dugouts and raked them from behind. In their haste to press forward, the Americans hadn't made sure all these snipers and machine gun crews were mopped up before continuing, and they paid a severe price for their negligence. Soldiers fell in windrows as the slow-moving line of olive drab continued, reaching the Malancourt woods, where "a withering fire of hidden machine guns and [more] snipers" cut them down.

The frontline troops slowly slugged their way through the woods and out into more open country that separated the Bois de Malancourt and the Bois de Cuisy. The ground sloped upward for about half a mile, and it was here at about 9:00 a.m. that the Germans made their first real stand.

An enemy map found later showed the positions for 113 machine guns that covered this area, not including another 50 guns that were added just before the attack. Most of them had overlapping fields of fire. The staccato patter of machine guns and the barrage from artillery on the heights of the Meuse to the far right blotted out nearly all other sounds. American casualties started to soar as the troops kept attacking. A major in charge of the Third Battalion was shot through both legs. Another major was fatally hit in the head. His adjutant had already been killed in the woods.

The captain in charge of Johnson's D Company had been badly wounded trying to clean out snipers and had been carried to the rear, where he died. A lieutenant with E Company lost practically his entire platoon in a matter of minutes. According to one history, "A temporary halt had to be made and an organized attack was started against the machine guns that were blocking the way. Only a few of these were in the immediate vicinity, as the woods and trenches on all sides were hiding places of the machine gunners and snipers."

Although considered second-rank troops by American intelligence, the German soldiers were mostly veterans who had been ordered to hold to the last. Their ranks included many older men—some in their midforties—and plenty of teenagers and the recently wounded. They fought with skill and tenacity. As one historian described it, "When cut off and surrounded they came forward yelling, 'kamerad!' then suddenly threw bombs, and in the ensuing disorder yelled in English, 'Retire! Retire!' as if American officers were ordering it."

The Americans began attacking the pillboxes one at a time, but lacking the necessary tactical skills, they made deadly mistakes, approaching the guns in clusters, moving into the streams of lead while standing up straight instead of crawling on their stomachs until they got close enough to kill the occupants with rifle fire or grenades. They failed to call in artillery fire because they didn't have the communications or the training to do so. The carnage continued for hours, and the 313th wasn't even close to Montfaucon. Around noon, Colonel Sweezey, the regiment's commanding officer, moved to a forward position and was bent over a map with a lieutenant from his intelligence section when the lieutenant was shot through the hip. Officers continued disappearing fast.

The loud drone of laboring engines suddenly broke through the crashing artillery fire. Johnson saw them, eight French tanks rolling forward toward the Bois de Cuisy. Most of his men had never seen a tank in action before, but here they were, crazy-looking contraptions bristling with short-barreled cannons and riding on tractor threads. "Suddenly, a black rattling monster loomed up before us almost filling the road," one of the soldiers remembered. "This was the first time we had seen one of those gigantic tanks we had heard so much about." It was six o'clock by then, and after advancing nearly two and a half miles, the battalion finally halted after reaching the Bois de Cuisy. Any thought that the woods would provide cover was quickly discarded as machine gun fire and high-explosive shells continued to sweep over them, the shrapnel lashing the remaining trees.

Peering out from cover at the mile of open ground that separated the woods from Montfaucon, Johnson could only hope they'd get a breather and that the German fire would slacken. His men were out of water and had already eaten their rations. The chocolate bars were always the first to go, then the cigarettes.

An order arrived from the colonel to dig in for the night. They'd been fighting for nearly twelve hours and had taken severe losses, including the deaths of two of three battalion commanders; they'd also lost communications with the brigade and were out of support range of friendly artillery.

Johnson's men had just started working with their shovels when another order arrived from their tough colonel. Forget about digging in. They'd been ordered to keep going and attack Montfaucon.

The troops must have been shocked. They'd taken a pounding and needed a rest. About 3,600 men from the 313th had attacked at H hour. Most of the casualties that the unit suffered in the Meuse-Argonne—1,122 wounded and nearly 300 killed—would occur in the first two days. They'd been bled badly, and some men were showing signs of shell shock, but they regrouped and headed back out into the killing zone.

They were still about a mile from Montfaucon, and much of the intervening distance was open ground. Moving forward with the tanks, the men ran into another wall of machine gun fire. More of them dropped, including the major in charge of the First Battalion, who was shot in the head. Against this withering fire, the 313th managed to eke out another half mile, and one company actually penetrated to the outskirts of Montfaucon before the tanks suddenly turned around. Their French commander didn't want to risk fighting in the dark over unfamiliar ground and had ordered a pullback.

That was enough for Colonel Sweezey, who recalled his troops. Some of them dug in out in the open, but most fell back to the woods, which offered only minimal cover. The hard-boiled colonel was the only field officer left for the entire regiment. With D Company's senior officers dead or wounded, Lieutenant Johnson found himself in charge during a cold, miserable night when they held their precarious position and tried to catch a few minutes of sleep. Montfaucon rose in front of them stump-like in the darkness. Whenever they dozed off for a few moments and opened their eyes, it was always there, tauntingly close. They had plenty of ground to cover come dawn, and the men were wondering what had happened to their artillery support, all those French 75s massed behind their lines. It had all but disappeared as the day progressed.

The lieutenant and the regiment's surviving officers had no idea how unhappy Pershing and other commanding officers were with their performance. The division's slow progress in front of Montfaucon was holding up the advance of the entire Meuse-Argonne offensive. Their French and English counterparts were also weighing in with a vengeance. It didn't matter that these conclusions were reached by officers totally removed from the fighting, or that the men dying in the field faced skilled German soldiers often willing to die where they stood. The scapegoating had begun and would only become more fierce.

THE ATTACK RESUMED at 7:30 a.m.

The machine guns opened up on them, but the drizzle and gloom threw off the German aim, and the battered 313th was able to get into the open and spread out in fairly good order. This time they had artillery backup; American guns were providing a rolling barrage, shielding the advance as Johnson and his men scrambled into a ravine and then hit the final slope to Montfaucon, where they were rejoined by the French tanks, now reduced in number to six. German artillery fire started falling on them from at least three positions, as concealed spotters directed the guns with deadly accuracy. It was probably during this period of intense bombardment that Royal Johnson was struck by shrapnel from a German 7.7, a cannon that fired a three-inch shell of high explosives. The fragment tore off a chunk of his right shoulder, knocking him unconscious. The regiment's assault line moved passed him, the survivors of D Company pressing forward into the outskirts of the shattered village. By 11:00 a.m., the men were moving through the streets of Montfaucon, often fighting house to house and eliminating the snipers who'd stayed behind, sometimes taking them prisoner, often not.

When Johnson recovered enough to try to stand up, his uniform was soaked with blood, but there wasn't much pain—at least not yet. He knew he'd been badly hit, but he tried to make a wisecrack: "I'd give one hundred dollars for a cigarette." A soldier on his way forward handed him his pack and kept going. (A few years later, Johnson would track the man down and repay him with a full carton.)

Although unable to use his right arm, the lieutenant helped lead two other wounded men from his company toward the rear. When they reached an advanced medical station, he made sure there was room for them in an ambulance before he took a place himself. The war was over for him, and he was soon on his way to a hospital at Bordeaux.

By 11:45 a.m. Montfaucon was captured. The view of the surrounding countryside from the concrete-reinforced observation point once used by the crown prince was breathtaking, even more so when the Americans realized the scope of the task still before them—the fortified and reinforced Hindenburg Line was still out there, beckoning and bristling with guns. The American attack slowed to a halt as the Germans started shelling the town they'd just evacuated, hitting it hard throughout the afternoon and evening with more high explosives and gas. Some troops hurried forward to the next stand of woods, running "into extremely heavy machine-gun and H.E. and shrapnel fire," but most dug in along the Montfaucon ridge as the shells kept falling.

News that the stronghold had been taken was sent back by carrier pigeon number 47, a plucky little bird that covered fourteen miles in one hour and forty-three minutes, "arriving with its left wing torn and bleeding." Somehow the message attached to its leg was lost, so headquarters didn't learn that Little Gibraltar had fallen until later in the day.

Complaints intensified about the performance of the Seventy-Ninth Division, which included the 313th and six other regiments, and in another two days the Meuse-Argonne attack appeared to have come unglued. Criticism from the French high command and officials like Clemenceau was stinging, as the most important offensive of the war pressed forward with increasing success by the French and English armies in other sectors while the critical American effort in the Meuse-Argonne lagged far behind.

The Eve of the Flu Voyage

ALREADY CONCERNED ABOUT the likelihood of an influenza outbreak aboard the *Leviathan*, Captain Phelps must have been seriously worried when the first men from the Fifty-Seventh Pioneer Infantry began stumbling up to the ship. The Vermont regiment had started lining up on the Hoboken pier shortly before sunrise on September 27, nearly two days before they were to sail for Brest. The regiment, the largest of the military units scheduled to travel on the *Leviathan* on her ninth round-trip of the war, was lucky to have made it that far.

Earlier that night the Fifty-Seventh had set out under a bright moon from Camp Merritt, an army base in New Jersey about ten miles north of New York City, the first leg of the trip that would bring them to the docks. Carrying their packs and weapons, men began falling out of rank almost immediately, collapsing on the side of the road; others stripped off their knapsacks as they struggled to keep up. Forced to call a halt, the officers summoned the camp surgeon. His diagnosis came as no surprise—the entire regiment had been hit with influenza, which recently had sent hundreds of soldiers to the base hospital, where the number of cases would hit one thousand within a week. Yet no one dared cancel the march to Alpine Landing, a Revolutionary War site near the Palisades where the troops were scheduled to board ferry boats for a two-hour cruise down the Hudson River to Hoboken. That option wasn't even discussed.

The men slowly fell back in formation, the sick and healthy alike helping one another as they continued their march. More of them started passing out, so many that ambulances and trucks were called to pick up all the sick. A hike to the landing that normally took an hour took twice as long. When they arrived, most of the men were able to cram into the barges for the trip to Pier 4, where they lined up alongside the *Leviathan*. More men were collapsing now, dropping in their tracks even as they were handed coffee and rolls by Red Cross volunteers. The decimated regiment started boarding the ship at 8:15 a.m. on Saturday, September 28.

This was far worse than anything Phelps had expected, and the *Leviathan* hadn't even shoved off yet. Many of these men couldn't even stagger up the gangways, and some of those who'd boarded were already being carried back down to the pier on stretchers as ambulances started to arrive. The captain and the ship's medical officers had to have known this was only the beginning. Help was coming with the arrival of nearly two hundred nurses from two base hospitals, but how many of them would be sick? The *Leviathan* continued to load troops and supplies right up to its departure the following afternoon. Phelps wanted throat sprays given to the crew, officers, and enlisted men at least twice a day.

One of these young hospital corpsmen was the first to die.

CHAPTER 19

"Kamerad! Kamerad!"

By late afternoon on Friday, September 27, ambulances with red crosses painted on their sides were bumping along the road from the village of Ripont, where hard fighting had raged all morning. Dozens of these French-made vehicles raced along the twisting road at dangerous speeds, finally slowing down as they came through the lines of the 371st Infantry. These daredevil drivers, most of them American volunteers, had rolled straight through a bombardment.

As the ambulances crawled through the village, Corporal Freddie Stowers or any other soldier with a strong stomach could have glanced inside at the wounded—many of them Moroccan troops, fierce-looking men who'd attacked the day before waving wickedly long knives over their heads and screaming curses as they went into battle. Blood seeped through the wooden floorboards, and the hastily applied bandages covering the wounds were soaked crimson. Attached to the French Red Hand Division, the African Americans stood somberly on both sides of the road as the caravan moved between them on the way to first aid stations a few miles in the rear. Worn out from an all-night hike to get to this position close to the front, the men said little as the ambulances passed by.

That same day they also had their first encounter with large numbers of German prisoners, as a wave of men in field gray came down the road, hundreds of them escorted by grinning French and Moroccan soldiers. Many of these prisoners were very young or

very old and seemed happy to be out of it. The gaunt expressions of
the officers told a different story as they plodded along, their blood-
shot eyes focused on the ground.

Artillery kept firing all morning a few miles in front of them.
The day before, Moroccans and the 369th Infantry, another African American unit attached to the French Fourth Army, had
attacked Ripont, where the Germans made a strong stand. The
enemy had been driven north to high ground designed on French
maps as Côte, or Hill, 188. The Argonne Forest was to the east, and
when the wind came from that direction, it carried the rumble of
artillery.

Stowers and the 371st moved into trenches recently held by
the Germans, which meant they were cleaner, deeper, and more
strongly fortified than the French variety. The men had just enjoyed
their first hot meal in days, the food sent up from rolling kitchens
far to the rear. The unit's location was just south of the village of
Ardeuil in the Champagne region. The drizzling rain that never
completely stopped was falling, and a foggy mist hung in the low
places. It was cool, almost cold, the stinging wind coming all the
way from the North Sea. Far to the south, the snow-covered peaks
of the Alps were obscured in a wall of menacing black clouds.

The men had already stripped down to battle gear, leaving their
packs in large warehouses near the village of Hans. They had their
weapons, extra ammunition, grenades, extra rations, a blanket,
and nothing else. As was his habit, Stowers would have been en-
couraging his men, quietly telling them to check their equipment,
especially the balky bolt actions on their three-shot M1886 Lebel
rifles that everyone disliked. At least it had an excellent bayonet, a
slender steel blade eighteen inches long and well suited for trench
fighting.

Some of the men tried to sleep, and a few might have taken
another look at the German propaganda leaflets picked up off the

ground in the villages they'd passed through. Written in English, one was entitled "How to Stop The War" and offered the following advice: "Do your part to put an end to the war! Put an end to your part of it. STOP FIGHTING! That's the simplest way. You can do it, you soldiers. Just stop fighting and the war will end of its own accord. You are not fighting for anything anyway. What does it matter to you who owns Metz or Strasburg; you never saw those towns nor knew the people in them, so what do you care about them? But THERE IS A LITTLE TOWN HOME IN LITTLE OLD UNITED STATES you would like to see and if you keep on fighting here in the hope of getting a look at those German fortresses you may never see home again."

This kind of propaganda didn't do anything but raise smiles.

There were times during the day when the sky was filled with a dizzying array of German and French airplanes locked in spectacular dogfights. Many of the French fighters were flown by Americans. The brightly painted German planes had large black iron crosses on the wings and were the easiest to recognize. The men heard the machine guns hammering as the planes twisted, dived, and climbed far overhead. Aircraft went into plunging spins, trailing flames and smoke and crashing far out of view. Some of the men had already seen the grotesquely charred and twisted bodies of fallen aviators lying near the wreckage of their planes. No one ever cracked jokes about something like that, even if the dead were German.

As they watched, three German planes streaked toward the gray sausage-shaped French observation balloons that hung low in the sky a few miles to the east. The planes were driven off before they could shoot down the balloons, which were always positioned near the front lines. Another fighter manned by a pilot and a machine gunner in the rear seat buzzed the American lines, firing at the men in the trenches, then made a wide looping turn and came in for another pass at two infantry companies. The men were told to tilt their machine guns toward the sky and fire when the officers blew their whistles. "When it was directly overhead and very close to the ground, the whistles began blowing and both infantry companies and four machine guns poured their fire into it," according to the regiment's history. "It lurched out in front of the lines, hit the ground with its wheels, bounded up in the air and turned over striking on its wings. The pilot was thrown out and did not move." The rear gunner escaped to the German lines. "The pilot had been shot through the face, throat and chest and evidently instantly killed."

The regiment was marched in double lines later that afternoon to a point near the jump-off for the attack that everyone expected to make early the next morning. The hills there climbed in a long, steady grade to a distant tree line. They were somewhere west of Ripont, and during their hike they'd encountered the dead and wounded from the earlier attack still lying out in the open. The bodies were everywhere, the figures often bent up and contorted. As one participant described it, "Groans of agony, curses, prayers and all manner of heartrending cries rose up from the lips of the wounded and dying." Chilling, yet not as bad as at the Somme, where just over two years earlier it had taken days before the sounds made by the wounded lying in no-man's land finally stopped.

Stowers and his men kept going. There was nothing they could do here. Maybe the ambulances would return later, but it was getting dark, and coming up the dirt roads at night would be difficult with troops moving into position. No one stopped or slowed down to attend to the wounded. Everyone was focused on the task at hand, turning into himself, preparing for what was coming in the morning.

At midnight, they took positions just below the crest of a hill, wrapped themselves in their blankets, and waited. Côte 188 rose in front of them.

*   *   *

AT FIVE THIRTY in the morning on Saturday, September 28, the wet fog was thick in the low places as the men assembled and crossed a road that connected the villages of Gratreuil and Fontaine-en-Dormois. The company commanders gathered in an abandoned dugout and examined the map. Their objective, Côte 188, was clearly marked. They faced a steady climb of maybe one and a half miles to the crest, which was defended by four or more machine gun nests. The barbed wire in front of the guns was thick, but a predawn patrol that cost the life of an officer discovered that the wire was cut in at least two places, leaving gaps infantry could pour through if they made it that far.

As the final details of the attack were worked out, there was a sudden commotion when soldiers brought in a German *Feldwebel*, a high-ranking noncommissioned officer, who said he had thirty-five men with him willing to surrender. They'd abandoned their machine gun position at the extreme left side of the hill, taken advantage of the fog, and crawled down a shallow trench dug for a telephone line. "They had been left to defend the hill," the German told them, "and did not care to risk their lives any longer in a lost cause." The *Feldwebel* said that Hill 188 had been strongly defended, but no more. "The Germans," he said, "were withdrawing, and he doubted we would find the position occupied at all." The company commanders were thinking that if all these men had surrendered, maybe the coming attack wouldn't be so bad after all. They passed along the news to the NCOs as they gave them their final orders. They'd move out at the whistle at precisely 6:45 a.m.

Stowers and C Company would attack straight up the hill, moving out first as assault platoons with skirmishers in front. As the daylight improved, they saw that they'd have to cut through a thick line of barbed wire about five hundred feet below the crest and made sure they had wire cutters. B and D Companies would follow them on the way up.

Whistles signaled the attack at H hour, and Stowers and his men quickly moved into the open. A steep rise to their right offered some slight protection on that side from the incoming machine gun, mortar, and rifle fire that was sweeping down on them, kicking up trails of dirt. Two of the three companies that started up the hill were immediately pinned down, and men began falling. Stowers kept moving forward into the lashing hail of bullets, the others following in a crouch. The firing from the German position on the right suddenly stopped. Enemy soldiers scrambled onto the parapet of their trench, holding up their arms and waving their helmets.

"*Kamerad!*" they cried out. "*Kamerad!*"

Some of the platoon commanders shouted for a cease-fire. It looked like the Germans wanted to surrender.

The Americans started advancing cautiously. Soldiers who'd been pinned down jumped to their feet and moved forward with them. They were about one hundred yards from the enemy lines when someone blew a whistle. The Germans leaped back into their trenches and interlocking machine guns began raking C Company. Within seconds, half of the men were wounded or shot dead. The two platoon commanders, both lieutenants, were hit. They were also taking fire from machine guns farther up the hill.

Stowers and the remnants of C Company were pinned down out in the open with nowhere to find cover. Bullets were spattering all around them, a torrential murderous fire. Immediately taking charge, the corporal shouted out that they had to silence the gun immediately in front of them or they'd all be killed. They had to tear themselves out of the dirt. They had to move!

Crawling into the stream of bullets whipping over their heads, they got close enough to the machine gun nest to take it out with rifle fire and grenades. The Germans who didn't flee were killed. Ducking down into the enemy trench, Stowers rallied his men to attack a second trench as he made a quick body count. His men reloaded and grabbed their hand grenades as bullets thudded into the parapet all around them. The corporal surveyed the ground ahead of them. They'd have to slip through a break in the wire. They'd roll out on their bellies and crawl forward, then scramble to their feet and charge the guns. The machine guns kept sweeping them like a hose of molten lead, maybe one hundred bullets for every rifle shot they fired.

Stowers shouted out the orders: "Keep moving!"

The corporal led the attack. He was immediately hit in the side, a burning hammer blow, and went down. He lay there for a few moments, then got up and continued to direct the attack, moving on adrenaline. He didn't get far before he fell again and lay gasping. Soldiers stopped to help. He waved them on.

His men crashed into the German trench, bayoneting anyone who hadn't fled. Other companies had come up by then, working their way along that telephone line trench that ran up the far side of the hill. They began enfilading the enemy positions, destroying the other machine guns. Abandoning their trenches, Germans began running across an open field as the Americans poured fire into them. Others stood their ground fighting until they were killed. Members of the 371st later reported seeing gunners chained to their machine guns.

Some dropped their weapons and shouted, *"Kamerad!"*

Most of those who tried to surrender—for real this time—died at the end of a French bayonet driven into their chest or throat by African American infantrymen. One after another, then another, anyone still alive. It didn't matter if they raised their hands or fell to their knees. "The final phase of this assault," the regimental history recounts, "was extremely gruesome as our men could not be restrained from wreaking their vengeance upon the enemy who had so shamefully entrapped their comrades earlier that morning."

Côte 188 had fallen about half an hour after the attack began. The toll was severe, an estimated 40 percent of the total number engaged in the first battalion—29 men killed and another 170 wounded. In another two days, the count would jump to 403 wounded.

Freddie Stowers bled out and died in the soaking mist, a dome of gray sky above him as big guns pounded in the near distance. Some of his men were with him and probably pleading for the corporal to hang on, telling him that help was coming and that he'd be all right. Someone would have examined his wounds and checked his pulse, maybe tried to slap on a bandage while they waited for a medic, but there was no need. The corporal was beyond help. He died far from his home in South Carolina, near the captured German machine gun and with soldiers he'd inspired and led to victory on Côte 188.

The fight wasn't going anywhere near as well in the Meuse-Argonne, where the American First Army continued to take a beating. General Pershing visited his corps and division commanders and tried to energize them and buck them up and urge more "push," but it didn't seem to do much good. The very next day, September 29, the Germans hit the Americans hard, all but decimating one division, which fled the battlefield.

Pandemic at Sea

So many sick and feverish soldiers were lurching down the ship's pitched gangways that it interfered with the lines of troops still trying to make their way on board. Men were falling over in mid-stride, dropping their rifles and packs and having to be carried to the pier while others tried to squeeze by them, pressing up against the side of the ship. Over two hundred soldiers and nurses stricken shortly after boarding were sent back ashore, stumbling down the gangways they'd just climbed. Several hundred other flu cases also should have been taken off the ship, but time ran out and they were stuck there. The *Leviathan* was under strict orders to sail on time, and when the mooring lines were cast off under clear skies at 1:40 p.m. on the afternoon of September 29, Captain Phelps understood the chilling dimensions of the disaster he faced. The influenza epidemic sweeping the country had broken out all over the ship; men were fainting on the decks by the dozens right before his eyes.

Phelps had another worry. His most recent information on German submarine movements in the North Sea indicated that as recently as four days earlier at least two U-boats had been operating in waters the *Leviathan* was expected to cross. Several mines were also reported adrift in the same area. The captain decided to change course, heading farther south into the Gulf Stream, almost as far as Florida, before turning eastward for the long run to France. He'd worked out the details in advance and was standing near the helm with the ship's pilot as the *Leviathan* passed Ellis Island and Staten Island and headed out to sea.

At first, the only medical case cited for that date was a sailor who'd concealed that he had a venereal disease, a serious infraction that cost him ten days in the brig on bread and water. All that soon changed. Within a few hours of reaching the open Atlantic, many of the 183 beds in the sick bay were already filled with soldiers suffering with the flu. The inpatient lines kept getting longer as men keeled over before they even reached their troop compartments. By the next morning the sick bay was filled to capacity, and hundreds of men—many of them so delirious they couldn't remember their own names—littered the passageways.

During that second day, Monday, September 30, the first death was recorded—a young navy hospital corpsman from Glen Ridge, New Jersey, named John Rawson, who died at 1:00 p.m. of what was entered in the log as pneumonia. It was possible, though not certain, that Rawson had contracted his fatal illness before he boarded the ship. The young sailor passed away suddenly after having a brief conversation with the chaplain about how much he looked forward to seeing his parents again. His voice hoarse, he told him he didn't want to die "because of the great need of his help at home."

Only two other sailors—an officer and an enlisted man—died during the journey to Brest, a testament to the rigidly enforced protective orders devised by the ship's medical officer and enforced by the captain. The soldiers, crammed in by the thousands, bore the brunt of the onslaught.

To make room for more sick patients, men were moved to quarters far below deck that originally had been declared off limits because of poor ventilation. Improvised sick bay space was created on E deck for 878 men, and by the third day out, all those bunks were filled. Many of the most seriously ill were from Appalachia. They were away from home for the first time in their lives and had been in the army barely a month. They were "extremely poor specimens physically. . . . Large numbers of them were unable to read or write and did not know their right from their left," according to the ship's history. They collapsed by the scores and were badly frightened, their fear heightened because of the strangeness of their surroundings. Most of these young men had never seen a ship before, much less traveled on one, and the *Leviathan*'s labyrinth of confined, dark spaces only added to their terror.

The chief medical officer, Lieutenant Commander H. A. May, briefed Phelps repeatedly on the disaster unfolding belowdecks. The doctor estimated that by October 2 there were nine hundred cases of influenza, and there was no way of telling how many of these men had also developed pneumonia. An isolation ward with seventy-five beds was set aside for the worst cases, and most of the patients in those beds died. With sick room space at a premium, doctors sent anyone whose fever fell below 100 degrees back to his regular bunk.

"The conditions . . . cannot be visualized by anyone who has not actually seen them," May wrote later. The *Leviathan* was carrying a crew of 2,482 and 9,327 soldiers for a total of 11,809, and it was estimated that as many as 2,000 of the doughboys had influenza. Most of them lay in their bunks unable to lift themselves up, even to relieve themselves, which meant the scenes belowdecks were appalling—hundreds of men leaning over the sides of their bunks, spitting and vomiting, drenching those in the bunks below them. Many had "severe nasal hemorrhages" and pools of blood mixed with the rinds of lemons and oranges given to the men to help quench their thirst were scattered throughout the troop compartments. The decks were slippery with all the pulp and bodily fluids. Added to the scene were the constant moans of the dangerously ill and dying. "The groans and cries of the terrified sick added to the confusion of the clamoring applicants for treatment, and altogether a true inferno reigned supreme."

Navy doctors manned the sick bay, but it was the army's responsibility to care for all the sick men belowdecks and those lying in the expanded infirmary. It didn't help that the army's top medical officer and two key subordinates were down with the flu and confined to their cabins. Only eleven army doctors were still on their feet and capable of tending to hundreds of desperately ill soldiers as well as forty nurses who were also lying sick in their cabins. Every day the body count rose—seven, then ten, then twenty-four, then thirty-one. After the first forty died, the ship ran out of caskets, and the embalmers who were working around the clock had exhausted the supply of embalming fluid. The navy required that an autopsy be performed on anyone who died at sea, so dissection tables were set up on B deck, where the work was performed and where "a succession of skeleton like soldiers [were] laid out naked, entrails piled on their chests, big toes tied together with string and another piece of string around the penis."

Sewn into canvas sacks, some of the bodies were stored in the refrigerators, but with the death toll still rising, the ship was quickly running out of room. As the dead continued stacking up, the unmistakable odor of decomposition wafted through the storage spaces. Captain Phelps discussed what to do about the smell with May, who suggested sprinkling the bodies with chloride of lime. Adding to the misery and confusion was the frequent difficulty identifying the men who'd died. Hundreds of soldiers wore name tags but hadn't filled them in yet.

THE BEDLAM INTENSIFIED as the *Leviathan* sailed into rough weather on the fourth day at sea. Hundreds of men became violently ill as the ship pitched and rolled, and inexperienced army doctors, unable to tell the difference between seasickness and influenza, admitted many seasickness cases to the flu wards, exacerbating the critical shortage of bunks and exposing more men to the virus.

Phelps also learned of an increasingly dangerous situation developing in the troop compartments, where soldiers were refusing direct orders to tend to the sick and clean up the mess. They were on the brink of mutiny, and no threat of severe punishment seemed to have the slightest impact. Everyone knew that a highly contagious and deadly disease was out of control, and that hundreds of men were sick and dying in indescribable filth. Phelps couldn't order army personnel to do their duty, and senior army officers, for whatever reason, weren't forcing their men to carry out cleaning details. Only a few soldiers responded to the orders, and most of these soon wandered away "never to be seen again."

The captain and Lieutenant Commander May worked out a solution, asking navy personnel to volunteer to go belowdecks with mops and buckets of hot water and start policing the infirmary areas, bunk spaces, and soiled passageways, where a fetid mixture of vomit, blood, and human waste needed to be cleaned up. It took several days of nonstop, backbreaking, dangerous work, but gradually these volunteers—the navy rightly considered them heroes—brought things under control. Over one hundred army nurses, remembered later in the ship's history as "ministering angels," also pitched in, working twenty-hour shifts and going from bunk to bunk as they cared for the sick. All these efforts seemed to have a calming effect on the soldiers, who watched the sailors and nurses attend to the sick without falling ill. There were no new refusals to obey orders, and the threat of mutiny abated.

Yet the deaths continued. The ship's log was punctuated with the names of soldiers who died from "pneumonia lobar" intermingled with the more mundane record of course changes, zigzag maneuvers, and, early in the voyage, a round of target practice. The entries from October 6 were typical: from six to eight o'clock in the evening, four men died; and during the eight-to-midnight watch, seven more expired, all influenza-pneumonia cases.

On October 7, with a bank of clouds rising over Brest, the influenza-haunted *Leviathan* finally steamed into the deep harbor. Ninety-six men had died during the voyage, including the thirty-one who expired on that final day. The medical officers calculated that nearly one thousand soldiers were still infected with the flu virus, and many of these men needed to be helped off the ship. It was obvious that the illness hadn't run its course and that hundreds of soldiers who'd escaped death during the voyage would probably find it waiting for them in the French port.

The men started to disembark at noon, thousands of soldiers slowly descending the gangways, many of them still weak and feverish. Brought ashore in large flat-bottomed barges called lighters, those who could walk had to hike several miles to the Pontanezen Barracks, which had no room for those who were sick. The flu pandemic had exploded at the army camp two weeks earlier, and already caring for an estimated 1,700 cases—most of them soldiers who'd fallen ill on troopships—the base hospital was no longer accepting patients. During their long march up through the hills of the city to the camp, many of the survivors from the *Leviathan* passed out. Some of those who dropped out of line died where they fell, and their bodies were picked up by ambulances. Increasing everyone's misery, a raging thunderstorm drenched the soldiers. "In the next few days," according to one history, "probably hundreds of the men who crossed on the *Leviathan* died. . . . Nearly 200 of the flu victims of the 57th [Pioneer Infantry] were buried in the American cemetery at Lambezellec, overlooking the ocean."

When it was finally time for the nurses to disembark, the *Leviathan*'s crew lined the decks and railings and cheered as the young women started down the gangways. The sailors knew what they'd accomplished during the height of the outbreak and what they'd risked descending into the chaos on the troop decks time and time again. Many of the nurses waved back, smiling through their tears. Some were ill themselves and had to be supported as they left the ship.

As he watched the soldiers and the white-capped nurses head for shore, Captain Phelps had to be thinking about the nearly two hundred men who remained behind in the sick bay and the improvised wards. The army would be coming for these men later, although no one seemed to have a clear idea where to take them. They might have to be sent to other military hospitals or to temporary first aid stations. Over ninety bodies also remained on board, over two dozen of them stored in coolers and another forty stacked in caskets. The rest were sewn up in canvas shrouds and kept in a guarded storage area.

The army wasn't giving Phelps any guidance on what to do with the bodies. His orders directed him to leave Brest for New York in three days without fail. In the meantime, they'd have to clean the soiled and polluted vessel as much as possible—and keep applying chloride of lime. A massive burial at sea looked inevitable.

CHAPTER 20

"Funny Little Smile"

THE FLU OUTBREAK aboard the *Leviathan* helped make Brest probably the most likely place in Europe to contract the deadly illness during the late summer and early fall of 1918. The epidemic decimated the American Expeditionary Force, forcing General Pershing to scramble to fill ranks thinned by the virus. In the first week of October, sixteen thousand new cases were reported and seventy thousand men were placed in hospitals. The death rate in the camps, Pershing was astonished to learn, often rose to 32 percent, far worse than on the troopships.

Those appalling numbers didn't stop or even slow the Meuse-Argonne slugfest, in which the American offensive was going badly. The fighting raged through dense woods, over shell-scarred hills, and up deep, mud-laced ravines as the Germans skillfully contested every inch of ground, a resistance that prompted F. Scott Fitzgerald to say later that they "walked very slowly backward a few inches a day, leaving the dead like a million bloody rugs." Prospects were bleak, and the weather equally miserable—sodden skies and a chilling rain. The first weeks of October, Pershing said years afterward, were the worst of the war.

Pershing was confronted almost daily by Foch, who stung him on October 13 with the remark that the French and English armies were making progress while the Americans were lagging behind. "No more promises," he snapped at Pershing during a meeting at Foch's headquarters at Bombon. "Results."

When the American commander started to describe the difficult, heavily defended terrain his men were facing, the French gen-
eralissimo stopped him cold. "Results are the only thing to judge
by," he said. "If an attack is well planned and well executed it suc-
ceeds . . . if it is not . . . there is no advance." It was obvious to Foch,
therefore, that the American attack wasn't well planned. Left un-
said was the question: Whose fault was it?

Around this time, officers and friends began to comment among
themselves that General Pershing wasn't looking well.

At such a dark moment it was fortunate perhaps that a widely
reported military operation diverted the attention of the US public
from the bloody quagmire the First Army found itself mired in in
the Meuse-Argonne. Two of the principal players in the drama of
the so-called Lost Battalion were a soft-spoken New York City law-
yer named Charles Whittlesey, who commanded the unit, and the
sportswriter turned war correspondent Damon Runyon.

Advancing too far into the Ardenne Forest, Major Whittlesey's
battalion was cut off and surrounded. From October 2 until October 7, he and his men held out against snipers, machine guns,
artillery fire, and flamethrowers until they were finally rescued.
Near the end of their epic fight, when all looked hopeless, the be-
spectacled Whittlesey turned down a German offer of surrender.
His men—an eclectic assortment of New Yorkers—fought off one
attack after another. When his battalion finally trudged off the hillside where they'd been trapped, nearly 70 percent of the 675 men
who'd set out with him were either dead, wounded, or captured.

The unit's heroic resistance was widely reported in the press, and
Runyon, no doubt helped by his long-standing personal friendship
with Pershing, was one of the first given a chance to interview the
survivors. His stories about the battalion and the shy, unassuming
Whittlesey, "a tall, lean-flanked fellow around forty years old" with
a "funny little smile" were a sensation. Runyon, then thirty-eight,
had followed Pershing into Mexico two years earlier during the

abortive hunt for the bandit-chieftain Pancho Villa. The reporter had uncovered a plot orchestrated by the American army to poison Villa by having someone slip him poison-laced food when he visited an iron ore mine in Chihuahua. Pershing asked Runyon not to publish the story—then or later—and the writer dutifully agreed. Payback came in France, where Runyon was sent as a special correspondent for Hearst's Universal Service in September 1918, arriving just in time to catch up with the Meuse-Argonne offensive. He'd been covering the New York Giants and primo boxing matches, but the press baron wanted his ace assigned to the main event.

Runyon and fifty other American journalists were working from a smoky, cramped press office located on a dark side street in Bar-le-Duc, a short drive from the front. They'd all been briefed on the scope and objective of the battle, how it fit with Foch's strategy and was aimed at a critical hinge in the German line. One of Pershing's aides, Major General Fox Conner, laid it all out for them on a wall-size map, then asked the reporters how public opinion in the United States might run if the attack bogged down and the body count kept increasing.

After an awkward silence, one of Runyon's colleagues spoke up. "Well, General," he said. "I think the people at home are just beginning to find out there's a war."

A few days later, on October 3, the press office received vague reports that Whittlesey's battalion had been cut off in a pocket of thick woods, underbrush, and ravines, giving birth to the legend of the Lost Battalion. Over the next few days, suspense mounted, and no one seemed bothered by the fact the battalion wasn't really lost. Everyone knew its men were running dangerously low on ammunition and were out of food and that snipers were picking them off whenever they tried to fill their canteens at a nearby spring. American planes swooped down to drop bundles of supplies, but the few packages that landed close to the battalion's position came under intense enemy fire. Then the reporters learned that the Germans had sent a message to the battalion leader pleading with him to surrender.

Without knowing how Whittlesey responded to the enemy's ultimatum, the journalists quickly reported as fact what they hoped he'd say: "Go to hell!"

When American troops finally pushed the Germans out of the Argonne Forest and relieved the unit on October 7, Runyon and another reporter were allowed to visit the hospital where the wounded had been taken and interview Whittlesey and the other survivors. It was the perfect story for Runyon, who loved the unit's "polyglot" makeup and how it reflected the rich diversity of New York, his favorite city—Jews, Italians, Ivy Leaguers, stockbrokers, truck drivers, and waiters. The *New York American's* headline on his story datelined October 12 "at the American Argonne front" underscores the writer's prominence: "Runyon Sees Return of Lost New York Battalion."

The journalist pressed Whittlesey on what happened when the German commander sent him a neatly typewritten note asking for his surrender. Did he really say "Go to hell"?

"Whittlesey says he did not say it, but that it covered his thoughts at the time," Runyon wrote, admitting that it would have made his story "more dramatic to say that Whittlesey sent back some stirring phrase in answer to the Germans." Instead, he stuffed the paper in his pocket, smiled his funny smile, and had his men give their answer with bullets. Runyon also described where the fighting had taken place, a thicket of woods and ground cover that some had likened to the Battle of the Wilderness.

"The Argonne forest in which the Seventy-Seventh Division is fighting is a mass of trees," he wrote. "They are not big trees, but stand close together like stalks in a wheat field. Woven through them in the undergrowth are vines.

"It is impossible for a man to walk through the woods straight for any distance in any direction. It is impossible to see through them to any great depth." It was said, he added, that the French had lost sixty thousand men trying to capture the Argonne Forest since the war started.

Runyon's stories and those of other reporters made Whittlesey and his men national heroes at a time when Pershing and the First Army badly need them. It didn't matter that their dispatches neglected to mention that some of the battalion's casualties were the result of friendly fire by the American artillery, or that Whittlesey suffered serious remorse for leading his troops into a death trap. The major had to smile his funny little smile repeatedly after he was sent back to the United States, where he received the Medal of Honor and campaigned for Liberty Loans. He never escaped his misgivings about his battlefield decisions and was troubled that he was allowed to return to New York while the survivors of his unit were sent back to the front. "Whittlesey was leaving the regiment," the historian Richard Slotkin wrote, "because of an achievement whose value he questioned, to face a fame he did not want and a public celebrity for which he was temperamentally unsuited, bearing with him the survivor's guilt and unresolved doubts of a man who had led hundreds of his comrades to maiming or death."

Runyon remained in France as the Meuse-Argonne fighting intensified. His work often focused on well-known New Yorkers, including sports celebrities such as the former New York Giants third baseman Eddie Grant, who was commanding an infantry company when he was struck by a shell as his men tried to rescue Whittlesey's battalion. Grant was killed a few moments after another shell killed or wounded all of the more senior officers in his unit. He was buried near where he fell. "His grave," Runyon wrote, "is marked by some stones and a rude little cross tenderly reared by his men."

As Pershing continued to press the Meuse-Argonne attack despite a succession of bloody reversals, Runyon and other reporters sensed that the war's climax was approaching and wanted to be there at the end. The German pullback from the hell of the Argonne Forest—"a duel in a dark room"—was an indication that they were nearing the end of their long resistance on the western front.

Burials at Sea

B ARELY TWO HOURS before the *Leviathan* was scheduled to cast off, the army had finally sent a crew to pick up the bodies of the soldiers who'd died from the flu during the crossing to Brest. Phelps and other senior officers had been pressing the port authorities to remove the dead for several days, to no effect. Thirty-three bodies would be returned in caskets to the United States, but that left sixty-three still on board that the army was now coming to retrieve at the last moment.

Determined to leave on schedule at 5:00 p.m., Phelps likely had to restrain himself from confronting the army officer in charge of the burial detail. The backbreaking job of carrying the dead off the ship seemed to be progressing at a snail's pace. Over a dozen soldiers, their faces flushed and dripping sweat, brought the bodies down the gangway to the lighter, then headed back on board for more. On this sunny fall afternoon of October 9, there was no memorial service, though a navy honor guard standing at rigid attention was posted near the railing.

The army detail kept at it until the clock ran out, and when it was time to cast off, seven bodies still remained on board. Phelps passed along his apologies to the army, allowed the men to disembark, and gave orders to cast off from the mooring buoy at 5:01 p.m., right on schedule. He wished it could have been otherwise, but it couldn't be helped. His orders set a rigid timetable for meeting the destroyer escort. The seven men would have to be buried at sea.

The ceremony occurred at six thirty the following morning as the *Leviathan* cut through the water at just over twenty-one knots, nearly top speed. The usual protocol was to stop the engines, which wasn't possible with the ship still in the submarine danger zone. They wouldn't even slow down. The starkly elegant formality of a naval burial at sea had remained largely unchanged for several centuries. When the hour came, the ship's bells rang out and the boatswain piped the call "All hands bury the dead."

Most of the 2,500 sailors on board lined up along the starboard side of the rear deck. The bier was already mounted there and draped with American flags. A short gangway was attached to the railing, a slide over which each body would be dropped into the sea. The flag was lowered to half mast, and the flags on the four destroyers accompanying the *Leviathan* were also brought down. The only sound was of the wind whipping across the decks as the pallbearers, moving at "slow time" and followed by the chaplain, carried out the bodies—each encased in a canvas shroud—and placed them side by side on the bier. The armed escort following the procession came to a rigid present arms. The crew stood at attention as the chaplain read the prayers for the dead in a loud, clear voice that carried across the deck.

"I am the resurrection and the life saith the Lord. He that believeth in me, though he were dead, yet shall he live. And whosoever liveth in me shall never die. Know that my redeemer liveth and that he shalt stand at the latter day upon the earth. And though after worms destroy this body, yet in my flesh shall I see God."

Continuing, the chaplain said, "He brought nothing into this world and it is certain we can carry nothing out. The Lord gave, and the Lord hath taken away. Blessed be the name of the Lord."

The ship's band played the slow cadences of "Nearer, My God, to Thee."

At the conclusion of the hymn, the crew was ordered to "off hats!"

The names of the dead were read and the boatswain piped out

another long, shrilling note, and one by one the bodies were lifted from the bier, carried to the gangway, and slid over the side, the canvas sacks weighed down by iron gratings. There was a small splash as each body hit the water. The escort fired three rifle volleys and the bugler, standing somewhere out of view, played taps.

After a long pause, Captain Phelps gave the word. "Carry on."

The crew quickly filed back to their duty stations, and the flags were raised to full staff. The heartbeat of the ship quickly returned to normal. A gunnery drill was held as the *Leviathan* continued on her course to New York. The sailors and their captain were eager to get back home. For most of them it had been the worst trip of their lives. Even now they weren't finished with the deadly attacks of influenza. On their third day at sea a navy ensign died from pneumonia, the third and last of the ship's crew to die from the disease during the round-trip. Phelps had good reason to be proud that his medical staff had successfully protected the overwhelming majority of the *Leviathan*'s sailors and officers from the outbreak, and he wanted to do everything possible to make sure the wounded weren't infected.

The captain was moved by the resilient spirit of these soldiers when he inspected the sick bay, usually with his fox terrier, Lord Nelson, trotting at his side. No matter how badly injured, the men never failed to smile. "Instances will never be forgotten," Phelps wrote later, "how the hopelessly maimed and paralyzed lay for forty-eight hours in clothing and life belts patiently, cheerfully . . . enduring discomfort" that he personally would have found unbearable. Their faces radiated "some holy sublime light. There seemed to be the glory and pride of sacrifice permeating the sick bay."

How much longer would the war last?

The question hovered over everyone as the *Leviathan* held to her zigzag course under blue-gray skies, remarkably fine weather for the start of the fall storm season on the North Atlantic. The ship's new eight-page newspaper warned that the fighting wasn't going well. "It is madness to consider the Germans losers while their armies are fighting everywhere on Allied soil," an editorial said. "The German army has not been broken. It still holds immense areas of conquered territory. . . . The Huns must be crushed and humiliated to the dust. They must be made to realize that they are beaten and beaten to a pulp."

CHAPTER 21

The U-Boats Go Home

GUIDED BY HER usual flotilla of a dozen tugboats, the *Leviathan* eased up to Pier 4 in Hoboken, where Captain Phelps and the other officers on the bridge were shocked to see a big ship wallowing in the mud near the adjoining wharf, her two stacks tilted toward the sky at a sickening angle. It was the *America*, another former German liner converted into a troopship. The vessel looked ridiculous sitting so low in the oily water, which lapped over her rear deck.

An inexcusable accident had occurred the day before when the *America*, ready to sail for France with five thousand troops on board, was being loaded with coal. The ship's coal ports were barely four feet above the waterline, and when the tide rose and the Hudson River started pouring in, it became clear that someone had forgotten to close them, and the vessel was soon scuttled.

Work crews were still pumping her out as the caskets of thirty-three soldiers who had died of the flu aboard the *Leviathan* were carried down her gangway.

There wasn't much time to get the ship ready for her next crossing—at the top of the list was a thorough cleaning and fumigation, especially in the hard-hit troop compartments and sick bays. Even after an intense scrub down in Brest, the ship was a disaster scene. All the troop compartments were scoured and washed with a strong cresol solution. So were the decks, bulkheads, ventilator ducts, washrooms, latrines, and urinals. Every washbasin was soaked for hours in a solution of chlorine of lime and water. Thousands of bunk bottoms were removed and sent to the laundry for sterilization. Every cabin was swabbed with the same cresol mixture. All the pillows and blankets—thousands of them—were sterilized. The few carpeted areas on the ship were vacuumed and sprinkled with cresol. The work took days, and the cleanup crews were still at it as the next sailing later that month rapidly approached.

The exterior also needed attention, but that would have to wait. Streaked with rust, her camouflage paint long eroded by months of sailing in the North Atlantic, the *Leviathan* was overdue to have her hull cleaned, and there were some mechanical problems. Recent vibrations when the ship was cruising at top speed meant the propeller bushings probably needed to be replaced—a major overhaul.

Meanwhile, rumors of impending peace were intensifying even as pressure increased on the German army all across the western front. The mood at the front and back home in Germany was ominously dark. On September 29 the German High Command recommended that fighting stop immediately. "There is now no longer any possible hope of forcing peace on the enemy," Field Marshal Paul von Hindenburg told the German chancellor. "The situation grows more desperate every day." Barely two weeks later, General Erich von Ludendorff somberly confessed that "our bravest men lay on the bloody battle-field." And on October 27, the leftist *Arbeiter-Zeitung* newspaper of Vienna noted that ten thousand American troops were arriving every day. "Do the people wish to continue war under such circumstances," it asked, "to sacrifice the lives of many hundred thousand men thereby destroying the remainder of the Nation's manhood and imperiling their future?"

When the *Leviathan* cast off at 11:10 a.m. on Sunday, October 27, on her tenth trip of the war, Captain Phelps had a surprise up his sleeve. Carrying the fewest number of troops of any crossing—8,123 and a crew of 2,327—the ship was heading for Liverpool instead of

Brest. The *Leviathan* needed to be put in dry dock for those much-needed repairs, and the only one large enough to accommodate her great size remained the Gladstone, where she'd been once before.

After a few good days, the weather turned rough, then awful. The seas were crashing over the bow on October 30 when the ship picked up a wireless report that Turkey, a German ally, had surrendered. Even better news was delivered a few days later by the captain of the *Stevens*, the lead ship of the four-destroyer escort that met the *Leviathan* at the edge of the danger zone. The weather, the worst yet, had delayed the rendezvous for nearly twelve hours. Scheduled for early on the morning of November 2, the meeting didn't occur until just before sunset, and Phelps recalled later how the destroyers suddenly emerged out of the heaving ocean and clustered like pups around the larger ship. "The little boats," the captain wrote, "would rear and plunge, would pound and flood themselves until it appeared that everyone on the bridge was drenched. It was often necessary to slow down the convoy, for it has been known that destroyers in such conditions have pounded their seams open and sprung leaks."

The captain of the *Stevens* talked to Phelps over the new wireless telephone recently installed on the *Leviathan*. Germany had recalled her submarine fleet to its home ports, he said. There were also unconfirmed reports that on October 30, crews of the High Seas Fleet had armed themselves and mutinied rather than put to sea in a final face-saving sortie against the English fleet.

Phelps didn't dare ease up on their vigilance. The gun crews were ordered to their stations round the clock as the *Leviathan* steamed into the danger zone. The crew still had no idea where they were heading until they neared the familiar Irish coast, and the sailors realized their destination was gloomy Liverpool, famous for its gray skies, dark streets, and unfriendly citizens.

The familiar fog that usually shrouded the English coast was almost impenetrable on November 3 when the ship headed up the channel of the Mersey River. With her foghorn blasting out a loud warning every few minutes, the *Leviathan* was slowly groping her way toward the entrance of the Gladstone Dock when she suddenly came to an abrupt stop. Even with the engines still churning, the ship made no headway, and Phelps knew immediately that they'd run aground. The *Leviathan*, listing slightly, remained stuck on the sandbar for nearly seven embarrassing hours. All the soldiers were disembarked onto troop lighters and taken upriver into Liverpool, where they boarded trains for the coast.

When the high tide rolled in—the Mersey tides were powerful and dramatic—the channel depth shot up twenty-seven feet and the ship was refloated. The following morning, the fog cleared and the *Leviathan* safely entered the dry dock chamber under her own power. Although no one realized it at the time, she'd reached the end of her wartime adventures.

There were more reports suggesting that the end was rapidly approaching. German navy mutineers seized the port of Kiel, and on November 3 Austria-Hungary surrendered. Pressure was mounting for the kaiser to abdicate. For Captain Phelps, these momentous and cascading events came in quick succession as he focused on the extensive repair work that needed to be performed on the *Leviathan* in Liverpool.

The Eleventh Hour of the Eleventh Day of the Eleventh Month

PERSHING'S DARKEST HOURS had come earlier in October when his recently organized First Army, battered and decimated, ground to a near standstill during the troubled Meuse-Argonne offensive. British prime minister Lloyd George and French premier Georges Clemenceau were both openly critical of the "quite ineffective" general. The French leader, whose drooping walrus mustache quivered when he railed about Pershing, insisted that President Wilson should be informed of the general's stubborn incompetence. Clemenceau paid no mind when Marshal Foch tried to point out that the Americans, far from doing nothing, were attacking over difficult terrain, admittedly moving forward more slowly than the French would have liked, and had suffered about fifty-five thousand casualties since late September. Nearly one million American soldiers were committed to the attack along the eighty-mile front of the Meuse-Argonne. Clemenceau, the steely French leader who was nicknamed Le Tigre for good reason, kept insisting the American army would never meet expectations until its mulish commander was removed—the sooner the better.

Frustrated, working alone at his desk well into the early-morning hours, Pershing was in a somber mood. "I feel like I am carrying the whole world on my shoulders," he said at one point. Another day, heading toward the front in his chauffeured staff car, he doubled over in grief. "Frankie . . . Frankie," he said, sobbing out his dead wife's name. "My God, sometimes I don't know how I can go on."

But he did keep going on, and in mid-October his luck changed dramatically. American soldiers finally broke through the Kriemhilde Stellung, the famous Hindenburg Line, the last and most pivotal of the German defensive strongholds that dominated the Argonne. The key to this crucial position was a fortified cluster of hills known collectively as the Côte-de-Châtillon. First-rate German troops who were dug in there had broken a pair of frontal attacks using innumerable machine guns and artillery, decimating two American divisions, the Thirty-Second and the First. After those debacles, the mission to take the position was given to the Forty-Second, or Rainbow, Division, which took over a three-mile front. From the outset, its commander, Douglas MacArthur, had his doubts the Côte-de-Châtillon could be taken.

The young brigadier general had learned some hard lessons in the few weeks since his division had served as a backup when the Seventy-Ninth Division attacked Montfaucon in late September. MacArthur recalled huddling in the wet, rain-soaked woods and watching one of the unsuccessful frontal attacks on the fortress. He'd acquired firsthand knowledge that such head-on assaults against fortified positions were usually a bloody disaster, and he'd also come to respect the daring of German aviators. "Without warning, a squadron of German planes dived out of nowhere and shot down every one of the dozen or more observation balloons the Army had in the air," MacArthur later wrote. "In leaving they flew not a hundred feet above me and I recognized the flowing yellow scarfs of the Richthofen Squadron—the famous 'flying circus' created by the German ace, Manfred Baron Von Richthofen."

So when the Forty-Second moved up to the Côte-de-Châtillon, MacArthur made his own reconnaissance of the cratered ground before committing his troops to what could be another costly defeat. He didn't like what he encountered. "There were rolling hills, heavily wooded valleys of death between the endless folds of ridges. Puffs of gas and shellfire broke like squalls of wind," he wrote. He ran into mustard and tear gas and paid the price for not carrying a mask, becoming so sick he almost had to be evacuated. His proposal to seize the Côte-de-Châtillon by attacking from a different direction was approved.

On the night of October 11, General Charles Summerall, the battlefield commander, entered MacArthur's candlelit quarters in a farmhouse two miles from the front. It was raining hard. Summerall looked worn out and drained, and MacArthur offered him a cup of throat-scalding black coffee. He was startled when the general suddenly blurted out an order in a strained, harsh voice.

"Give me Chatillon, MacArthur. Give me Chatillon, or a list of five thousand casualties."

"All right, General," MacArthur said after a moment. "We'll take it, or my name will head the list."

Summerall departed too overwhelmed to speak.

After several more days of reconnaissance and seizing a pair of adjoining hills at a stiff price—"death, cold and remorseless, whistled and sung its way through our ranks"—the final American advance started on the last defenses of the Côte-de-Châtillon. Instead of ordering a frontal attack, MacArthur moved his men around to the flanks, where the barbed wire wasn't as thick. The squads and platoons started crawling uphill from both slopes, searching out any cover they could find, cleaning out machine gun nests, and engaging a determined enemy in hand-to-hand fighting. They were coming up like pinchers, the First Battalion of the 168th regiment under Major Lloyd Ross moving in from the right; a battalion of the 167th regiment coming from the left toward a break in the wire. "Officers fell and sergeants leaped to the command," MacArthur wrote later. "Companies dwindled to platoons and corporals took over. At the end Major Ross had only 300 men and 6 officers left out of 1,450 men and 25 officers. That is the way the Cote-de-Chatillon fell."

MacArthur, who'd personally led his men during the attack, afterward received his second Distinguished Service Cross. His citation concluded, "On a field where courage was the rule, his courage was the dominant factor." MacArthur's biographer William Manchester wrote: "For the rest of his days, he would be unable to speak of the Cote-de-Chatillon without visible emotion."

The enemy was in retreat, and Pershing was elated, calling it "a decisive blow." By the end of the month, he was ready to begin what became the final phase of the Meuse-Argonne offensive. For the first time in the war, Pershing wrote later, the Americans were able to prepare for "an offensive with some deliberation, under reasonably normal conditions, and more nearly on an equal footing with the other armies." And for the first time in weeks, the fog and cold rains had given way to blue, late-fall skies. The seven American divisions participating in the attack consisted of nearly all battle-tested veterans by then and represented the fighting core of the 1.8 million soldiers in the AEF. Pershing added even more punch to his usual pep talk, telling all of his commanders that he'd hold them personally responsible if they failed.

By the November 1 jump-off date, the AEF's lines extended four to six miles beyond Montfaucon and the Argonne Forest, and the American army was facing similar ground as during the first abor-tive attacks on September 26: the Meuse River on the east; thick woods on the west, this time the Bois de Bourgogne; and in the cen-ter another hillcrest stronghold, Barricourt Ridge. The plan called for a head-on attack against the ridge with a flanking movement into the woods on the west, where the Americans would link up with the French Fourth Army and press forward for the main ob-jective, Sedan. The city held special significance as the place where the Germans had defeated and demoralized the French in 1870.

During the week before the attack, three batteries of fourteen-inch naval guns mounted on railway flatcars shelled German rail-road hubs, road intersections, and supply depots, some as far as twenty-five miles away, with 1,400-pound shells. American artillery, greatly improved, also plastered the Bois de Bourgogne with green clouds of mustard gas. Pershing had made special arrangements to secure the gas and hoped to have several hundred tanks participate in the attack. It shocked him that only eighteen were available, an inexcusable shortage that he knew meant more infantrymen would lose their lives. "It seems strange," he said, "that with American genius for manufacturing from iron and steel, we should find our-selves after a year and a half of war almost completely without [the tanks] which had exercised such a great influence on the western front in reducing infantry losses."

Another sky-rending barrage opened up at 3:30 a.m. on November 1, a dark, moonless night turned into day by the artillery flashes, the barrels of the guns glowing red from nonstop firing that continued until 5:30 a.m., when the troops headed into no-man's land. Crossing a front nearly a mile wide, they were closely supported by American pilots, who repeatedly strafed enemy positions.

During the assault, as with the attack on the Côte-de-Châtillon, extreme courage became ordinary. In his memoirs Pershing singled out the Medal of Honor exploits of John Barkley of the Fourth Infantry. The twenty-three-year-old private from Kansas City, Missouri, quickly repaired and mounted a captured German machine gun in a disabled French tank, and "holding his position under a hostile barrage and against direct artillery fire, he broke up two counterattacks against [the American] lines." The tank took a point-blank hit from a German gun, but Barkley kept firing, waiting until the enemy was almost abreast of him before opening up.

After enduring weeks of deadly attrition warfare, the American First and Second Armies were fighting with skill borne of harsh experience, and this time everything was going their way. By nightfall the lead units had advanced five miles and taken all the first day's objectives. When the attack resumed the next morning, troops found the fields and roads littered with dead German soldiers, horses, and scattered equipment dropped as the enemy retreated. By November 3 the Germans had been driven across the Meuse River and were still being pursued by American battalions, which used rafts and pontoon bridges to keep attacking. Towns and villages long held by the enemy were falling like dominoes— Tailly, Buzancy, Harricourt, Germont, Verriers—so many that the pages of Pershing's memoirs often read like a travelogue.

An objective that had seemed impossible only a few weeks earlier now appeared to be within the Allies' grasp—encircling and destroying the German army. Pershing ordered his troops to keep pressing "wherever resistance is broken, without regard for fixed objectives and without fear for their flanks." Energy, boldness, and open warfare tactics were emphasized.

By the morning of November 7, the Americans were on the heights overlooking Sedan, a critical rail hub and evacuation point for the German army. In less than a week, they'd pushed the enemy back twenty-four miles. The German government signaled that it was ready to discuss an armistice.

ARRIVING TWELVE HOURS late because of roads hopelessly clogged with retreating troops and equipment, the German delegation crossed the lines by automobile and boarded a special railway coach sent by the French. During the night, the car was pulled up next to Marshal Foch's personal rail car on an isolated, heavily guarded siding at Rethondes in the forest of Compiègne near Paris.

Foch greeted the German representatives coldly after they presented their credentials.

He curtly asked them why they had come.

We wish to discuss an armistice to end the fighting, one of the men said.

In full uniform—polished boots and red-striped trousers—and standing erectly at his desk, Foch stared hard at them. I haven't asked for an armistice and personally don't want one, he said.

The increasingly distressed German emissaries repeated they'd come to stop the fighting as soon as possible.

All right, the French general said. Here are the terms. He handed them a sheet of paper that contained the Allied demands. Reading them over, the Germans were staggered by their severity.

The document required that they withdraw from the western bank of the Rhine and all occupied territory, most notably Alsace-Lorraine, which France had surrendered in 1871. The German High Seas fleet and all submarines were to be turned over to the Allies, and the payment of war reparations was demanded, although the exact amount wasn't specified. Pershing noted that the Germans didn't object to turning over five thousand cannons, but deplored the requirement that they surrender over thirty thousand machine guns. With their government in shambles and Bolshevik-precipitated rioting occurring in the streets of Berlin, the Germans said that they might need some of those weapons to maintain order. "They finally succeeded in getting this reduced to 25,000 machine guns on the ground that they might have some left for riot duty."

When the members of the peace delegation explained they had no authority to sign an agreement stipulating to such demands, Foch gave them seventy-two hours—until 11:00 a.m. on November 11—for a final decision, which needed the German chancellor's approval. A messenger departed for Berlin to secure the required authorization. Meanwhile, the war continued, on the assumption that the Germans could always refuse and keep fighting.

The delegation that remained behind in the rail coaches presented a grim picture to the French of the conditions in Germany, where there were fears of starvation and famine because of critical food shortages. Pressure was building for Wilhelm II to abdicate, which would mean the end of the house of Hohenzollern. The kaiser had rejected "a suggestion that he should seek death in the trenches, as incompatible with his position as head of the German Lutheran Church."

Opposing the armistice, Pershing kept his army pressing forward and on Friday, November 8, received a telephone call from Foch, urging him to hold his troops' positions if and when hostilities ceased. American commanders were well aware of the armistice rumors and the November 11 deadline. At least one commander sought guidance after scheduling an attack for November 11.

He asked whether it should proceed.

The reply came quickly: Absolutely!

Acceptance of the armistice conditions arrived by a wireless message at about eleven o'clock on the evening of November 10, and Foch and the German envoys stayed up throughout the early-morning hours to decode the document and draft the final agreement. The work was completed at about five in the morning. Eager to speed the process and stop the killing, they first wrote and signed the last page, which laid out the conditions. This took a few minutes, then Foch sent a message by wire and telephone to the Allied commanders: Hostilities will cease on the entire front November 11th at 11:00 a.m. Telephone lines were kept open between Pershing's headquarters and the First and Second Armies, and at 6:00 a.m. American commanders and troops were told all fighting would stop at 11:00 a.m.

Despite the best efforts, a few advance units apparently didn't get the message, and even as the French carefully avoided any attacks that morning, Americans were wounded and killed right up to the moment the guns finally stopped firing. This needless slaughter later prompted outrage at home and a congressional investigation, but nothing came of it. The war was over. "I cannot express the horror we felt" at the waste of life, said one commander.

As the hour neared 11:00 a.m., Pershing stood before the large wall map in his office at Chaumont, tracking the final American advances. When the moment finally arrived and all was quiet on the western front for the first time in four years, he was proud of what his men and country had accomplished.

In a moment's exuberance later that evening, he did something totally out of character for someone usually so reserved in public—he danced a jig. The battle that had driven him to the edge of despair had raged from September 26 to November 11, forty-seven days during which twenty-two American and French divisions had battled forty-three often worn-down and depleted German divisions through some of the most difficult, fiercely defended terrain of the war. The US First Army suffered 117,000 casualties, including 26,277 killed, while the German losses were estimated at 100,000.

The armistice may have stopped the carnage, but the general believed that if the fighting had continued for ten more days, the Germans would have been forced to surrender. Pershing thought that would have served a better strategic purpose than an armistice. "We would have rounded up the entire German army, captured it, humiliated it," he said. "The German troops today are marching back into Germany announcing that they have never been defeated. . . . What I dread is that Germany doesn't know that she was licked. Had they given us another week, we'd have taught them."

Pershing was correct in his assessment of how some Germans viewed the end of hostilities. On November 11, a prominent general of the German Third Army reminded his men that they had finished undefeated, pointedly adding: "You are terminating the war in enemy country." For many Germans and for some of the victors, the gravest threat to the future was the brutal terms spelled out in the armistice, a precursor to an even harsher peace treaty, which almost guaranteed that there would be a round two. Shocked by the requirements of the armistice, the head of the German delegation, Matthias Erzberger, bitterly protested, saying they threatened ruin and anarchy in his country.

"A nation of seventy million," he said prophetically, "suffers but does not die."

For many soldiers, the reaction to the armistice was often raw and boisterous, and no more so than for the pilots of Eddie Rickenbacker's Ninety-Fourth Aero Squadron. "Shouting like mad, tumbling over one another in their excitement," he reported, the airmen grabbed anything they could shoot—pistols, machine guns, flares, rockets—and dashed outside to light up the night in one delirious semihysterical orgy of noise, laughter, and light. Setting gasoline drums afire, they danced around them holding hands.

"I've lived through the war!" shouted one man as he pirouetted in a mud hole.

Another grabbed Rickenbacker by the arm and yelled into his ear almost in disbelief, "We won't be shot at anymore!"

As the emotional reaction to the news spread, Pershing must have felt the oppressive weight of nearly eighteen months of command slipping away. Later that afternoon, he drove back to Paris, where the victory celebration was just warming up in all its glorious, zany pandemonium, and where he hoped to see Micheline.

BLOCK-LONG SNAKE DANCES twisted down the streets, growing steadily longer as more men and women joined hands and swayed along with those in front of them; soldiers kissed smiling young women; smiling young women kissed soldiers, then hugged them or jumped in their laps; men and women decked themselves out in glittering, beaded costumes that left little to the imagination; roving musicians played the "Marseillaise" at full bore; accordion players appeared on almost every corner surrounded by people singing their hearts out; soldiers in wheelchairs with cigarettes pressed between their lips were pushed down the middle of streets heaped with bouquets of flowers and sprigs of green; all the broad and famous avenues were flag bedecked and overrun with scores of thousands; convoys of slow-moving military trucks inched through the mobs, the men in back smiling, waving, many crying for joy; French, American, and British soldiers marched two, three, or four abreast with roses stuck in the muzzles of their rifles; every public square was filled to capacity; every monument in a city famed for monuments was decorated with flags; every care, regret, and fear was set aside or forgotten, at least for a few incomparable hours. And did someone mention wine? Peace had been declared, and after four years of a bloody war in which the German army had come within a whisper of marching down these very streets, Paris was celebrating.

Driven to the city that afternoon, Pershing found himself in the middle of the swelling, raucous celebration. As his car slowly made its way into the Place de la Concorde, he was recognized and surrounded, his vehicle invaded. Shouting, clapping, and slightly crazed men and women climbed on top of the vehicle, and a few managed to squeeze inside. "No amount of persuasion would prevail upon them to let us pass," Pershing wrote later. A group of American soldiers swept up in the celebration spotted the general's car and came to his rescue. Pershing was dumbfounded by the pent-up craziness that was sweeping across the city in waves of contagious gaiety. "If all the ridiculous things done during those two or three days by dignified Americans and French men and women were recorded the reader would scarcely believe the story. But this was Paris and the war was over."

Two days later, on November 13, Pershing wrote to Micheline that the war was, indeed, over, and that it was all "so glorious, so joyous!"

"My little one," he said, "there are many things to say to you. Now I will speak as before."

With the war over at last, the general was looking forward to reconnecting with his petite mistress, who was apparently still working on his portrait. The day he wrote to her, Wednesday, November 13, had been a busy one. He'd visited Marshal Joffre's quarters at the École de Guerre in Paris and had pinned the US Distinguished Service Medal on the Frenchman's rotund chest. Saying little, Joffre gripped Pershing's hand in gratitude. A few hours later, Pershing pinned the same decoration on his old friend General Pétain, driving out to Provins, where the French commander and several staff officers gathered in the courtyard outside their headquarters. The next day he also decorated Field Marshal Sir Douglas Haig, who met him at Cambrai as a brigade of Highlanders assembled in their bright tartans and leggings. A band of kilted bagpipers marched by, playing "a medley of Scottish airs" while the soldiers stood at rigid attention. Pershing was impressed by the spectacle.

Arriving back in Paris that afternoon, he had one more important call to make. He stopped to see Clemenceau. Despite their differences, he considered the French leader a remarkable personality, possessing at age seventy-six the vigor and fire of a man of fifty. It was the most emotional of his meetings with French officials, who not many days earlier were eager to have him removed. The two men started to say something, then reached out to each other, unable to speak. "We fell into each other's arms, choked up and had to wipe our eyes," Pershing wrote in the last lines of his war memories. "We had no differences to discuss that day."

CHAPTER 22

Partying in Liverpool

O N THE MORNING the long apocalypse finally ended on the western front, Captain Phelps received a terse message from the English workmen who were making extensive repairs on the dry-docked *Leviathan*: Sorry captain, but we're taking a break to join the party.

Dropping their tools and promising to return by the end of the week, the men poured off the ship and headed straight for the nearest pubs and the heart of Liverpool, which had exploded in the same wild street celebrations that were rocking Paris, London, and New York. The steam whistles on every ship lining both sides of the Mersey were blasting out the news—It's over! The *Leviathan* did the same, her foghorn adding to the cacophony as church bells rang out across the city.

In short order, most of the ship's crew was granted liberty and scrambled aboard lighters that took them ashore by the hundreds. They soon joined the crowds dancing and embracing on Lord and Church Streets and spilling onto sidewalks, and into parks and storefronts. Trucks filled with American soldiers rolled in from their camp a few miles outside the city, the men firing their rifles and pistols into the air.

The wild celebration continued rocking that Monday morning, and Liverpool's pubs were invaded and soon drained of beer, wine, and spirits. As in Paris, any American in uniform was likely to be kissed by one or more young women, or invited to dance or join a snake line or offered a swig of gin straight from the bottle.

Phelps, who stayed aboard, was already thinking about the role the *Leviathan* would play in returning nearly two million American soldiers to the United States. Right now his crew needed to celebrate and blow off a year's worth of steam, so the captain was quick to approve extended leaves, up to a week for many of the men. It wasn't long before the ship's log was punctuated with the same entry: "intoxicated while ashore in a foreign port." That was usually considered a serious offense, but this time the punishments were mild, a small fine and one month without liberty.

Besides, with critical repairs required on the propeller's screw bushings and on the hull, which needed a good barnacle scraping and repainting, the *Leviathan* would need to remain in dry dock for several weeks. Considering the need to precisely coordinate her departure with the high tide, the ship couldn't sail until December 3 at the earliest. With time on their hands, Phelps agreed to a diversion that he hoped would help the men cope with the long delay until they could get under way again and sail for Brest and then home: a football game.

And not just any football game. The matchup that pitted navy and army teams on Thanksgiving Day in a stadium in Liverpool just may have been the roughest game American servicemen played during the war. Notices were posted aboard the ship that 125 players were needed, and it didn't take long to assemble a team that probably included collegiate and semipro players as well as the ship's toughest physical specimens. For two weeks the teams practiced daily on a shin-and elbow-lacerating cinder field next to the dry docks. Going all out, they even found a Liverpool seamstress to make them football uniforms.

After a hearty Thanksgiving meal served aboard ship, the men played the game in a downpour. Army and navy bands belted out collegiate fight songs, and cheerleaders known as the "U Boat

Squad" performed before a sellout crowd that watched both sides slog to a 0–0 tie. When the final gun sounded, there were enough bloody contusions to satisfy everyone. "We were greatly surprised that there were not more casualties than there were," wrote an impressed English newspaper reporter unused to American football. "For the opposing teams went at each other as though they were deadly enemies about to destroy each other by brute force."

A few days later, the repairs on the *Leviathan* were completed. Repainted a drab navy gray—those eye-popping dazzle paint jobs had been discontinued—the ship slipped out of dry dock on December 4 and headed for Brest on what proved to be one of her shortest and scariest voyages. A powerful storm exploded as she headed into the English Channel, her bow slamming deep into the waves as she labored to make headway. Phelps tried to keep the speed at twenty knots, almost an impossibility in such roiling seas. Then he received an ominous report from one of his officers that something was hitting the ship's keel. He heard and felt the thuds himself, the sound of iron hitting iron, and sent an inspection party into the hold to find out what was going on. The pounding continued at irregular intervals, something huge hitting the ship from below like a giant hammer. Phelps was worried the hull would give way and that maybe they'd gotten off course and were in shallows and bumping along the bottom. The charts showed that was out of the question, but there was no other way to explain what was happening.

The answer finally came after a small party of sailors gripping hand lines slowly inched their way out onto the foredeck, which was rising and plunging in the wild seas. They discovered that the capstan had slipped, releasing one of the anchors and several fathoms of chain. Dragged below the ship, the massive anchor—it weighed several tons—was crashing into the bottom.

Phelps immediately ordered all engines slow.

With a work crew hanging on for dear life near the tip of the bow, the anchor was raised by an electric winch. The men stayed out there in the wind and seas all night keeping careful watch on the capstan to make sure it didn't slip again. When the ship pulled into the harbor at Brest the next morning, December 5, "a number of large fish were found on the foredeck."

A master by now of the fast turnaround, Phelps had the *Leviathan* ready to depart for New York early on the afternoon on December 8. Among the 13,558 on board—the largest number carried since the beginning of the war—were 1,421 wounded soldiers. Their voyage had some added excitement when, four days out, the lookouts spotted the *George Washington*, a German-made sister ship, carrying President Wilson to the Paris Peace Conference. The crew and passengers started lining the railings, and when the vessels finally passed each other later that morning at a distance of less than a mile, gun salutes were exchanged and flags hoisted. The smaller *George Washington* was escorted by a single battleship, the USS *Pennsylvania*, but when the convoy cruised into the French harbor on December 13 it had grown to include ten battleships and twenty-eight destroyers in a massive display of America's rapidly growing naval power.

Soon after the encounter, the *Leviathan* steamed into rough weather that hung on all the way to New York, where dense fog required the ship to anchor off Sandy Hook rather than risk a collision by trying to head into the bay. The fog finally lifted in the morning, and when the ship started up the Hudson on December 16, New York City was ready for a blowout. Tugboats and small craft came out to meet her by the swarming dozens as fire boats shot shimmering arcs of water high into the air in welcome. The long-anticipated landmarks were coming in rapid succession for the thousands of soldiers who watched from the railings, shouting themselves hoarse and waving their hats—Governors Island, the Statue of Liberty, the Manhattan skyline. American flags seemed to be draped from almost every window, and confetti was streaming down into the streets in long white trails.

Phelps had already given orders to stop the troops from rushing from one side of the ship to the other for fear that the sudden shift in weight might cause the *Leviathan* to run aground. One mishap occurred when she banged up against a police boat that got in the way as tugs eased the big ship into her slip. Dueling bands were playing on the army pier and aboard the *Leviathan*. Soldiers were peering from every porthole, some wearing German helmets and holding up captured rifles and flags. Thousands of relatives—wives, children, parents—who'd been waiting for hours in a line stretching into River Street cheered when the gangways started coming down. More cheers went up in a great roaring wave as the smiling doughboys began to descend carrying their packs and bundles of souvenirs, and more still when they started bringing off the wounded.

For the first time since the war began, reporters were allowed on board, and one of them soon found an upbeat young soldier from Brooklyn with most of his face shot away. Swathed in bandages, he was with a new friend he'd met on the ship: Ty Cobb, the legendary Detroit Tigers slugger who'd served at the front as a captain with a chemical warfare unit and had come back on the *Leviathan*. Cobb encouraged any soldier or sailor who went to one of his games to shout out to him that he'd sailed with him on the big troopship. "I'll run right off the baseline and over to wherever you are in the bleachers," Cobb promised, "and shake hands and sit down and have a talk about this trip."

Another passenger was a fourteen-year-old French orphan who'd somehow managed to hide out as a stowaway. He wore a soldier's blouse and was soon befriended by members of the crew, who smuggled food to him. The teen's father had been killed at Château-Thierry, and his mother and younger brother were dead.

A newspaper story reported that a soldier took the boy to Jersey City, "where it was hoped some family would adopt him."

As in Liverpool, half the crew was given an extended leave—ten days for most of the sailors. Those who remained on board pooled their money and at Captain Phelps's suggestion hosted a gala Christmas party for 1,200 orphans from the New York City area. The children were escorted on board and given a tour, and even before a bugler sounded the call for dinner—turkey with all the trimmings, pie, and three different kinds of ice cream—the fun started as small groups of boys and girls scurried off to explore things for themselves. Some of them wound up in the ductwork and coal chutes and tumbled out black with soot. Two others were tracked down deep in the engine room, where sailors were entertaining them.

The crew went all out. Standing before a twenty-foot tree trimmed with tinsel, stars, and ornaments in the galley, Santa gave each child a gift—for the girls often a doll with a separate high chair. Earlier, Santa caused a sensation when he descended in full red-and-white regalia from high atop one of the smokestacks. Charlie Chaplin movies and puppet shows followed dinner, and except for few children who were still hiding out, the fun and controlled mayhem was over by late afternoon. A photo, which haunts nearly a century later, shows over thirty children—boys wearing ties, girls in dresses—gathered in front of Santa, some holding American flags or clutching dolls and staring at the camera with brave, soulful faces. Another photo captured Captain Phelps in full uniform with four gold stripes on his sleeves holding up a child grinning broadly and clutching him around his neck. Phelps looks like he's thinking about smiling.

The *Leviathan* didn't sail again until nearly a month later, bound once more for Brest on her eleventh voyage. The ship was supposed to depart on December 31 with a former passenger aboard, Assistant Secretary of the Navy Franklin Roosevelt, who'd recuperated from his near-fatal flu attack and was heading back to France for the peace conference. But FDR had to book passage on another ship after one of the *Leviathan*'s stern turbines broke down. When the big ship finally sailed in January, the crew included scores of recently enlisted sailors who were making their first sea voyage. Among them was a teenager from New York City with a smooth face not yet molded to its later chiseled ruggedness.

A Sailor Named Bogart

GRIPPING HIS DUFFEL bag, a newly minted sailor named Humphrey DeForest Bogart boarded the *Leviathan* at 4:55 p.m. on December 17, according to the ship's log. A few weeks later, the young man's mother surprisingly called the ship at 6:50 a.m. to report that her son was "ill at home."

The seaman second class probably had been granted a short liberty sometime after reporting for duty—with the war over, that wasn't unusual—and had gone home to spend a little time with the parents he'd been feuding with for years. His room in their tony West End Avenue home would have been far better than a hammock berth aboard the *Leviathan*—and Humphrey Bogart was accustomed to the finer things.

Bogart was born December 25, 1899, the son of a prominent surgeon, Belmont DeForest Bogart. His mother, Maud Humphrey, was one of the most well-known magazine and children's book illustrators of that period. A talented artist, she'd studied with James Whistler in Paris and didn't have much time to spare for her son and two daughters. The parental plan for Bogart to attend Yale as had his father fell apart when the rebellious teen was asked to leave the Phillips Academy in Andover, Massachusetts. The dismissal letter was sent to his home in May 1918. Young Bogart, it seemed, much preferred drinking, partying, and socializing with wealthy pals to academics.

Probably looking for adventure, Bogart joined the navy a few weeks later aboard a Civil War–era training ship moored in the North River, the USS *Granite State*. He enrolled in the US Naval Reserve on May 28, 1918. At his physical he stood five feet seven and a half inches tall, weighed 136 pounds, and had a slight scar on his chin and another on the inner side of his left forearm and left leg. Called up for active duty, Bogart didn't have far to travel from home for his training at the naval reserve base in Pelham Bay Park, and in late November he was assigned to the *Leviathan*, which was still stuck in a Liverpool dry dock.

Traveling without a destroyer escort on her first peacetime voyage to France, the *Leviathan* left New York late on January 24 bound for Brest. The cruise almost called to mind the ship's brief experience as a luxury liner when she carried only a few thousand passengers instead of the ten to twelve thousand soldiers and sailors who had squeezed aboard during many of her wartime voyages. On this trip the ship sailed with only 1,073 servicemen, including several hundred Polish soldiers, so for the first time since the *Leviathan* had become a navy vessel, there was plenty of space, and considering it was the peak of the North Atlantic storm season, the voyage was remarkably smooth.

The international news was much rougher. Although fighting had stopped on the western front, the Russian Civil War had erupted, and Red Army soldiers were pushing back American and White Russian forces near Archangel, according to a story Bogart would have read in the ship's newspaper. Other stories predicted that Lloyd George's government in Britain would be voted out of office with the war over, and that the kaiser, who'd fled to the Netherlands, would to return to Germany. The later report was erroneous; Wilhelm II never left Holland. He'd already abdicated, and when he arrived at his new manor home, Huis Doorn, where he would die in exile, his first request was for a "cup of good English tea." There was also a puzzling story about when the recently approved Eighteenth Amendment instituting prohibition would take effect.

The *Leviathan* reached Brest on January 31 and sailed for New York three days later with 9,470 soldiers, including 2,122 who were wounded. "When I saw the suffering of these men, and even though I was just a teenager, the terror of war struck my heart," Bogart reportedly told a friend years later. "War no longer seemed the grand adventure it had when I first sailed."

Far less believable was a story about how Bogart allegedly acquired the scarred lip that gave him his distinctive accent. According to this version, a piece of shrapnel cut his mouth when he was at the helm of the *Leviathan* during a U-boat attack, a remarkable occurrence considering the ship never came under U-boat fire and the war was already over when Bogart came aboard. He also told the director John Ford that during his navy career he visited a Parisian bordello. That may have happened while he was serving on another ship, but on this trip there wasn't time. The *Leviathan* sailed for New York on February 3.

Bogart transferred to the USS *Santa Olivia* later that month and promptly got into serious trouble. He somehow managed to miss the troop transport's departure when it sailed from Hoboken in April bound for France and was turned in as a deserter. He wound up spending three days in confinement on bread and water for neglect of duty and was released from the service on September 30, 1919. Records show the desertion charge was later removed from his record as erroneous, but the matter wasn't cleared up until 1921, when he finally received an honorable discharge and the World War I Victory Medal.

CHAPTER 23

Journey of the Survivors

E XPLOSIONS ROCKED BAN-DE-LAVELINE as the withdrawing
Germans blew up ammunition dumps in the hills overlooking the village that was tucked in a valley in the Vosges Mountains.
Smoke from the blasts settled like ground fog, and streetlamps
were lit at night for the first time in years. The detonations were
also heard a few miles to the south in Plainfaing and Habeaurupt,
where the residents joined French *poilus* and the soldiers of the
371st Infantry in celebrating the end of the fighting. The local band
was called out, and the party roared on for several days, fueled by
copious amounts of wine and hard cider as the villagers, overjoyed
to welcome the African American troops, poured them drinks and
welcomed them into their homes. The raucousness finally reached
the point that enlisted men were ordered off the streets by 7:00
p.m. Drunks were arrested and the names taken of "all men found
creating a disturbance."

So began the war's epilogue for the 371st Infantry, an arduous,
nearly three-month journey that took them to Brest and then home
aboard the *Leviathan* with other African American units that had
been attached to the French army. On November 13, two days after
the armistice, Freddie Stowers's old regiment headed for Germany
as part of the army of occupation, but after two hours on the road
they were ordered to turn around and hike nearly twenty miles due
west to Bruyers and Leval, where they spent the next seven weeks.

The residents of Bruyers and Laval were delighted to have "*les soldats American Noirs"* in their communities. The two villages, as well as nearby Granges, where another black regiment was bivouacked, had largely escaped the war unscathed, and there were plenty of shops, markets, and comfortable homes where soldiers could rent rooms for their quarters. The Americans remained favorites with the young women, which happened so often in the Vosges and elsewhere that nervous army officials issued Order Number 40, declaring that "Negroes should not speak with or to French women." Military police officers were authorized to arrest any African American soldiers found violating this order, but not whites. The order and its enforcement apparently sparked "a number of brawls in which the white and black soldiers participated" and was part of a larger plan aimed at preventing African American soldiers from having social contact with French civilians. At the same time, French officers were advised "not to present any semblance of mixing socially with Negro officers, especially not to eat with them, and also not to praise the Negro in the presence of white Americans for any military action in which he participated."

The regiment had been fighting nearly nonstop since its arrival in France over half a year earlier. No leaves had been granted during that time, while white officers had received a seven-day pass to visit Paris, another glaring example of the sharp racial disparities in the army. The excuse, illustrative in itself, was given that a "leave area for colored troops had not been designated" in the French capital. Another reason was also alleged in the regiment's official history: the Secret Service reportedly had "discovered a movement to stir up race hatred among these troops." To make up for the blatant unfairness of the no-leave policy for African Americans, these regiments were given priority for their return to the states.

Adding to these stiffening racial tensions—and how quickly things started going badly after the fighting ended—African American regiments that had served with the French army also missed out on the Thanksgiving and Christmas meals provided to their white counterparts. The history of the 371st Regiment simply states: "Special provision was made for troops in the American armies for Thanksgiving and Christmas. We, as part of the French Army, did not rate anything. We did the best we could for the men with our own funds." The Christmas holiday celebrated in the charming Vosges region was peaceful and quiet by American standards, especially with the war over. Religious services were held in the village churches, and small groups of officers and men walked the streets that Christmas night singing carols.

The weather remained cold and clear, although that was about to change. The daily drilling and long marches were unpopular but considered necessary to maintain discipline until the departure from France, a moment everyone knew was coming soon. And at least the 371st wasn't subjected to one of the humiliations inflicted on the 369th Regiment from New York City. Decorated with a unit citation of the Croix de Guerre for bravery under fire, the men were still ordered to take rifle instruction from a young lieutenant who'd never been in combat.

The 371st also received a unit citation of the Croix de Guerre, and on December 16 at 10:30 a.m., the men assembled on an impromptu parade ground in Bruyères, where General Goybet, who commanded the 157th Division of the French Fourth Army, personally pinned the Legion of Honor and Croix de Guerre on the regiment's flag. With French and American flags snapping in the wind, he decorated 184 men for bravery. Addressing the survivors, Goybet spoke of their courage and self-sacrifice, how they'd lived for seven months "as brothers in arms, sharing the same burdens, the same hardships, the same dangers." He mentioned the great battle of the Champagne, in which Freddie Stowers had been killed. Nearly two months had passed since the corporal was cut down during the attack on the German machine gunners defending Hill 188, but through an oversight his medals wouldn't be awarded for another seventy years. "The most formidable defenses, the strongest machine gun nests, the most crushing artillery barrages were unable to stop them," Goybet said. "Our pure brotherhood in arms has been consecrated in the blood of the brave. These bonds will never be severed."

Two weeks later on January 1, the troops boarded French railway cars in a cold rain for a 350-mile trip to Le Mans. Arriving two days later, they were assigned to filthy tents, where they had to sleep on the ground and used bundles of tree branches as makeshift mattresses. The reason given for this uncomfortable ordeal was to delouse, a rite of passage for all American soldiers heading home. After taking hot showers, their first in weeks, the men were sprinkled with a powdery chemical disinfectant and issued new clothing and equipment. Some of them had to go through the process two or three times before they were lice free. The tiny bloodsucking insects spread highly contagious trench fever and typhus, and the inspections were rigorous and remorseless. It wasn't unusual to delay an entire regiment until everyone had received a clean bill of health.

On January 10, the 371st finally hiked to the Le Mans rail station. Whatever grumbling was still going on about the long, cold wait in the bath lines ended the moment the men spotted one of the big "American Jack" locomotives come around a curve pulling a string of large American boxcars. The train stopped in front of them with a whistle blast as clouds of steam rose up from the locomotive's massive wheels. The soldiers cheered, not believing their eyes or their good fortune. After they'd ridden all over France in those cramped forty men/eight horse boxcars, this was more like it. The American freight cars seemed almost as luxurious as Pullmans. The men crowded aboard—2,594 enlisted troops and 55 officers—stretched out in all the extra space, and prepared to enjoy their last ride in France.

The two-day trip through Normandy and Breton covered nearly 217 miles and passed through Rennes and half a dozen smaller towns. Along the way the men often leaned out of the boxcars to shout greetings to the French citizens who waved to them as the train passed. They also had fun with the fresh-looking soldiers they encountered at some of the rail stops—support troops who were usually white and hadn't been anywhere near the front. One African American unit, the 369th, made a point of gleefully reminding them of that fact from their slowly moving train.

"Who won the war?" they yelled derisively.

This same unit reached Brest around the time the 371st rolled in. The African American troops soon found out the French debarkation port had become a powder keg of racial tension. Within an hour of their arrival, a private in the 369th was clubbed in the head by a white MP after interrupting a conversation to ask directions to the latrine, according to one account. "His comrades instantly came to his aid and liberated the injured man from arrest. They knew what to expect from White troops [and] wanted to serve notice . . . that they would resist insult or assault." A white officer from the regiment hurried over and chewed out the MP, cooling down a tense situation when it wouldn't have taken much to set off a riot.

After a long march in the rain from the train station, the men were amazed when they arrived at the camp. Since their last visit in April, it had exploded in size and now sprawled for several miles, the muddy streets lined with hundreds of two-story prefabricated barracks, huts, and tents. The men never forgot the mud or how hard it was to cross a street without stepping into the ankle-deep muck. Cars and trucks sank to their axles, horses to their knees. They had to spend nearly a week in tents before they were assigned to barracks, which didn't have floors but at least were equipped with crude cots. And once again, they went through the hot delousing showers.

As they waited for their departure orders, the men occupied their time laying duckboard sidewalks, working on the docks, and helping coal and unload ships. Proud of their combat record, they weren't happy to work as laborers, especially when white regiments were usually spared such details, but they didn't dare complain for fear it would delay their leaving. The camp was filled with tens of thousands of veterans, all waiting their turn to go home.

On January 27, the 371st marched into Brest to receive a unit citation for valor from the French. Wearing American Army helmets and carrying slung rifles, the men lined up between a long double row of trees, standing at rigid attention as another Croix de Guerre was pinned to their regimental colors in final homage from the grateful French. The official citation noted the 371st had demonstrated "the very best qualities of bravery and audacity which are characteristic of shock troops. . . . It took [a heavily defended position] by terrific fighting under an exceptionally violent machine gun fire. It then continued its progression in spite of the fire of enemy artillery and its cruel losses, taking numerous prisoners, securing cannon, machine guns and important material."

The citation was signed: Pétain, Marshal of France.

After a few more days spent coping with the mud and rain, the men were finally told that they'd be leaving France on February 3 aboard the *Leviathan*. They got their first close look at the monster on February 1, when they marched into Brest wearing new blue denim work outfits and helped coal the ship along with the 372nd regiment. Setting the tone and pace, their bands broke out with some hot jazz numbers, and the ship's vast coal hoppers were loaded in record time. Many of the men couldn't believe the size of the ship, on which sailors could be seen walking about on the main deck nearly one hundred feet over their heads.

A Famous Shoreline

WHAT WERE YOU doing on the eleventh hour of the eleventh day of the eleventh month?"

It was a common question as soldiers three months removed from the slaughter of trench warfare mingled on the wide decks of the *Leviathan* during the raucous voyage home.

As they shared stories during the eight-day trip to New York, the men knew there was much to be grateful for. They'd come through while so many others—friends, comrades, and quiet leaders like Freddie Stowers—were now buried somewhere in France. Of the 2,284 men who'd started the attack with him in Champagne on September 28, 1918, 1,065 had been killed or wounded. Most of them fell during the first three days of what was one of the pivotal battles of the war.

In quiet moments aboard ship, the survivors of C Company certainly must have spoken about their corporal—where and how he died and their memories of him and how he'd wanted to get all of them back home alive. Other names would have been mentioned as well, among them Private Burton Holmes, who also died on September 28 on Hill 188. When his rifle jammed he picked up another one and continued the attack in the face of withering machine gun fire. Another private, Robert Lee, was killed on the same day, caught in a cross fire as he helped take out a machine gun nest. Private Charlie Butler crawled two hundred yards under grass-clipping fire to rescue one of his white officers who lay mortally wounded in a shell hole. The survivors of the 371st Infantry had these and so many other stories to tell, enough to fill a long voyage home, or a lifetime.

As the *Leviathan* steamed on a southerly route seeking calmer seas for the many sick and wounded on board—2,122 of them—the ship offered plenty of other diversions. The African Americans accounted for about two-thirds of the 9,470 troops and other passengers and were delighted with the spacious, well-ventilated *Leviathan*, especially after their recent experiences in the mud baths of Brest. They held boxing matches, played volleyball on the deck, and hit the ship's canteens as often as possible, buying ice cream and soda in record amounts, items they hadn't enjoyed or seen in months. At night, jazz wafted up from below deck.

The white and black soldiers were kept apart as much as possible, and there were none of the provocative encounters that had occurred with the white MPs in Brest. The weather cooperated, with only two squalls that marred the otherwise smooth seas. Perhaps inevitably, two soldiers from the 371st died from flu-related pneumonia on their way home. One of them, a private from F Company, had survived all the fighting in France but passed away at 4:00 p.m. on February 11, just as the ship was approaching Long Island.

When the famous shoreline emerged from the haze on the western horizon, cheering broke out from one end of the *Leviathan* to the other. Entering Ambrose Channel at 3:40 p.m., the ship was greeted by a harbor ferry with a big sign on the upper deck proclaiming in a single word, "Welcome." They passed the Statue of Liberty on the left as the army bands on deck boomed out one song after another while bands on shore did the same. By 6:15 p.m., the *Leviathan* was made fast to her moorings at Pier 4. Too late to disembark, the men spent their last night aboard the ship and in the morning started coming down the gangways as thousands loudly welcomed them home. They lined up for pictures, proud of how they looked in their olive-hued uniforms and overcoats and prouder still of what they'd accomplished. The photographs show small groups of smiling young men clutching Red Cross sandwiches and doughnuts and drinking steaming coffee from their mess-kit cups. They were waiting for the ferries that would take them a few miles up the Hudson River to board trains for Camp Upton on Long Island; from there the next stop would be Camp Jackson in South Carolina.

The crowd that had cheered their arrival at the pier quieted as the regiment's wounded were carried off the ship, many of them on stretchers, so many it took much of the morning to bring them all down. Some were heavily bandaged or were missing arms or legs or had been gassed. The luckier ones managed to limp down the gangway on crutches to the army ambulances that were pulled up alongside the ship to take them to military hospitals.

Similar scenes were playing out in England, France, and Germany—the joyous, often mournful return of the living and wounded to places that would never be the same. In Paris they were already placing placards on the Métro trains reserving seats for the *mutilés de guerre*. The casualties of the Great War were almost too monstrous to calculate, the numbers of maimed and emotionally broken men too vast to comprehend. The American hospitals in France and new ones opening in Germany were full of them, taxing exhausted medical staffs to the maximum even as they prepared for another flu epidemic.

CHAPTER 24

"Amid a Silence That Hurt"

THE *LEVIATHAN* SAILED from Brest in the rain on Thursday, April 18. On the previous trip from New York, the ship had carried a special passenger, nine-year-old Warren Pershing, who joined his famous father in Paris for their first extended visit in nearly two years. Also on board was Secretary of War Newton Baker, on his way to the Paris Peace Conference. For the return voyage, most of the twelve thousand passengers were members of the famous Rainbow Division, including the young brigadier general of the 84th Infantry Regiment, Douglas MacArthur, who strode the decks in all weathers wearing a long purple scarf knitted by his mother and an oversize raccoon coat.

It was the big ship's fourteenth Atlantic crossing since America entered the war—and with the fighting over, the *Leviathan* was at the forefront of the massive effort to return two million troops to the United States. To help speed the effort, fifty-eight cargo vessels were converted to troop transports, in addition to the scores of ships that had been used to ferry doughboys to France. As part of the peace proceedings, Germany was required to provide nine ships to help the United States bring her soldiers home, this in addition to German liners such as the *Leviathan* that had been seized in American ports when the US declared war. The navy was also using battleships and cruisers in a massive logistical undertaking that by June would be moving as many as 314,000 soldiers a month and was aimed at returning nearly all American soldiers by September.

The *Leviathan* remained the gold standard for these crossings, and for the rest of his life Douglas MacArthur would recall the splendor of the trip and the bittersweet arrival in New York. He compared his accommodations on board to one of New York's finest hotels. "I gracefully occupied a $5,000 suite consisting of four rooms and three baths," he wrote a former aide. "It filled me with excitement to change my bed and bath each evening."

MacArthur was introduced to the new skipper of the *Leviathan*, Captain Edward Durell, another sea-hardened veteran, who'd replaced Captain Phelps earlier that month. A navigator on the around-the-world cruise of the Great White Fleet during the presidency of Theodore Roosevelt, the aging captain had a "high forehead and small mustache" that gave his face a softer, friendlier look than the more angular, tight-lipped Phelps. Unfortunately, there's no record of what Durell, who was nearing the end of his career, discussed with the brigadier general just getting started on his path to becoming an American icon.

By wartime standards, the crossing was an uneventful trip, the only brief excitement the sighting of what looked like a barnacle-encrusted floating mine, which was passed at a safe distance. The weather was often foggy, and there were two deaths—army privates who apparently shot each other during an argument. The passengers were in a buoyant mood, and the ship's newspaper was filled with announcements for band concerts, athletic events, and vaudeville shows. The movies that played every evening in the F deck mess hall included Charlie Chaplin's *The Adventurer.*

The *Leviathan* entered Ambrose Channel at 3:43 p.m. on April 25 and by six o'clock was tied up at her dock. Unlike previous arrivals greeted by noisy, shoving crowds, competing bands, and fire boats, the mooring this time was subdued. Wearing his oversize raccoon coat, MacArthur was the first down the gangplank. The only spectator, he was shocked to discover, was "one little urchin" who asked what troops were on the ship.

"We are the famous 42nd," the general gaily said.

"Have you been to France?" the boy asked.

The question jolted MacArthur and left him crestfallen. He later wrote an aide: "Amid a silence that hurt—with no one—not even the children—to see us—we marched off the dock—to be scattered to the four winds—a sad, gloomy end of the Rainbow. There was no welcome for the fighting men—no one wanted us to parade—no one even seemed to have heard of the war."

MacArthur had been awarded seven Silver Stars for gallantry in action, the last for his leadership in the capture of Côte-de-Châtillon in the Meuse heights. He was gassed twice and taken prisoner at gunpoint once by American troops who encountered him at night "leaning over a map and wearing a floppy hat, muffler, riding breeches, and polished boots [and] assumed that he must be a German." General Pershing, no fan of MacArthur's flamboyance but an admirer of his courage and leadership skills, pinned a second Distinguished Service Cross to his tunic during a ceremony in Remagen, where the young general was part of the occupation force. This time—and no doubt in deference to Pershing's wishes—MacArthur was wearing a doughboy helmet tightly strapped under his chin instead of his famously nonregulation smashed-down cap.

When he strode off the *Leviathan* on that April afternoon in New York, the cap was back on his head.

In the letter written to his aide on May 13, he expressed surprise at the prices in New York. "Paris is certainly a cheap little place after all." He also judged that clothing prices were exorbitant because the girls he met at a play "were absolutely unable to wear any."

MacArthur also offered a prophetic warning about the peace terms proposed for Germany. "They look drastic," he wrote, "and seem to me more like a treaty of perpetual war than of perpetual peace."

CHAPTER 25

Farewell to Arms

GENERAL PERSHING STOOD with a cluster of victorious generals in the Hall of Mirrors at the Palace of Versailles as President Wilson signed the peace treaty that ended the Great War. It was a long, narrow room, more like a corridor, and Pershing and the other military leaders, decked out in the red sash of the Legion of Honor, drew appreciative stares. One by one, other representatives of thirty-two nations walked to the three signing tables and affixed their signatures—some using quill pens—in the same resplendent room where Louis XIV, the Sun King, held court and where the defeated French had signed a peace treaty with Germany in 1871. With another, far-greater war over, the scene that Saturday afternoon, June 28, 1919, glittered with pomp and pageantry carefully orchestrated by the victorious French and meant, at every level, to humiliate the Germans. Hundreds of journalists and photographers pressed in as the two German representatives, their faces drained white, signed the document "under duress" after complaining bitterly about the treaty's terms and the threat that the Allied troops massed on the west bank of the Rhine would march for Berlin.

Whether Pershing agreed with American concerns that the severity of the treaty would guarantee continued strife in Europe isn't clear, but there's no question that he often found himself in bitter disagreement with the French. He resented what he considered to be Marshal Foch's efforts to downplay America's pivotal role in winning the war. It came as no surprise to him that soldiers stationed in Germany increasingly preferred the clean, polite, and well-organized Germans to their "slipshod, temperamental, exploitive and dirty" ally. Pershing told Britain's Field Marshal Haig that "it was difficult to exaggerate the feeling of dislike for the French which existed in the American Army."

By the time the treaty was signed early that summer, Pershing was all but finished with his long service in France. The AEF had greatly shrunk in size, and most of the two million doughboys sent Over There had already returned home aboard the *Leviathan* and a fleet of other transports.

On Memorial Day Pershing spoke at a cemetery dedication near Montfaucon, where the remains of 14,246 soldiers would be buried, most of them killed during the Meuse-Argonne fighting. Accompanied by his son, Warren, Pershing stood on a hillside that overlooked acres of simple white crosses with an oversize American flag at their center. Modeled after Lincoln's Gettysburg Address, his short remarks ended with the words: "Dear Comrades, Farewell. Here, under the clear skies, on the green hillsides and amid the flowering fields of France, in the quiet hush of peace, we leave you forever in God's keeping." A few hours earlier he'd broken into tears when he stopped at a small cemetery near Beaumont and encountered the village mayor and a group of children decorating the graves of American dead with wildflowers. The mayor assured him they would always care for these young men "sleeping so far away from their homes."

On Bastille Day, July 14, came the Victory Parade led by one thousand wounded French soldiers, many missing arms, legs, or eyes, the *mutilés* who limped, hobbled, or were wheeled under the Arc de Triomphe and then seated in a place of honor. Watched by an estimated two million cheering Parisians, who jammed the seven-mile parade route along the Champs-Élysees, the grand boulevards, and the vast Place de la République, the procession featured contingents from the victorious nations marching in alphabetical order—A for Americain through P for Polonais—with the French bringing up the rear. The American "Composite Regiment" of 1,500 handpicked soldiers—each had to be at least six feet tall—was selected from the best units in the army. Faded newsreels of the parade still capture the powerful impression these men made as they swung in perfect step up the Avenue de la Grande Armée wearing their doughboy helmets and cartridge belts, rifles over the right shoulder and carrying nearly ninety regimental flags in a blaze of color.

Pershing, a superb horseman since his cavalry days on the western frontier, rode in straight-backed elegance on a dark bay named Kidron. He wore glistening black boots, jodhpurs, and a Sam Browne belt and was followed by a lone rider carrying a large flag emblazoned with the four gold stars of his rank. Uncustomarily smiling, he acknowledged the cheers with crisp salutes as he led his men down the wide avenues and past French infantrymen standing at attention at the curbs and holding their rifles at port arms. His most fervent admirer, after his son, Warren, watched him ride by from an apartment window overlooking the Champs-Élysees.

Micheline Resco.

"I Have Made Plans for Us"

THE CANNONS STARTED booming as General Pershing approached the *Leviathan* aboard a navy lighter—a seventeen-gun salute fired from a French shore battery at Brest and answered by an American destroyer in the harbor, the USS *Bridgeport*. Pershing came aboard at 9:26 a.m. on Monday, September 1, accompanied by his son, Warren, the Composite Regiment, and an honor guard of one hundred marines. The cannons roared again at 11:00 a.m. when Pershing's frequent adversary Marshal Foch boarded the ship to say farewell. The two men had often fought bitterly over how and where American troops should be used, encounters sometimes punctuated with red-faced anger and table pounding. This time they embraced, the white-mustached French commander kissing Pershing on both cheeks and the taller American warmly taking his hand, forgetting their arguments and his more recent outbursts that the French were trying to downplay America's scale-tipping role in the war.

Foch, who later visited Pershing in the United States, was deeply moved. "I never saw him show so much feeling," he remembered. The marshal left the ship at 12:10 p.m., and his launch followed the *Leviathan* as she made her way out of the harbor, Foch standing on the deck and giving Pershing a final salute before the ship put out to sea.

The general occupied the kaiser's former luxury suite on C Deck—nine rooms including two bathrooms, a fireplace, and a private veranda overlooking the ocean. The cruise started off well enough, with fair skies and calm seas, but squalls rolled in two days later and Pershing was laid low. A queasy stomach didn't stop him from writing a short, plaintive message to Micheline: "I have sea sickness and have not been outside my room." Despite his mal de mer, he was still focused on their future together. "I have thought about you a lot, my Cherie, and I have made plans for us in New York."

On that same day, September 3, President Wilson signed an order granting Pershing the four-star rank of "general of the armies of the United States." Wilson signed the promotion shortly before departing on his doomed whistle-stop trip out west to promote the Paris Peace Treaty and the League of Nations. The journey was cut short when Wilson fell ill two weeks later in his blue presidential railcar as the train neared Wichita, Kansas. A few days after arriving back in Washington, Wilson suffered a severe stroke that paralyzed his left side.

Pershing's son, Warren, delivered the news about the promotion when the *Leviathan* was more than halfway across the Atlantic. The boy jumped up in his father's bed and read the radio message bearing the good news. The seas had become calm again and, feeling better, the general went out on deck, where he was congratulated by the Composite Regiment as the band broke out in "Over There."

This was the final crossing for the big ship as a troop carrier, and so it was fitting that Pershing was on board. Since the armistice, she'd made nine round-trips between New York and Brest, and another nine and one-half before the peace. The ship looked much the worse for wear after so many battering voyages across the unforgiving North Atlantic, her dull gray paint faded and showing patches of rust, but the sleek lines of what had once been the world's largest, most luxuriously appointed ocean liner were still unmistakable. Life aboard for the sailors went on as usual. The ship's log shows the usual list of deck courts and summary courts-martial for a variety of offenses. The day before the *Leviathan* reached New York, sailors were fined and assigned extra duty for offenses that included "failing to get up when called and for using profane language." Another sailor, who'd probably visited Paris on leave, was fined $18.50 and assigned extra work details for "failing to take venereal treatment."

At seven o'clock in the morning on September 8, Pershing was suddenly awakened by a medley of sirens, whistles, foghorns, and bells as the *Leviathan* approached the harbor. Four hours earlier, the ship had been joined by the USS *Calhoun* and other destroyers that formed an honor escort. Shortly before Pershing was jolted from his sleep, the ship entered Ambrose Channel; a seventeen-gun salute was fired from Fort Wadsworth as the vessel slowly steamed through the Narrows and passed the Statue of Liberty. Dressing quickly, Pershing and his closest staff members enjoyed the show from the bridge, doffing their hats and smiling everywhere they looked. With tugs and fire boats circling them, a destroyer pulled alongside carrying Secretary Baker and other dignitaries, who came aboard to welcome the returning AEF commander. Another vessel brought out Pershing's brother and two sisters. A seaplane flew overhead, while another swooped low and dropped a stack of newspapers on the *Leviathan*'s deck.

Pershing had expected a welcome, but nothing like this—and it was only the opening act.

The New York City victory parade held on September 10 matched the gaudy celebration in Paris, with the magnificent Composite Regiment and the storied First Division marching down Fifth Avenue to Washington Square, twenty-five thousand soldiers wearing battle gear and led by Pershing, who once again was on horseback. The street was almost covered in places with laurel as he rode by on a tough-to-handle mount provided by the New York City Police Department. He was showered with roses and clouds of white confetti that rained down from the tall buildings. One of the memorable moments of the three-hour parade came when he dismounted in front of Saint Patrick's Cathedral and shook hands with Cardinal Mercier of Belgium, who was famous for resisting the German occupation of his country and for his efforts to raise money to rebuild the destroyed library at Louvain.

The final victory parade occurred a week later on September 17 in Washington, DC, a repeat of the same moving street scenes, with Pershing joining President Wilson on the reviewing stand as the First Division marched by. The general made a short speech the following day praising the AEF to a joint session of Congress, then departed on his first vacation in nearly four years. The getaway included a three-week stay at a private lodge in the Adirondacks, where he took a quick look at the mountain views and sky, tossed off his hat, and vowed never to leave.

At about the same time, the curtain was coming down on the wartime career of the *Leviathan*. It happened quietly, with none of the fanfare and news flashes that had accompanied the seizure of the ship in April 1917. The last entries in the log were made on October 29 as the vessel was tied to her moorings at Pier 4. Totally ignoring or missing the quiet end to her naval career, the New York papers devoted their front pages that day to the ongoing Senate fight over the peace treaty, a looming national coal strike, and how the prohibition amendment would be enforced when it went into effect in January. There was no mention of the *Leviathan*.

The crowds that had pushed their way onto the pier to welcome Pershing home a month earlier had long departed, and only a skeleton crew remained on board. The ship's log had been filled for days with the names of scores of men relieved from active duty and sent home. Those discharged on the twenty-ninth included a lieutenant commander who'd wrapped up the task of "closing out accounts of the U.S.S. *Leviathan*." On that same day four men who'd been in the brig were freed by "order of CO."

Dutifully recorded in the log, the weather was "clear, slightly hazy [with] light SW airs."

At 4:05 p.m. came this final entry: "The U.S.S. *Leviathan* was placed out of commission this date by order of Commander of Third Naval District."

EPILOGUE

A T LOOSE ENDS after leaving the army, **General John Pershing** flirted with running for president as a Republican, but nothing came of it. Though he disliked the job intensely, he had better luck as a writer. After working on his autobiography for over a decade, Pershing finally published his memoirs in 1931, *My Experiences in the World War*, which won the Pulitzer Prize.

During his annual pilgrimages to France to research his opus, Pershing and Micheline renewed their love affair, preferring as always to keep it scrupulously low key and out of the spotlight. For years they'd discussed whether to get married, yet never made the commitment. That changed when the general's health began failing, and on September 2, 1946, they were married in his apartment at Walter Reed Hospital.

Pershing was buried in Arlington Cemetery on July 19, 1948, thirty years to the day after the soldiers he commanded counterattacked out of the rain at Soissons, one of the first big steps on the road to victory. George C. Marshall Jr. was one of the sixteen generals who marched in a downpour at Pershing's funeral, along with Dwight Eisenhower and Omar Bradley. A key member of Pershing's staff in France, Marshall recalled the American commander's decision to keep his men attacking during the darkest hours of the Meuse-Argonne battle. Despite severe casualties, green troops, a raging flu epidemic, a determined enemy holding "one of the strongest positions of the Western Front, pessimism on all sides and the pleadings to halt the battle made by many of the influential members of the army," he persisted in fighting through until victory, Marshall said, adding, "nothing else in [Pershing's] leadership throughout the war was comparable to this."

Royal Johnson's service ended on December 20, 1918, when he was discharged from the army, the recipient of the Distinguished Service Cross and the Croix de Guerre for gallantry. He needed extensive treatment for his shattered right shoulder and suffered pain for the rest of his life. Returning to Congress, he quickly earned a reputation as an advocate for veterans.

Johnson served in the House until 1932, resigning to open a law office. Six years later a speeding police car struck him as he crossed a street in downtown Washington. Still hobbling on crutches, he'd just started getting back to work when he suffered a heart attack at his home. He died the following morning, on August 2, 1939. Johnson, who was fifty-six, was buried in Arlington Cemetery. A decade later, a Veterans Administration hospital was named in his honor in Sioux Falls.

Elizabeth Weaver returned to the United States in August 1919. She later became the head nurse at a veterans hospital in Tacoma, Washington, and died at age eighty-eight in 1962. The war was the defining moment of her life, and her arrival back home remained one of her greatest memories. She joyfully marked the moment in her diary:

"Finie la guerre pour moi!"

Over the next two decades, **Irvin Cobb** continued writing books, short fiction, and magazine articles. He also became a successful Hollywood actor, appearing in movies with Will Rogers, Bing Crosby, and W. C. Fields. He died in 1944 at age sixty-eight.

A few months after returning from France, Cobb spoke at the Circle for Negro War Relief benefit at Carnegie Hall in New York. Considering that lynchings were still commonplace, his views toward African Americans were far ahead of the existing social norms, especially coming from an avowed southerner who'd often caricatured blacks. "The color of a man's skin hasn't anything to do with the color of his soul," he told his audience. "The value of your race has been proven over there and your value here at home is unquestioned."

The hill that **Freddie Stowers** and his men climbed in the face of machine gun fire on September 28, 1918, is now a pasture near the village of Ardeuil in the Champagne region of France. The outlines of the German trenches are faintly visible, and shell fragments still litter the ground. The survivors of the 371st Regiment paid to erect a stone obelisk in honor of their dead comrades on the crest of Côte 188. On the left side of the monument, nineteen spaces down, is the name CORP. FREDDIE STOWERS. The lettering is in gold paint, the sign of a Medal of Honor recipient.

Stowers was recommended during the war for the nation's highest award for valor, but for unknown reasons the paperwork was never processed. Seventy-three years passed before he received the medal. In a ceremony at the White House on April 24, 1991, President George H. W. Bush presented the award to Stowers's two surviving sisters.

Bush recounted how the young soldier took charge in the midst of "bloody chaos" and continued to urge his men forward even after he was mortally wounded. "On that September day," the president said, "Corporal Stowers was alone, far from family and home. He had to be scared; his friends died at his side. But he vanquished his fear and fought not for glory but for a cause larger than himself: the cause of liberty."

Captain Henry Bryan, the *Leviathan*'s skipper for seven of her nine wartime round-trip voyages through the submarine zone, received the Navy Cross and retired as a rear admiral, as did the ship's two other wartime captains. Bryan was named the governor of American Samoa, and for once in his long career was able to take his wife with him for two sun-drenched years in the South Pacific. He died in 1944.

After serving seven tumultuous years as assistant secretary of the navy, **Franklin D. Roosevelt** resigned in August 1920 to enter politics. Crippled from the waist down by polio, Roosevelt fought back against a cruel disease and was elected governor of New York, then president of the United States. He died in April 1945 during his fourth term in office. FDR never lost his love of big oceans and big ships.

Damon Runyon returned from Europe aboard the *Leviathan*. Many of his short stories were made into movies, including probably the most enduring of his works, the musical comedy *Guys and Dolls*. He died of throat cancer in 1946. **Captain Eddie Rickenbacker**— the World War I fighter ace—released his friend's ashes from the window of a DC-3 as it flew over Broadway's Great White Way. Like Runyon, **Humphrey Bogart** died of throat cancer. A Hollywood legend, the former seaman second class drew on his navy experiences for two of his most memorable roles—as rough-cut Charlie Allnut in *The African Queen*, for which he won an Academy Award for best actor, and as the unstable Captain Queeg in *The Cain Mutiny*. He died in 1957.

THE *LEVIATHAN'S* THIRD and final act started in July 1923, when the ship set sail for Cherbourg as America's largest and fastest luxury liner, a breathtaking transformation from her long months as a troopship. "An army of two thousand workers" completed the $10 million overhaul at a Newport News shipbuilding company. The prize of the new American-owned passenger fleet, her tall stacks painted red, white, and blue, the *Leviathan* was just in time to catch a wave. The Roaring Twenties were taking off, and the Charleston and hot jazz blended with the staccato of high heels as women in gowns and men wearing tuxedos again swept across the ship's spacious dance floors.

Despite her opulence and speed, problems soon surfaced. During Prohibition, the government-owned ship was bone dry, while booze flowed freely on English and French liners. The first trip set the tone for what followed, and over the next decade, few crossings made money.

The inevitable end finally came in September 1938, when the *Leviathan* was sold for $800,000 to an English company to be cut up for scrap iron at a shipyard in Rosyth, Scotland. An entire generation of veterans remembered how the ship survived a killer flu pandemic, dodged German U-boats, and helped change the outcome of a war the Allies risked losing. On January 26, 1938, a single tugboat helped the former troopship down the Hudson as a cold rain fell and ice floes swept along in the fast-moving current. A dirge of wailing horns, bells, and whistles followed her down the river to the Battery, Ellis Island, and the Statue of Liberty, and out to the open sea. A newspaper headline that morning tolled out the final leave-taking of an iconic ship: "*Leviathan* Sails Away Forever."

ACKNOWLEDGMENTS

I STUMBLED ACROSS the history of the USS *Leviathan* compiled by her crew in 1919 and was struck by the names of some of her passengers. The first one that jumped out was Damon Runyon, and then I spotted Ty Cobb, Douglas MacArthur, John Pershing, and FDR—and so the journey began.

I was helped at the outset by Chris Killillay, an archivist with the National Archives and Records Administration in Washington, DC, who determined that the collections were rich in material related to the ship's wartime cruises.

Dieter Stenger, a professional researcher, mined those resources, spending days photocopying the *Leviathan*'s logs and war diaries. Fluent in German, he also translated the logs of the U-90. I couldn't have written this book without his patience and skill.

Ken Stewart of the South Dakota State Historical Society assembled records on Royal Johnson, as did Carol Jennings, a researcher based in Pierre. Chip Johnson of Orlando, Florida, helped broaden the portrait of his grandfather, the former congressman-soldier.

Alexandra McCallen of the Naval History and Heritage Command located material on the ship's wartime captains. Helen Kimball of Dalton, Pennsylvania, graciously tracked down the invaluable history that her uncle Charles Bryan had written about his father, Captain Bryan, and the *Leviathan*.

My thanks to Indiana University Press for allowing me to quote from the fine biography on Pershing by the late Donald Smythe:

Pershing: General of the Armies. And thanks to Judy Stowers Siddoway, who shared her research on the Freddie Stowers family history.

Laurene DiCillo, an archivist at John Carroll University where Smythe taught, steered me to Saint Louis. Smythe was a Jesuit, and the John Pershing–Micheline Resco letters that he acquired are located there in the Jesuit Archives, Central United States. David R. Miros, PhD, the archivist, and Cass Coughlin, an administrative assistant, helped me work my way through the Pershing-Resco material.

Marc E. Kollbaum gathered personnel records at the NARA facility in Saint Louis—and a special thanks to him for tracking the information on a sailor named Bogart.

Taylor Beattie, a former Special Forces officer, graciously invited me to his home in Norfolk, Virginia, where he shared his research on Freddie Stowers. I owe him the deepest gratitude.

The same goes for the military historian Dwight R. Messimer, whose excellent book *Escape* is rich in details about U-90. I can't thank him enough for sharing his insights.

Likewise, a special thanks to Noelle Braynard for her advice and encouragement, and for allowing me to quote from her late father's book. Frank O. Braynard's six-volume epic, *Leviathan: The World's Greatest Ship*, is the final word on the subject. No ship ever had a more dedicated biographer.

Christy Gutowski, an investigative reporter I was fortunate to work with at the *Chicago Tribune*, helped fill in the blanks in the life of Elizabeth Weaver.

I also want to thank members of the Freddie Stowers family who took the time to talk to me during the emotional unveiling of the corporal's statue in Anderson, South Carolina—at precisely the eleventh hour of the eleventh day of the eleventh month in 2015.

This book wouldn't have been written without the help and encouragement of Larry Weissman and Sascha Alper, two exceptional agents, who sharpened the early drafts with spot-on suggestions. And somehow I had the good fortune to work with Luke Dempsey, my editor at HarperCollins.

Lastly, a special thanks to my wife, Janice, for her excellent advice—and to the other two loves of my life: my daughters, Margaret Tucker, a doctoral candidate in English literature at Washington University, and Clair Dimmig, an officer in the US Navy.

NOTES

CHAPTER I

2 First-class passengers: Frank O. Braynard, *World's Greatest Ship: The Story of the "Leviathan,"* vol. 1 (New York: South Street Seaport Museum, 1972), 78.

3 "Pork Chops in Jelly": Ibid., 83.

4 a black marble statue: Ibid., 68.

4 Deck space was reserved: Ibid., 10.

5 Under bleak skies: Barbara W. Tuchman, *The Guns of August* (New York: Bantam Books, 1976), 115.

6 A headline in the: Ibid., 87.

7 Tickets had been sold: *History of the U.S.S. Leviathan, Cruiser and Transport Forces, United States Atlantic Fleet,* complied by ship's log and the history committee (Brooklyn, NY: Brooklyn Eagle Job Department, 1919), 16.

8 The kaiser immediately instructed: Tuchman, *Guns of August,* 93.

8 Hoboken police officers: *History of U.S.S. Leviathan,* 16.

8 Besides the *Vaterland:* Ibid.

9 "in visible distress": Tuchman, *Guns of August,* 145.

9 crew members from the interned ships: *History of the U.S.S. Leviathan,* 16.

9 "The lamps are going out": Sir Edward Grey, *Twenty-Five Years,* vol. 2, (New York: Frederick A. Stokes Company, 1925), 20.

10 "her terribly expensive rest": Braynard, *World's Greatest Ship,* 98.

11 "Boom! Boom!": Irvin S. Cobb, *Exit Laughing* (New York: Bobbs-Merrill, 1941), 519.

11 The line of refugees: Irvin S. Cobb, *Paths of Glory: Impressions of War Written at and Near the Front* (New York: George H. Doran, 1915), 14.

11 "Seems like this here war": Anita Lawson, *Irvin S. Cobb* (Bowling Green, OH: Bowling Green State University Popular Press, 1984), 113.

12 a passport, a stack of: Ibid., 113–15

12 "The Germans are coming!": Cobb, *Paths of Glory*, 14.

12 "You Americans, you come from": Ibid., 17.

12 "a tall, lean, blond": Ibid.

13 At the same time: Tuchman, *Guns of August*, 43.

14 "The sun," he wrote: Cobb, *Paths of Glory*, 169.

14 "They came and came": Ibid., 19.

14 "in Brussels and its suburbs": Lawson, *Irvin S. Cobb*, 116.

14 the face of one: Cobb, *Paths of Glory*, 7.

15 A young lieutenant took Cobb: Ibid., 29.

15 "The enemy lost many men": Ibid., 30.

15 "Who are you?": Lawson, *Irvin S. Cobb*, 119.

15 "If one of those journalists": Ibid., 120.

16 "a business proposition": Elisabeth Cobb, *My Wayward Parent: Irvin S. Cobb* (New York: The Bobbs-Merrill Company, 1945), 139.

16 "a gorgeous military figure": Ibid.

16 "a row of tiny scarlet dots": Cobb, *Paths of Glory*, 100.

17 "those ants were not": Ibid.

17 "looked like a bed": Ibid., 102.

17 "Remember to keep your mouth": Ibid., 117.

18 "they can stand": Ibid., 120.

18 "I aided at setting": Cobb, *Exit Laughing*, 304.

19 "Please buy some pictures,": Cobb, *Paths of Glory*, 169–70.

19 "Within the first three": John Keegan, *The First World War* (New York: Vintage Books, 1998), 82.

CHAPTER 2

21 "It was raining": Braynard, *World's Greatest Ship*, 108.

22 "I protest": Ibid., 113.

23 they were given a choice: *History of U.S.S. Leviathan*, 16.

23 Similar scenes: Josephus Daniels, *Our Navy At War* (New York: George H. Doran, 1922), 92.

23 "You will never run": Braynard, *World's Greatest Ship*, 115.

24 "Ten thousand": Albert Gleaves, *A History of the Transport Service: Adventures and Experiences of United States Transports and Cruisers in the World War* (New York: George H. Doran, 1921), 189.

24 "engine room, fire room": *History of U.S.S. Leviathan*, 19.

24 "to remove and probably destroy": Ibid.

25 William Randolph Hearst: Braynard, *World's Greatest Ship*, 106.

25 "which were carried off": *History of U.S.S. Leviathan*, 16.

26 Johnson, a Republican serving: The sources for Johnson's boyhood, education, marriage, and congressional career are mainly derived from news clippings and Royal C. Johnson's biographical file from the South Dakota Historical Society State Archives.

27 "I have called the Congress": Kenneth S. Davis, *FDR: The Beckoning of Destiny* (New York: Capricorn Books, 1975), 455.

27 Other ships soon followed: Daniels, *Our Navy at War*, 30.

27 Wilson had polled: Geoffrey C. Ward, *A First-Class Temperament: The Emergence of Franklin Roosevelt, 1905–1928* (New York: Vintage Books, 2014 [1989]), 341.

27 "a warfare against mankind": Davis, *FDR*, 455.

28 "we cannot make": Ibid.

28 "made safe for democracy": Woodrow Wilson, War Messages, 65th Cong., World War I Document Archive.

28 "no quarrel": Ibid.

28 "God helping her": Ibid.

28 "arms ostentatiously folded high": Davis, *FDR*, 456.

32 The war resolution was rushed: Thomas Fleming, *The Illusion of Victory: America in World War I* (New York: Basic Books, 2003), 42.

CHAPTER 3

33 Their mission: check for bombs: *History of U.S.S. Leviathan*, 19.

33 "attempts to smuggle small bombs": Ibid., 20.

34 Cigar-shaped bombs: Howard Blum, *Dark Invasion, 1915: Germany's Secret War and the Hunt for the First Terrorist Cell in America* (New York: HarperCollins, 2014), 176.

34 During the last six months: Jules Witcover, *Sabotage at Black Tom: Imperial Germany's Secret War in America, 1914–1917* (Chapel Hill, NC: Algonquin Books, 1989), 134.

35 "the engines of all": Daniels, *Our Navy at War*, 20.

35 "Cylinders had been broken": Ibid., 91–92.

36 "numerous floods were caused": *History of U.S.S. Leviathan*, 14.

36 "The big ship was never": Ibid., 18.

36 "Bathtubs were broken": Braynard, *World's Greatest Ship*, 119.

37 Space also was found: *History of U.S.S. Leviathan*, 78.

38 "That's easy": Braynard, *World's Greatest Ship*, 125.

39 "D.E. McCarthy": Donald Smythe, *Pershing: General of the Armies* (Bloomington: Indiana University Press, 2007), 13.

39 "artillery salute fired": John J. Pershing, *My Experiences in the World War*, vol. 1 (New York: Frederick A. Stokes, 1931), 42.

40 When America declared war: Smythe, *Pershing*, 8.

40 "Hardly an hour passed": Ibid., 14.

41 "severely condemned the German": Pershing, *My Experiences in the World War*, 1: 47.

41 "The Kaiser, God damn him": Smythe, *Pershing*, 17.

41 "expressed a desire": Pershing, *My Experiences in the World War*, 1: 54–55.

42 "did not seem to be": Ibid., 54.

42 "I am sure": Ibid., 57.

43 "Danced every dance but one": National Park Service Publication, Presideo of San Francisco.

43 "cool as a bowl": Smythe, *Pershing*, 2.

43 'All the promotion in': Ibid.

44 "Each of you must": Ibid., 4.

44 "if I can be of help": Jimmy Breslin, *A Life: Damon Runyon* (New York: Ticknor & Fields, 1991), 170.

44 "Women climbed into": Pershing, *My Experiences in the World War*, 1: 59.

45 "I hope," he said: Ibid., 60.

45 "twenty-four to forty-eight hours": Smythe, *Pershing*, 21.

45 "We have had enough": Ibid., 22.

45 "I shall wait for": William Manchester, *American Caesar: Douglas MacArthur, 1880–1964* (Boston: Back Bay Books, 2008), 83.

46 "of whom twenty-one thousand [were]": John Keegan, *The Face of Battle* (New York: Vintage Books, 1977), 255.

46 "long docile lines": Ibid., 255–56.

47 "quite simply, the worst thing": Manchester, *American Caesar*, 81.

47 "It looks as though": Daniels, *Our Navy at War*, 42

48 "attractive but not beautiful": Smythe, *Pershing*, 296.

49 "Later they were to tell": Henry Wales, "The True Story of Famous General's Romance with a Charming Young Portrait Painter," *Chicago Tribune*, 30 November 1952.

CHAPTER 4

51 "this vessel is in all respects": *History of U.S.S. Leviathan*, 22.

51 "All reverse slow": Ibid.

52 "When will the *Vaterland*": Braynard, *World's Greatest Ship*, 125.

53 Oman was from rural: Biographical material based on personnel files at the National Archives and Records Administration (NARA), Record of Officers of the US Navy, Saint Louis.

53 "more like a Methodist": Braynard, *World's Greatest Ship*, 137.

56 "The machine shop was invaded": *History of U.S.S. Leviathan*, 23.

57 "In a short time": Ibid.

59 "grab the children": Hazel Rowley, *Franklin & Eleanor* (Carlton, Australia: Melbourne University Press, 2011), 77.

60 "would end in the murdering": Braynard, *World's Greatest Ship*, 132.

CHAPTER 5

63 Captain Oman watched: *Leviathan Log Book*, 15 December 1917. Most of the descriptions of the *Leviathan*'s wartime sailings come from the ship's log book and war diaries contained in the US National Archives and Records Administration (NARA): Records of the Bureau of Naval Personnel, Record Group (RG) 24; Navy Records Collection, Record Group 45; General Records of the Department of Navy, Record Group 80; and Records of the Office of the Judge Advocate, Record Group 125.

63 "prehistoric gorge": Robert Wilson and Benedict Crowell, *The Road to France: The Transportation of Troops and Military Supplies, 1917–1918*, vol. 2 (New Haven, CT: Yale University Press, 1921), 345.

65 As recently as December 6: Daniels, *Our Navy at War*, 64.

66 Every man on deck: *History of U.S.S. Leviathan*, 25.

67 "Down below it seemed": E. Keble Chatterton, *Danger Zone: The Story of the Queenstown Command* (Boston: Little, Brown, 1934), 313.

68 "We Wish You a Merry Christmas": *History of U.S.S. Leviathan*, 26.

70 "It took our bluejackets": Ibid., 27.

70 "was helplessly drunk": Log Book, Jan. 5, NARA, RG45.

71 Working around the clock: *History of U.S.S. Leviathan*, 28.

72 The destroyers shepherding: Ibid.

73 "front-line trenches": Chester D. Heywood, *Negro Combat Troops in the World War: The Story of the 371st Infantry* (New York: Negro Universities Press, 1929), 19.

74 "The first intimation we": Ibid., 3.

75 "the laughing stock": Ibid., 10.

76 "Why We Are at War,": Charles F. Horne, *The Great Events of the Great War,* vol. 5 (The National Alumni, 1920), 123.

77 "Everyone simply 'knocked'": Heywood, *Negro Combat Troops*, 13.

CHAPTER 6

79 "something was very wrong": Admiral William Sims, NARA, RG125.

79 "While he may be": Ibid.

80 "Sims," he wrote: Oman to secretary of navy, 20 March 1918, NARA, RG125.

80 "present at the bombardment": Fitness report, September–December 1899, NARA, RG125.

81 "daily expectation of meeting": Ibid.

81 "a great reader": Ibid.

81 "He would show me around": Charles Bryan, letter to niece, Helen Kimball, 21 May 1975.

81 "rough bedsprings fastened": Braynard, *World's Greatest Ship*, 146.

82 "sustained in upright posture": Cobb, *Exit Laughing*, 535.

83 "what looked like a woman's": Irvin S. Cobb, *The Glory of the Coming* (New York: George H. Doran, 1918), 28.

84 "one of those phony": Cobb, *Exit Laughing*, 306.

84 "a feeling of security": Cobb, *Glory of the Coming*, 28.

85 "What the devil": Cobb, *Exit Laughing*, 536.

85 After night fell: Ibid., 537.

86 "it [would] only add": Cobb, *Glory of the Coming*, 31.

87 "Where Do We": Ibid., 34.

CHAPTER 7

90 The captain had been directed: War Diary, 2 March 1918, NARA, RG45.

90 "latest enemy information": Ibid.

90 "at best speed": Ibid.

91 Each passenger was also: *History of U.S.S. Leviathan*, 29.

92 The bulletins notified: War Diary, 21 March 1918, NARA, RG45.

92 "very thick, the visibility": War Diary, 15 March 1918, NARA, RG45.

92 "from stem to stern.": *History of U.S.S. Leviathan*, 29.

92 "We've hit a mine!": Ibid.

93 "destruction of two U-boats": "Two U-boats Sunk in Raid on Leviathan," *Chicago Tribune*, 7 June 1918.

93 "Undesirable press reports.": War Diary, 16 July 1918, NARA, RG45.

94 "the heaviest German bombardment": Smythe, *Pershing*, 96.

94 British losses numbered: Ibid.

95 The Pennsylvania unit: University Archives and Record Center, the University of Pennsylvania.

95 A member of a well-known: Information on Elizabeth Weaver primarily comes from public records and from the meticulous diary she kept during the war and which is on file at the US Army Heritage and Education Center.

96 Cortland Scott Weaver: *New Holland Clarion*, 16 May 1891.

97 "We flocked to the windows": Emma Elizabeth Weaver, *U.S. Army Nurse Journal* (Carlisle, PN: Army Heritage Center Foundation, 2006), 5.

97 "clear and beautiful": Ibid., 7.

99 "boomeranged" back over the deck: "Nurses Killed by Boomerang of Shell Part," *Chicago Daily Tribune*, 22 May 1917.

99 "for any length of time": Weaver, *U.S. Army Nurse Journal*, 7.

CHAPTER 8

102 "dead water": War Diary, 15 March 1918, NARA, RG45.

102 advanced eighty miles: Keegan, *First World War*, 349.

104 "Mothers are no longer": Bryan, letter to son Charles, 7 May 1918, Navy History and Heritage Command.

107 "most pathetic": Pershing, *My Experiences in the World War*, 1: 359.

108 "I come to tell you": Ibid., 364–65 (translated from the French by the author).

108 "scrambled forward": Douglas MacArthur, *Reminiscences: General of the Army* (New York: McGraw-Hill, 1964), 55–56.

109 "No," she said: Pershing, *My Experiences in the World War*, 1: 339.

110 "garishly furnished in the style": Smythe, *Pershing*, 45.

110 "There was a great": Pershing, *My Experiences in the World War*, 1: 391.

111 "There is no": Smythe, *Pershing*, 106.

112 "sat in front of": Ibid., 297.

112 "quips and ribald jokes": MacArthur, *Reminiscences*, 59.

CHAPTER 9

114 "for the lost souls": *History of U.S.S. Leviathan*, , 31.

114 "Kamerad!": Daniels, *Our Navy at War*, 59.

115 "Iceberg!": *History of the U.S.S. Leviathan*, 31.

116 "I must always think": Braynard, *World's Greatest Ship*, 152.

116 "I propose to get the men": Smythe, *Pershing*, 90.

116 At 9:30 a.m., seaman: Ship's Log, Records of Bureau of Navy Personnel, 18 April 1918, NARA, RG24.

119 "This incident restrained": Monroe Mason, *The American Negro Soldier with the Red Hand of France* (Boston: Cornhill, 1920), 42.

119 "A feeling of disdain": Ibid., 44.

120 "had been turned over": Heywood, *Negro Combat Troops*, 32.

120 "Unfortunately, they soon": Pershing, *My Experiences in the World War*, I: 291.

122 "The practical lessons": Richard Slotkin, *Lost Battalions: The Great War and the Crisis of American Nationality* (New York: Henry Holt, 2005), 131.

123 "The first time the French": Haywood, *Negro Combat Troops*, 35.

123 "The colored men were given": Emmett J. Scott, *Scott's Official History of the American Negro in the World War* (Chicago: Homewood Press, 1919), 238.

124 antiaircraft fire burst: Heywood, *Negro Combat Troops*, 40.

CHAPTER 10

126 sometimes hit 73 degrees: *History of U.S.S. Leviathan*, 31.

126 "We don't know where": Ibid., 32.

127 "Black and white buoy": Ibid.

127 table number five: Weaver, *U.S. Army Nurse Journal*, 13.

128 "very fine looking man": Ibid., 15.

128 "The jackets," Elizabeth wrote: Ibid., 17.

129 "sun [was] on one side": Ibid., 12.

129 "a good omen": Ibid., 18.

129 "Vive la France!": Ibid., 19.

130 "sailor boys": Ibid., 15.

130 "I wonder where": Ibid., 21.

132 "I'm going to be": "Royal C. Johnson Ex-Congressman," *New York Times*, 2 August 1939.

133 The regiment's commander: Descriptions of the regiment and its commanding officer are drawn from Henry C. Thorn Jr., *History of 313th US Infantry, Baltimore's Own* (New York: Wynkoop Hallenbeck Crawford, 1920).

134 "Tell your Americans": Tim McNeese, *World War I and the Roaring Twenties* (New York: Chelsea House, 2010), 49.

135 "Royal," he said, smiling: "A Genuine Red-Blooded American," unidentified newspaper, 12 December 1921, South Dakota Historical Society State Archives.

135 "few paid attention": Alfred W. Crosby, *America's Forgotten Pandemic: The Influenza of 1918* (New York: Cambridge University Press, 2003), 18.

CHAPTER 11

137 1,066 employees were sent: *Influenza: Annual Report of the Secretary of Navy* (Washington, DC: Navy Department Library, 1919), 2424.

138 "the flu epidemic": Crosby, *America's Forgotten Pandemic*, 19.

138 "a suspicious outbreak": *Influenza: Annual Report*, 2423.

139 "so abnormal that pieces": Crosby, *America's Forgotten Pandemic*, 8.

139 Germans called it *"Blitzkatarrh"*: Ibid., 26.

140 "For most [victims]": Ibid.

140 "At that time": *Influenza: Annual Report*, 2414.

140 A second sailor died: Ship's Log, 15 May 1918, NARA, RG24.

141 Surprised that he'd been: Gleaves, *History of the Transport Service*, 162.

142 "in all probability": Ibid., 161.

143 "turn in and out": Gleaves, *History of the Transport Service*, 88.

143 From July until the Armistice: Ibid., 90.

143 One-third ahead: Ship's Log, 22 May 1918, NARA, RG24.

144 a German submarine: Gleaves, *A History of the Transport Service*, 111.

144 "Get too close to one": Dwight R. Messimer, *Escape* (Annapolis, MD: Naval Institute Press, 1994), 1.

144 major technological surprises: Description of U-boat characteristics drawn from John Terraines, *The U-Boat Wars, 1916–1945* (New York: G. P. Putnam's Sons, 1989), chapter 2.

145 His crew consisted: Messimer, *Escape*, 10.

145 the ace of aces: Terraine, *The U-Boat Wars*, 19.

CHAPTER 12

147 At one point it: Messimer, *Escape*, 2.

147 Somehow he'd turned: *History of U.S.S. Leviathan*, 33.

148 Bryan ordered a change in course: Ibid., 34.

148 "Recommend sending after dark": Report of Signals Changed, 31 May 1918, General Records of the Department of Navy, NARA, RG80.

149 "Unable to catch": Messimer, *Escape*, 3.

149 "Moonlight held no charms": *History of U.S.S. Leviathan*, 34.

150 "I saw the break": Submarine attack on Leviathan, 30 May 1918, General Records of the Department of Navy, NARA, RG80.

150 Their crews fired three: *History of U.S.S. Leviathan*, 34.

151 Taking positions along: Ibid., 35.

152 "The exact number": Ibid.

152 "Spies Put U-Boats": Braynard, *World's Greatest Ship*, 160.

153 "outside of the zone": John G. Pershing, *My Experiences in the World War*, 2: 90.

154 smashing into four French: Ibid., 61.

154 "everything was quiet": Ibid., 62.

154 hysterical officer: Smythe, *Pershing*, 128.

155 compared with the fifty killed: Ibid.

156 "It would be difficult": Pershing, *My Experiences in the World War*, 2: 65.

156 "You are to die east": Smythe, *Pershing*, 132.

156 "a beaten, routed Army": Ibid., 137.

157 "We will dig no": Ibid., 138.

157 "effectively stopped the German": Pershing, *My Experiences in the World War*, 2: 64.

157 "The battle, the battle": Ibid., 71.

158 "Refer it to the": Smythe, *Pershing*, 135.

158 "The whole discussion": Pershing, *My Experiences in the World War*, 2: 76.

158 "to build up the armies": Ibid., 83.

158 "very grave . . . one of depression": Ibid., 82.

159 "a temporary and exceptional": Ibid., 79.

159 "fleeing from their homes": Ibid., 85.

159 "Men with a hand": Smythe, *Pershing*, 139.

160 "Come on, you sons-o-bitches": Ibid., 138.

160 "The individual soldiers": Ibid., 140.

160 "I have time for": Pershing to Resco, 6 June 1918, Donald Smythe–Micheline Resco collection, Jesuit Archives, Saint Louis, MO.

160 "I recall it as yesterday": Pershing to Resco, 13 June 1918, Donald Smythe–Micheline Resco collection, Jesuit Archives, Saint Louis, MO.

CHAPTER 13

161 One day earlier: Daniels, *Our Navy at War*, 78.

162 "Eleven medium depth charges": Remy's log, 1 June 1918, Records of U-boats and T-boats, 1914–1918, NARA.

162 When Remy ordered: Messimer, *Escape*, 49.

163 "Submarine on starboard quarter!": Submarine attack on *Leviathan*, 1 June 1918, General Records of the Department of Navy, NARA, RG80.

163 "Range 3,000, numbers five": Ibid.

164 "We saw periscope": *History of U.S.S. Leviathan*, 36.

164 "Remember most gracious Virgin": Ibid., 37.

165 "The drill went off": Braynard, *World's Greatest Ship*, 171.

165 "There was alarm": Daniels, *Our Navy at War*, 189.

165 On June 2, the U-boat: Ibid., 190.

166 "He was a ballsy bastard": Dwight Messimer, e-mail communication with author, 18 July 2015.

167 "I heard her falling": Cobb, *Glory of the Coming*, 224.

167 During six months: Pershing, *My Experiences in the World War*, 1: 352.

168 "I saw them caught": Cobb, *Glory of the Coming*, 124–25.

169 "I wonder," he asked: Fred G. Neuman, *Irvin S. Cobb: His Life and Achievements* (Paducah, KY: Young Publishing, 1934), 182.

169 "Almost without exception": Cobb, *Glory of the Coming*, 287.

170 "Kernul, suh, we don't": Ibid., 290.

170 "I'd take a chance": Ibid.

170 "At the call of": Cobb, *Glory of the Coming*, 291.

171 "were familiar with Cobb's": Slotkin, *Lost Battalions*, 146.

171 "They were apt": Cobb, *Glory of the Coming*, 294.

172 "Mammy's Chocolate Soldier": Slotkin, *Lost Battalions*, 151.

172 "a Southerner with all": Cobb, *Glory of the Coming*, 295.

172 "As a result": Ibid., 295.

173 "One torpedo passed": Cobb, *Exit Laughing*, 540.

173 "a straight white line": 4 June 1918, General Records of the Department of Navy, NARA, RG80.

173 "Hello," he said: Elisabeth Cobb, *My Wayward Parent*, 174.

CHAPTER 14

175 handed him a sandwich: Thorn, *History of 313th U.S. Infantry*, 18.

177 The ship's stern batteries: Ship's Log, 25 June 1918, NARA, RG24.

177 They were nearing an expansive field: *History of U.S.S. Leviathan*, 38.

178 a "rest camp": Thorn, *History of 313th U.S. Infantry*, 19.

178 A luckier group: Ibid., 20.

179 sustained an incredible 66 percent turnover: Paul B. Mitchell III, MA thesis (US Army Command and General Staff College, Fort Leavenworth, Kansas, 2011), 70.

180 heading straight at them: Gleaves, *History of the Transport Service*, 125.

181 The *Covington* sank: Ibid., 127.

181 During a trench fight: *History of U.S.S. Leviathan*, 39.

182 "stump speech": Ibid.

183 German air raids: Weaver, *U.S. Army Nurse Journal*, 32.

183 Working twelve-hour shifts: Ibid., 36.

184 One of the patients: Ibid.

184 "Very often," she remembered: Ibid., 37.

CHAPTER 15

188 "Man overboard!": *History U.S.S. Leviathan*, 39.

188 an apparent suicide: Ibid.

188 The man had disappeared: Braynard, *World's Greatest Ship*, 182.

189 "large destroyers": U.S.S. *Leviathan* Operation, 10 June 1918, NARA, RG80.

190 "The American Troop Transport": Report *Leviathan* Sunk, War Diaries, NARA, RG45.

190 "must have the greatest": Ibid.

191 "our opponents have suffered": Ibid.

191 "laboring under the impression": Censorship of photographs, 29 July 1918, General Records of Department of Navy, RG80.

191 They were one day: *History of U.S.S. Leviathan*, 39.

191 Edgar Rubin died: Ship's Log, August 8, 1918, NARA, RG24.

192 Assistant Secretary of the Navy Roosevelt: Pershing, *My Experiences in the World War*, I: 229.

192 "with his party": Smythe, *Pershing*, 169.

192 "khaki riding trousers": Ward, *First-Class Temperament*, 386.

192 "rusty bayonets, broken guns": Davis, *FDR*, 523.

193 "danger and glory": Ibid.

193 "toward the German": Ibid.

193 "Within a five-minute": Ibid., 519.

193 "for a good deal": Ward, *First-Class Temperament*, 393.

193 "a lively tour": Ibid., 398.

194 "As he told me": Davis, *FDR*, 522.

194 "like undergraduates": Ward, *First-Class Temperament*, 407.

194 "a line of French": Ibid., 405.

195 "Somehow I don't believe": Ibid.

195 "For weeks on end": Davis, *FDR*, 529.

CHAPTER 16

197 The ship's ensign: Braynard, *World's Greatest Ship*, 187.

197 reminding him to notify: Message, 16 September 1918, General Records of Department of Navy, NARA, RG80.

198 The men who died: Gleaves, *History of the Transport Service*, 143.

199 "collision mat": Ibid., 147.

199 "Within the iron walls": Davis, *FDR*, 529.

200 "Roosevelt, in mid-Atlantic": Ibid.

200 Eleanor discovered a stack: *Chicago Tribune*, 17 October 1971; *New York Times*, 20 April 2008.

201 "Capt. H. F. Bryan": Ship's Log, 21 September 1918, NARA, RG24.

201 watching the flashes: Thorn, *History of 313th U.S. Infantry*, 23.

202 "The sky over": Pershing, *My Experiences in the World War*, 2: 267.

203 two black-and-white: Thorn, *History of 313th U.S. Infantry*, 23.

204 "American success": Smythe, *Pershing*, 186.

206 "The crown prince's": William Walker, *Betrayal at Little Gibraltar* (New York: Scribner, 2016), 28–29.

208 "A man," he said: Heywood, *Negro Combat Troops in the World War*, 85.

209 "The exterior marks": Ibid., 86.

209 They sought protection: Ibid., 108.

210 "to all concerned": Ibid., 75.

211 "accidental woundings": Ibid., 91.

211 Graves mentions a soldier: Robert Graves, *Good-Bye to All That* (New York: Doubleday, 1957), 110.

212 "Men who are accidentally": Heywood, *Negro Combat Troops in the World War*, 92.

213 "The flashes from the": Ibid., 160.

213 "It was wondrous": Ibid.

CHAPTER 17

215 ON NE PASSE PAS: Pershing, *My Experiences in the World War*, 2: 287.

216 "Worse by far was": Keegan, *First World War*, 285.

216 The grand offensive: Manchester, *American Caesar*, 103.

216 "Everyone attack as soon": Ibid.

217 "a wild Hans Christian": Ibid., 104.

218 "Incredibly": Smythe, *Pershing*, 192.

218 "aggressive spirit of our troops": Pershing, *My Experiences in the World War*, 2: 293.

219 "The amount of confusion": Smythe, *Pershing*, 192.

219 "They were all alert": Pershing, *My Experiences in the World War*, 2: 294.

219 "the most gorgeous thing": "War Flier Recalls Battle's Splendor," *New York Times*, 24 March 1931.

220 He also ordered that: Gleaves, *History of the Transport Service*, 190.

220 On the same day: Crosby, *America's Forgotten Pandemic*, 122.

221 "which under present conditions": Ibid., 123.

221 Lord Nelson: War Diaries, undated news article, Navy Records Collection, NARA, RG45.

221 "The blanked old captain": Ibid.

221 "through inattention and negligence": Court of Inquiry, 5 July 1917, General Records Department of the Navy, NARA, RG80.

222 The sailors soon discovered: Ibid.

CHAPTER 18

223 "To the men waiting": Thorn, *History of 313th U.S. Infantry*, 27.

225 "a withering fire": Ibid., 29.

225 An enemy map found: Mitchell, MA thesis, 79.

225 "A temporary halt": Thorn, *History of 313th U.S. Infantry*, 30.

226 "When cut off": Smythe, *Pershing*, 197.

226 "Suddenly, a black rattling": Mitchell, MA thesis, 87.

227 shot in the head: Thorn, *History of 313th U.S. Infantry*, 31.

227 Their French commander: Mitchell, MA thesis, 88.

229 The fragment tore off: News clip, 29 December 1921, South Dakota Historical Society State Archives.

229 "I'd give one hundred": Undated clip from American Legion News Service, South Dakota Historical Society State Archives.

230 "into extremely heavy": Thorn, *History of 313th U.S. Infantry*, 32.

230 "arriving with its left wing" Mitchell, MA thesis, 99.

231 Earlier that night: Crosby, *America's Forgotten Pandemic*, 126.

232 the arrival of nearly two hundred: *History of U.S.S. Leviathan*, 73.

CHAPTER 19

233 As the ambulances crawled: Monroe, *American Negro Soldier*, 119.

234 Stowers and the 371st: Heywood, *Negro Combat Troops*, 161.

235 "How to Stop": Mason, *American Negro Soldier*, 116.

236 "When it was directly overhead": Heywood, *Negro Combat Troops*, 173.

236 "Groans of agony": Mason, *American Negro Soldier*, 116.

237 "They had been left": Heywood, *Negro Combat Troops*, 163.

237 As the daylight improved: Ibid., 164.

238 "Kamerad!" they cried: Ibid.

239 Stowers shouted out: Paraphrase drawn from the description of the

battle offered in Taylor V. Beattie, "Seventy-Three Years after His Bayonet Assault on Hill 188, Freddie Stowers Got His Medal of Honor," *Military History,* August 2004, 76.

239 The corporal led: Ibid. Description of the battle also drawn from "Remarks (by President George Bush) at a Ceremony for the Posthumous Presentation of the Medal of Honor to Corporal Freddie Stowers, 24 April 1991." Citation posted on Congressional Medal of Honor Society online site, www.cmohs.org.

239 Members of the 371st: Scott, *Scott's Official History,* 236.

239 "The final phase": Heywood, *Negro Combat Troops,* 168.

240 In another two days: Ibid., 170.

240 Over two hundred soldiers and nurses: *History of U.S.S. Leviathan,* 43.

241 The captain decided: War Diary, 29 September 1918, Navy Records Collection, NARA, RG45.

241 a serious infraction: Ship's Log, 29 September 1918, NARA, RG24.

241 littered the passageways: War Diaries, Epidemic of Influenza, Oct. 11, 1918, Navy Records Collection, RG45.

242 His voice hoarse: *History of U.S.S. Leviathan,* 43

242 The soldiers, crammed in: Ibid.

242 "extremely poor specimens": Ibid.

242 An isolation ward: *History of U.S.S. Leviathan,* 75.

242 "The conditions . . . cannot": War Diaries, Epidemic of Influenza, 11 October 1918, Navy Records Collection, RG45.

243 "severe nasal hemorrhages": Ibid.

243 "a succession of skeleton like": Braynard, *World's Greatest Ship,* 193.

244 sprinkling the bodies: War Diaries, Epidemic Among Troops, 14 October 1918, Navy Records Collection, RG45.

244 "never to be seen again": War Diaries, Epidemic of Influenza, 11 October 1918, Navy Records Collection, RG45.

244 "ministering angels": *History of U.S.S. Leviathan,* 43.

245 Ninety-six men had died: Ibid., 75.

246 "In the next few days": Crosby, *America's Forgotten Pandemic,* 135.

246 Many of the nurses: *History of U.S.S. Leviathan,* 43.

CHAPTER 20

247 Pershing was astonished: Pershing, *My Experiences in the World War,* 2: 327.

247 "walked very slowly backward": F. Scott Fitzgerald, *Tender is the Night* (New York: Charles Scribner's Sons, 1933) 57.

247 The first weeks of October: Smythe, *Pershing*, 206.

247 "No more promises,": Ibid.

248 "Results are the only": Ibid.

248 Around this time: Ibid., 208.

248 "a tall, lean-flanked fellow": Damon Runyon, "Runyon Sees Return of Lost New York Battalion," *New York American*, 12 October 1918.

249 Pershing asked Runyon: Breslin, *A Life*, 168–69.

249 They'd all been briefed: Emmet Crozier, *American Reporters on the Western Front* (New York: Oxford University Press, 1959), 251.

249 "Well, General": Ibid., 252.

250 "Go to hell!": Ibid., 255.

250 "Runyon Sees Return": Damon Runyon, "Runyon Sees Return of Lost New York Battalion," *New York American*, 13 October 1918.

250 "Whittlesey says he did not": Ibid.

250 "The Argonne forest": Ibid.

251 "Whittlesey was leaving": Slotkin, *Lost Battalions*, 367.

251 "His grave," Runyon wrote: Runyon, "Eddie Grant Died Leading His Battalion," *New York American*, 22 October 1918.

252 that left sixty-three still: *History of U.S.S. Leviathan*, 43.

252 seven bodies still remained: War Diaries, 9 October 1918, Navy Records Collection, RG45.

252 The ceremony occurred: Ibid.

253 "All hands bury the dead": Gleaves, *History of the Transport Service*, 192.

253 "slow time": Ibid.

253 "Nearer, My God": Ibid.

253 "off hats!": Ibid.

254 "Carry on": Ibid.

254 "Instances will never be": Braynard, *World's Greatest Ship*, 193.

255 "It is madness": Ibid., 194.

CHAPTER 21

258 "There is now no longer": Smythe, *Pershing*, 219.

258 "our bravest men lay": Ibid.

258 "Do the people wish": Ibid.

259 Scheduled for early: War Diaries, 2 November 1918, Navy Records Collection, RG45.

259 "The little boats": Braynard, *World's Greatest Ship*, 197.

259 Germany had recalled: *History of U.S.S. Leviathan*, 44.

260 Even with the engines: War Diaries, 23 November 1918, Navy Records Collection, RG45.

260 "quite ineffective": Smythe, *Pershing*, 216.

261 "I feel like I am carrying": Ibid., 208.

261 "Frankie . . . Frankie": Richard O'Connor, *Black Jack Pershing* (Garden City: Doubleday and Company, 1961) 182.

262 "Without warning, a squadron": MacArthur, *Reminiscences*, 65.

262 "There were rolling hills": Ibid., 66.

262 "Give me Chatillon, MacArthur": Ibid.

263 Summerall departed too overwhelmed: Manchester, *American Caesar*, 106.

263 "death, cold and remorseless": MacArthur, *Reminiscences*, 66.

263 "Officers fell and sergeants": MacArthur, Ibid., 67.

263 "For the rest": Manchester, *American Caesar*, 107.

263 "a decisive blow": Ibid., 106.

263 "an offensive with some": Pershing, *My Experiences in the World War*, 2: 370.

264 hold them personally responsible: Smythe, *Pershing*, 223.

264 "It seems strange": Pershing, *My Experiences in the World War*, 2: 374.

265 "holding his position": Ibid.

266 "wherever resistance is broken": Ibid., 378.

266 He handed them a sheet: Ibid., 394.

267 "They finally succeeded": Ibid., 395.

267 "a suggestion that he": Keegan, *First World War*, 419.

268 "I cannot express": *Quarterly Journal of Military History* (Winter 2005).

268 he danced a jig: Smythe, *Pershing*, 232.

269 "We would have rounded": Ibid.

269 "You are terminating": Ibid.

269 "A nation of seventy million": Gideon Rose, *How Wars End* (New York: Simon & Schuster, 2010), 16.

269 "Shouting like mad": Eddie Rickenbacker, *Fighting the Flying Circus*, (Philadelphia: J. B. Lippincott, 1919), 359–60.

269 "I've lived through": Ibid., 360.

270 "We won't be shot": Ibid.

271 "No amount of persuasion": Pershing, *My Experiences in the World War*, 2: 395.

271 "If all the ridiculous": Ibid.

271 "So glorious, so joyous!": Pershing to Resco, 13 November 1918, Donald Smythe–Micheline Resco collection, Jesuit Archives, Saint Louis.

271 "a medley of Scottish": Pershing, *My Experiences in the World War*, 2: 397.

272 "We had no differences": Ibid.

CHAPTER 22

274 "intoxicated while ashore": Ship's Log, 12 November 1918, Records of the Bureau of Navy Personnel, NARA, RG24.

275 "We were greatly surprised": *History of U.S.S. Leviathan*, 45.

276 "a number of large fish": Braynard, *World's Greatest Ship*, 204.

276 Among the 13,558: War diaries, Navy Records Collection, NARA, RG45.

277 "I'll run right off": Braynard, *World's Greatest Ship*, 209.

278 "where it was hoped": Ibid.

278 hosted a gala Christmas: *History of U.S.S. Leviathan*, 45.

279 sailor named Humphrey DeForest Bogart: Ship's Log, 17 December 1918, Records of the Bureau of Navy Personnel, NARA, RG24.

279 A few weeks later,: Ship's Log, 13 January 1919, Records of the Bureau of Navy Personnel, NARA, RG24.

279 The parental plan for Bogart: Biographies in Naval History, Naval History Heritage Command.

280 At his physical he stood: Humphrey DeForest Bogart file, National Personnel Records Center, Saint Louis.

280 according to a story: "The Transport Ace," Jan. 28, 1919.

281 "cup of good English": Keegan, *First World War*, 419.

281 "When I saw the suffering": Darwin Porter, *The Secret Life of Humphrey Bogart* (New York: Georgia Literary Association, 2003), 39.

281 He wound up spending: Humphrey DeForest Bogart file, National Personnel Records Center, Saint Louis.

281 received an honorable discharge: Ibid.

CHAPTER 23

283 "all men found": Heywood, *Negro Combat Troops*, 227.

283 "*les soldats American Noirs*": Mason, *American Negro Soldier*, 138.

284 "Negroes should not speak": Ibid., 140.

284 "a number of brawls": Scott, *Scott's Official History*, 442.

284 "leave area for colored troops": Heywood, *Negro Combat Troops*, 231.

284 "discovered a movement": Ibid.

285 "Special provision was made": Ibid., 234.

285 Decorated with a unit citation: Slotkin, *Lost Battalions*, 396.

285 "as brothers in arms": Heywood, *Negro Combat Troops*, 239.

287 "Who won the war?": Slotkin, *Lost Battalions*, 396.

287 "His comrades instantly came": Ibid., 397.

288 "the very best qualities": Heywood, *Negro Combat Troops*, 250.

289 Private Burton Holmes: Ibid., 305.

290 a private from F Company: Ship's Log, 11 February 1919, Records of Bureau of Navy Personnel, April 18, 1918, NARA, RG24.

290 a single word, "Welcome": Mason, *American Negro Soldier*, 153.

CHAPTER 24

293 The navy was also: Gleaves, *History of the Transport Service*, 99.

294 "I gracefully occupied a $5,000": Letter, 13 May 1918, General Douglas MacArthur Foundation, Norfolk, VA.

294 "high forehead and small": Braynard, *World's Greatest Ship*, 242.

294 there were two deaths: Ship's Log, 17 April 1919, Records of Bureau of Navy Personnel, April 18, 1918, NARA, RG24.

294 "one little urchin": Letter, 13 May 1918, General Douglas MacArthur Foundation.

295 "leaning over a map": Manchester, *American Caesar*, 109.

295 "Paris is certainly": Letter, 13 May 1918, General Douglas MacArthur Foundation.

CHAPTER 25

297 "under duress": Davis, *FDR*, 570.

298 "slipshod, temperamental": Smythe, *Pershing*, 245.

298 "it was difficult": Ibid., 247.

298 "Dear Comrades, Farewell": *Infantry Journal*, July 1919–June 1920, US Infantry Association, Washington, DC.

298 "sleeping so far": Smythe, *Pershing*, 257.

299 His most fervent admirer: Henry Wales, "The True Story of Famous General's Romance with a Charming Young Portrait Painter," *Chicago Tribune*, 30 November 1952.

299 Marshal Foch boarded: Ship's Log, 1 September 1919, Records of Bureau of Navy Personnel, NARA, RG24

300 "I never saw him": Smythe, *Pershing*, 259.

300 "I have sea sickness": Pershing to Resco, 3 September 1919, Donald Smythe–Micheline Resco collection, Jesuit Archives, Saint Louis.

301 broke out in "Over There": Edward Kneass, "Pershing's Son Climbs on Bed to Tell Dad of Rank," *Chicago Tribune*, 6 September 1919.

301 "failing to get up": Ship's Log, 7 September 1919, Records of Bureau of Navy Personnel, NARA, RG24.

301 seventeen-gun salute was fired: Ship's Log, 8 September 1919, Records of Bureau of Navy Personnel, NARA, RG24.

302 tossed off his hat: Smythe, *Pershing*, 261.

303 "closing out accounts": Ship's Log, 29 October 1919, Records of Bureau of Navy Personnel, NARA, RG24.

303 "The U.S.S. *Leviathan*": Ibid.

EPILOGUE

305 "one of the strongest" Smythe, *Pershing*, 209.

306 "Finie la guerre": Weaver, *U.S. Army Nurse Journal*, 283.

307 "The color of a man's skin": Lawson, *Irvin S. Cobb*, 164.

307 "On that September day": Bush, "Remarks at a Ceremony."

308 released his friend's ashes: Damon Runyon Jr., *Father's Footsteps: The Story of Damon Runyon by His Son* (New York: Random House, 1953), 176–77.

308 "An army of two thousand": Steven Ujifusa, *A Man and His Ship* (New York: Simon & Schuster, 2012), 80.

309 "*Leviathan* Sails Away": *New York Herald Tribune*, 6 December 1937.

SELECT BIBLIOGRAPHY

Blum, Howard. *Dark Invasion: 1915: Germany's Secret War and the Hunt for the First Terrorist Cell in America.* New York: HarperCollins, 2014.

Blunden, Edmund. *Undertones of War.* Chicago: University of Chicago Press, 2007.

Braynard, Frank D. *Leviathan: The World's Greatest Ship,* vols. 1–6. New York: South Street Seaport Museum, 1972.

Breslin, Jimmy. *A Life: Damon Runyon.* New York: Ticknor & Fields, 1991.

Cobb, Elisabeth. *My Wayward Parent: Irvin S. Cobb.* New York: Bobbs-Merrill, 1945.

Cobb, Irvin S. *Exit Laughing.* New York: Bobbs-Merrill, 1941.

———. *The Glory of the Coming: What Mine Eyes Have Seen of Americans.* New York: George H. Doran, 1918.

———. *Paths of Glory: Impressions of War Written at and Near the Front.* New York: George H. Doran, 1915.

Crosby, Alfred W. *America's Forgotten Pandemic: The Influenza of 1918.* New York: Cambridge University Press, 2003.

Crowell, Benedict. *The Road to France: The Transportation of Troops and Military Supplies, 1917–1918.* New Haven: Yale University Press, 1921.

Daniels, Josephus. *Our Navy at War.* New York: George H. Doran, 1922.

Davis, Kenneth S. *FDR: The Beckoning of Destiny.* New York: Capricorn Books, 1975.

D'Itri, Patricia Ward. *Damon Runyon.* Boston: Twayne Publishers, 1982.

Freidel, Frank. *Over There: The Story of America's First Great Overseas Crusade.* New York: Bramhall House, 1964.

Fussell, Paul. *The Great War and Modern Memory*. New York: Sterling, 2009.

Giddings, Robert. *The War Poets*. New York: Orion Books, 1988.

Gleaves, Albert. *A History of the Transport Service: Adventures and Experiences of United States Transports and Cruisers in the World War*. New York: George H. Doran, 1921.

Graves, Robert. *Good-Bye to All That*. New York: Doubleday, 1957.

Keegan, John. *The Face of Battle: A Study of Agincourt, Waterloo, and the Somme*. New York: Vintage Books, 1977.

———. *The First World War*. New York: Vintage Books, 1998.

———. *The Price of Admiralty: The Evolution of Naval Warfare*. New York: Viking, 1989.

Larson, Erik. *Dead Wake: The Last Crossing of the "Lusitania."* New York: Crown, 2015.

Lawson, Anita. *Irvin S. Cobb*. Bowling Green: Bowling Green State University Popular Press, 1984.

Luciano, Lorraine and Casandra Jewell, eds. *Army Nurses of World War One*. Carlisle: Army Heritage Center Foundation, 2006.

MacArthur, Douglas. *Reminiscences: General of the Army*. New York: McGraw-Hill, 1964.

Manchster, William. *American Caesar: Douglas MacArthur, 1880–1964*. New York: Back Bay Books, 1978.

Mason, Monroe. *The American Negro Soldier with the Red Hand of France*. Boston: Cornhill, 1920.

Messimer, Dwight R. *Escape*. Annapolis: Naval Institute Press, 1994.

Neuman, Fred G. *Irvin S. Cobb: His Life and Achievements*. Paducah, KY: Young Publishing, 1934.

Pershing, John J. *My Experiences in the World War*, vols. 1–2. New York: Frederick A. Stokes Co., 1931.

Scott, Emmett J. *Scott's Official History of the American Negro in the World War*. Chicago: Homewood Press, 1919.

Slotkin, Richard. *Lost Battalions: The Great War and the Crisis of American Nationality*. New York: Henry Holt, 2005.

Smythe, Donald. *Pershing: General of the Armies*. Bloomington: Indiana University Press, 2007. Bloomington & Indianapolis. Reprinted with permission of Indiana University Press.

Terraine, John. *The U-Boat Wars: 1916–1945*. New York: G.P. Putnam's Sons, 1989.

Thorn, Henry C. *History of 313th U.S. Infantry, Baltimore's Own*. New York: Wynkoop Hallenbeck Crawford, 1920.

Tuchman, Barbara W. *The Guns of August*. New York: Bantam Books, 1976.

Ujifusa, Steven. *A Man and His Ship*. New York: Simon & Schuster, 2012.

Walker, William. *Betrayal at Little Gibraltar: A German Fortress, a Treacherous American General, and the Battle to End World War I.* New York: Scribner, 2016.

Ward, Geoffrey C. *A First-Class Temperament: The Emergence of Franklin Roosevelt, 1905–1928.* New York: Vintage Books, 1989.

Witcover, Jules. *Sabotage at Black Tom: Imperial Germany's Secret War in America, 1914–1917.* Chapel Hill: Algonquin Books, 1989.

INDEX

accidental (self-inflicted) wounds, 211–12

Adriatic (British liner), 9–10

Adventurer, The (film), 294

African American troops. *See also* 371st Infantry Regiment; 372nd Infantry Regiment

  Circle for Negro War Relief and, 306–7

  Cobb visits, 169–73

  discrimination vs., 284–85

  French and, 120, 123–24, 283–88

  Pershing and, 43

  racial tensions and, 118–19, 287

  segregation of, 74–75, 117–19, 123–24, 290, 306–7

  sent to France, 158–59

  South Carolina and, 73–74

  work duty and, 103, 118–19

African Queen, The (film), 308

Aisne River, 154

Aix-la-Chapelle, 16

Albatross aircraft, 124

Albert, King of Belgium, 195

Algonquin (steamship), 27

Allied Supreme War Council, 156–59

Allies

  armistice and, 266, 268

  early war and, 21

  shipping and, 23, 59

  submarines and, 92

Alpenkorps (German-Austrian), 102

Alsace, 13

Alsace-Lorraine, 266

Ambrose Channel, 5, 142

Ambrose Lightship, 89–90

America, USS (troopship), 257

American Expeditionary Force (AEF), 39, 77, 109. *See also* Meuse-Argonne Offensive; Spring Offensives; *and specific battles; locations; military units; and transport ships*

  first combat deaths of 1917, 61

  segregation, 74–75, 117–19, 123–24, 290, 306–7

  training of, 40, 75, 77, 109, 122–24, 131–35, 159, 170–71, 179–80, 202, 208–13, 218–19, 226

  transport to Europe, 61, 105, 110–11

  trucks and tie-ups, 219

amputations, 184–85

antitoxin injections, 98–99

Arbeiter-Zeitung (newspaper), 258

Ardenne Forest, 13, 248

Ardeuil, 234, 307

Argonne Forest, 168, 206, 212, 216–18, 234, 250–51, 264

Arizona, 29

Arlington Cemetery, 305–6

armed neutrality, 27

armistice, 266–79

Arnauld de la Periere, Lothan von, 145

Attila the Hun, 215

Austria-Hungary
declares war on Serbia, 5
surrenders, 260

Avocourt ruin, 205

Axel, Prince of Denmark, 197

Azores, 142

Baccarat, 108–9

Badger, Charles J., 81

Badger, Oscar, 81

Baker, Newton, 105–6, 293, 302

Baltic, SS (British troopship), 38–41, 82–86

Ban-de-Laveline, 283

Barbarossa (German liner), 8

Barkley, John, 265

Bar-le-Duc, 201, 249

Bar Light Vessel, 68

Barricourt Ridge, 217, 264–65

Base Hospital 12, 99

Base Hospital 18, 182–83

Base Hospital 20, 97, 128–29, 183

Base Hospital 33, 128

Bastille Day Victory Parade, 298–99

Battleship Division Nine, 194

Baylis, John, 21–24

bayonet, 75, 121, 133, 234

Bazoilles-sur-Meuse, 183

Beebe, John, 150

Begum, SS (British freighter), 149

Belgium, 9–14, 19, 46–47, 183
FDR visits, 195

Belleau Wood, 156–57, 159–60, 192

Belle Isle, 142

Berlin riots, 267

Bernstorff, Count Heinrich von, 2, 24–25, 34–35

Big Bertha (Paris Gun), 153, 166–67, 183

Black Tom munitions plant bombing, 34

Bogart, Belmont DeForest, 279

Bogart, Humphrey DeForest, 279–81, 308

Bois de Bourgogne, 264–65

Bois de Cuisy, 224–27

Bois de Malancourt, 224, 225

Bolsheviks, 61, 267

Bordeaux, 153

Boulogne, 42

Bouresches, 156

Bradley, Omar, 305

Brazil Naval Commission, 200–201

Brest, 65, 94
American expansion in, 101–4, 118
black troops in, 117–19
Bryan visits, 101–5
Cobb visits, 166–67

Leviathan and, 94, 102, 104, 111, 142–45, 176–78, 180–82, 191, 293
    U-boat attacks near, 150–53
Bridgeport, USS (destroyer), 299
Britain
    food shortages and, 23, 42, 59
    outbreak of war and, 5, 7, 9
    Pershing in, 41
British Army, 17, 45–46, 106, 111, 216. *See also* specific military units
    casualties, 76, 94
    flu and, 139
    self-inflicted wounds and, 211
British dirigibles, 68
British Fifth Army, 107
British Grand Fleet, 5, 139, 194
British intelligence, 29
British merchant ships, 47, 65
British passengers ships, 9–10
British submarines, 68
British Tommy helmet, 121–22
Browning Automatic Rifle (BAR), 131–32
Brussels, occupation of, 14
Bruyers, 283–84
Bryan, Charles (son), 81, 104
Bryan, Elizabeth Champlin Badger (wife), 81
Bryan, Elizabeth (daughter), 104
Bryan, Helen (daughter), 104
Bryan, Henry, 221
    background and family of, 80–81, 104
    becomes captain of *Leviathan*, 80–82
    Carlton SOS and, 148–49
    FDR and, 195, 197–201

flu and, 197–98
icebergs and, 115–16
Leviathan voyages to Brest and, 94, 101–5, 115–16, 125–28, 142–45, 176–78, 180–81, 187–88
Leviathan voyages to Liverpool and, 89–94, 113–16
Lincoln sinking and, 161–62
postwar career of, 307–8
reassigned to Brazil, 199–201
U-boats and, 141–42, 147, 149–53, 162–66, 190–91
Bryant, S.W., 65, 67, 69, 72
Buffalo Soldiers, 76
Bull Run, Battle of (Civil War), 204
Bush, George H.W., 307
Butler, Charlie, 289
Buzancy, 265

Cain Mutiny, The (film), 308
Calhoun, USS (destroyer), 301
Camp Funston, 137–38
Camp Jackson, 73–76, 121, 290
Camp Lewis, 220
Camp Meade, 131–32, 135, 175, 179
Camp Merritt, 231
Campobello Island, 59
Camp Upton, 290
Canadian troops, 85
Cannon, Joe, 26, 32
Cantigny, 154–56, 159, 183
Cantor, Eddie, 172
Caporetto, Italian retreat at, 102–3
Carlton, SS (British tanker), 148–49
Carrel, Alexis, 185
Carrel-Dakin solution, 184–85
carrier pigeon number 47, 230

Cerny, 17

Champagne, 207, 212–13, 234, 285

Champlitte, 178–80, 201

Chaplin, Charlie, 70, 294

Chasseurs Alpins (French mountain corps), 208

Château-Thierry, 153–59, 192–93, 202, 277–78

Châtel-Buyon, 183

Chauchat machine gun ("cho-cho"), 122

Chaumont (Pershing Headquarters), 110, 112, 154, 159, 268

Chemin des Dames, 154

Chicago, flu and, 139

Chicago Tribune, 10, 92–93, 160

Churchill, Winston, 5, 47

Circle for Negro War Relief, 306–7

City of Memphis (steamship), 27

Civil War, 74, 76, 81, 184

Clark, James Beauchamp "Champ," 135

Clemenceau, Georges "Le Tigre," 105, 107, 111, 134, 157–58, 193–94, 230, 260–61, 272

Clermont-sur-Oise (Foch headquarters), 107

Cliveden (Astor estate), 193

Cobb, Irvin, 10–19, 21, 48, 82–87, 89, 166–73, 306

Cobb, Laura, 173

Cobb, Ty, 168, 277

Collier's, 10

Columbus, Christopher, 56

Compiègne (Pétain headquarters), 106

Composite Regiment, 299, 301–2

Conner, Fox, 249

Connor, Ralph (Charles William Gordon), 98

Côte-de-Châtillon, 218, 261–63, 265, 295

Covington, USS (troopship), 176, 180–81

Croix de Guerre, 171–72

Cropley, Ralph, 60

Crosby, Bing, 306

Cuba, 52–59

Cummings, USS (destroyer), 151

Cunard Line, 58

Cunel, 217

Custer, George A., 30

Dakin, Henry, 185

Daniels, Josephus, 27, 35, 80

Davis, Kenneth, 195, 199

Dead Man's Hill, 170

Democratic Party, 31

Destroyer No. 533, USS, 21–22

diphtheria, 98–99

Distinguished Service Cross, 184

Dosch, Arno, 10

Downes, USS (destroyer), 67

Durell, Edward, 294

Dyer, USS (destroyer), 192

Edna (schooner), 165

Eighteenth Amendment, 281

Eighth Brigade, 43

84th Infantry Regiment, 293

Eisenhower, Dwight, 305

Eleventh Infantry, 125

Ellis Island, 21, 23, 95, 97–99

English Channel, 13, 27, 47, 90, 142

Erzberger, Matthias, 269

Fanning, USS (destroyer), 114

Farewell to Arms, A (Hemingway), 103

Fields, W.C., 306

Fifteenth Calvary, 140

Fifteenth Machine Gun Battalion, 125

Fifty-Fifth Infantry, 188

Fifty-Seventh Pioneer Infantry
      (Vermont) Regiment, 230–32,
      246

Finch, Tubby, 83, 86

First Army, 204, 212, 216, 240, 248,
      251, 260, 265, 268

First Division, 61, 105, 108–9, 155–56,
      261, 302

Fitzgerald, F. Scott, 247

Flanders, 46, 106

flu epidemic, 137–41, 185, 191, 195,
      197–200, 220–22, 230–32, 240–47
   FDR and, 195, 197–200
   history of, 139
   Leviathan and, 220–22, 230–32,
      240–46, 252–55, 290–91

Foch, Ferdinand, 48, 107–8, 156–58,
      192, 202, 216, 247–49, 261,
      266–68, 297–300

Fokker, 124

Fontaine-en-Dormois, 237

Ford, John, 281

Ford Motor Company, 137

Fortieth Parallel, 64

Fort McPherson, 115

Forty-Second (Rainbow) Division,
      108, 140, 168, 261–63, 293–95

Fourth Infantry, 265

France. *See also specific locations*
   African American troops and,
      118–24, 283–88
   armistice and, 266
   outbreak of war and, 7–9, 13–17
   Pershing travels to, 39–42, 44–49
   Schlieffen plan and, 13–15

Franco-Prussian War (1870–71), 5,
      107, 297

Franz-Ferdinand, Archduke, 5

French Adrian helmet, 121–22

French Army. *See also specific units*
   African American troops and, 120
   casualties, 103
   early war and, 15–19
   flu epidemic and, 139
   food rations, 122–23
   German Spring Offensive and,
      106–7
   Meuse-Argonne Offensive and, 216
   near collapse of, 45–46, 154, 156

French Fourth Army, 208, 212, 216,
      218, 234, 264, 285

French hand grenade, 170

French Indochina, 201

French Lebel rifle, 121, 234

French 157th (Red Hand) Division,
      207, 208, 233, 285

French POWs, 16, 18

Freya Stellung (German defense line),
      217

Friedrich der Grosse (German liner),
      8, 25

gangrene, 184

gas warfare, 108, 122, 133, 211
  chlorine gas, 98, 182
  mustard gas, 182–84, 264
  phosgene gas, 182

General Headquarters (GHQ), 219

General Staff College, 219

George V, King of England, 41, 193

George Washington (German liner), 8, 276

German Admiralty Staff, 190

German aircraft, 124, 207

German Army. *See also* Meuse-
    Argonne Offensive; Spring
    Offensives; *and specific military
    units*
  Belleau Wood and, 159
  Caporetto and, 102
  casualties and, 268
  early fighting in France, 14–18
  flu epidemic and, 139
  Meuse-Argonne Offensive and, 217
  outbreak of war and, 8
  success of, by 1917, 45–46
  transferred to western front, 105

German First Division Prussian
    Guards, 205

German High Command, 76, 134, 258

German High Seas Fleet, 91, 259, 266

German Naval Academy, 144

German Navy mutineers, 260

German passenger ships
  crews in New York, 22–23, 25, 35
  trapped in US ports, 8–9

German POWs, 103, 113–15, 204, 233–34

German propaganda leaflets, 234–35

German Seventh Army, 15

German spies, 24–25, 34, 53, 104

German storm troopers, 106, 154

German Third Army, 269

Germany
  American supporting, 25
  armistice and, 266–69
  food shortages, 267
  Mexico and, 29
  outbreak of war and, 5–9, 12–17
  Paris Treaty of 1919 and, 297–98
  Russian exit from war and, 61
  Schlieffen plan and, 13–15
  submarine warfare and, 27–28, 31

Germont, 265

Gibbons, Floyd, 160

Giselher Stellung (German defense
    line), 217

Gleaves, Albert, 24, 93–94, 189

Good-Bye to All That (Graves), 211

Gordon, Charles William (Ralph
    Connor), 98

Gotha bombers, 105

Goybet, Mariano, 208–9, 212, 285–86

Grandpré, 218

Granite State, USS (training ship), 280

Grant, Eddie, 251

Gratreuil, 237

Graves, Robert, 211

Great Northern, USS (troopship),
    187–90, 199

Great White Fleet, 294

Grey, Sir Edward, 9

Guantánamo Bay, 52–53, 56

Guys and Dolls (musical), 308

Guyton, 184

Haig, Sir Douglas, 46, 111, 271, 298
Hamburg-American Line, 2–4, 24
Hans, 234
Harricourt, 265
Harvard University, 138
Hasbrouck, R.D., 180–81
Haskell, Kansas, flu and, 137
Hattie Dunn (schooner), 165
Haudiomont, 202
Hauppauge (schooner), 165
Hearst, Millicent, 25
Hearst, William Randolph, 25, 44, 249
Heiltz l'Évêque, 207, 212
Hemingway, Ernest, 103
Hill 188, 218, 233–40, 285–86, 289, 307
Hindenburg, Paul von, 258
Hindenburg Line (Kriemhilde Stellung), 45, 217, 229–30, 261
Hippocrates, 139
Hoboken, 21
    departure of *Leviathan* for Cuba and, 52, 58–59
    departure of *Leviathan* for Europe, 63, 73
    German liners in, at outbreak of war, 8–10, 22–23
    Leviathan refitting in, 141
    sabotage in, 33–34
Holmes, Burton, 289
Housatonic (freighter), 27
Howell, Allan, 51
Humphrey, Maud, 279

icebergs, 115–16
Illinois (tanker), 27

Indian Ghost Dance, 43
"In Flanders Fields" (McCrae), 46–47
Irish Channel, 90, 142
Irish Sea, 64–65, 67, 82, 85, 90
Irwin, Will, 10
Italian Army, 102–3

Jackson, Andrew, 76
Jacob Jones, USS (destroyer), 65
Jellicoe, John, 47
Jersey City munitions plant bombing, 25
Joan of Arc, 215
Joffre, Joseph, 48, 105, 271
Johnson, Carl Frank, 116, 140
Johnson, Eli, 29–30
Johnson, Everett, 26
Johnson, Florence, 26
Johnson, Harlan, 26
Johnson, Henry, 171–72
Johnson, Philena, 30
Johnson, Royal, 26–32, 131–35, 175–80, 201–5, 207, 219, 223–30, 306
Justica, SS (British troopship), 190–91

Kansas, USS (battleship), 81
Keegan, John, 19, 46
Kiel mutineers, 260
Kriemhilde Stellung (Hindenburg line), 45, 217–18, 229–30, 261
Kronprinzessin Cecilie (German liner; later troopship *Mount Vernon*), 198

La Buissiere, Belgium, 15
La Follette, Robert, 29, 31, 84

La Guardia, Fiorella, 132

Laignes, 178

Lairesse, Gerard de, 3

Laval, 283–84

League of Nations, 300

Lee, Robert, 289

Leviathan, USS (troopship, *formerly*
    German liner *Vaterland*), 33

    armistice and, 259–60, 273–79

    Bogart and, 278–81

    Brest and, 94, 102, 104, 111, 143–45,
        176–78, 180–82, 191, 293

    Bryan as captain of, 80–82, 89–94,
        95, 199–201, 220–222

    camouflage paint and, 71

    Carlton SOS and, 148–49

    Christmas party for orphans and,
        278

    Cobb and, 169, 173

    convoys with *Great Northern* and
        Northern Pacific, 187–91, 199

    Cuban shakedown and, 51–59

    Durell as captain of, 294

    FDR and, 195, 197–200

    flu and, 197–98, 220–22, 230–32,
        240–46, 252–55, 257–58, 290

    German POWs and, 113–16

    icebergs and, 115–16

    Liverpool and, 68–73, 79, 89–95,
        101, 258–60

    MacArthur and, 293–95

    man overboard and, 188–89

    mistakenly reported sunk, 190–91

    nurses and, 64, 66, 69, 125–31, 151,
        243–46

    Oman as captain of, and missed
        rendezvous, 64–68, 79–82

    outfitted as troopship, 33, 35–38,
        60–61, 81–82, 111, 141–43

    Pershing and, 299–302

    Phelps as captain of, 200–201,
        220–222, 294

    pneumonia and, 116, 140–41, 191

    postwar career as luxury liner and,
        308–9

    postwar decommissioning of, 302–3

    runs aground, 260

    sold for scrap, 309

    speed and, 57–58, 181

    steering and, 55–56, 176–77

    troops first ship to Europe on,
        63–66, 105–6

    troops of 313th and, 175–76

    troops of 371st and, 288–91

    troops return to US on, postwar,
        293–94, 298

    U-boats and, 60, 92–93, 105, 147–53,
        161–66, 173, 190–91, 198, 241

Lewis and Clark expedition, 30

lice, 205, 286

Ligny-en-Barrois (Pershing
    headquarters), 216–17

Little Bighorn, Battle of, 30

Liverpool, 67–73, 79, 89–95, 101, 113,
    258–60, 273–75

Lloyd George, David, 41, 42, 111,
    157–58, 260, 280

Lodge, Henry Cabot, 26

London, bombing of, 105

Lorimer, George, 11

Lorraine, 13, 183

Lost Battalion, 248–52

Louis XIV, King of France, 297

Louis XV, King of France, 154

Louisiana, USS (battleship), 222

Louvain, Belgium, 10–14, 18–19, 302

Ludendorff, Erich von, 61, 134, 258

Lusitania (Cunard liner), 6, 9, 19
  sinking of, 25, 64, 114

Luther, Martin, 28

Luxembourg, 13

MacArthur, Douglas, 108, 112,
  261–63, 293–95

"Mammy's Chocolate Soldier" (song),
  172

Manchester, William, 47, 263

Manley, USS (destroyer), 92–93

Marat-la-Grande, 120, 123

March, Peyton C., 111, 116, 221

Mareuil-en-Dôle, 192

Marne River, 140, 154, 156, 170

"Marseillaise," 270

Marshall, George C., Jr., 219, 305–6

Martha Washington (German liner), 8

Massachusetts Colony, 139

Mather, Cotton, 139

Maubeuge, 18

Mauretania (Cunard liner), 58

May, H.A., 242–45

McAdoo, William, 60

McCrae, John, 46–47

McCutcheon, John, 10

McDouglas, USS (destroyer), 67

McGonigle (wounded soldier),
  181–82

McKinley, William, 60

Mennonites, 95–96

Mercer, Lucy, 200

Mercier, Cardinal, 302

Messimer, Dwight R., 149, 152, 166

Metropolitan Museum of Art, 37

Meuse-Argonne Offensive, 213,
  247–52, 305
  armistice and, 266–68
  Barricourt Ridge and, 264–65
  Côte-de-Châtillon and, 261–63
  final phase of, 263–66
  flu epidemic and, 247
  German defense lines and, 217–18
  Hill 188 and, 233–40
  Hindenburg Line broken in, 261
  lack of training and, 218–19
  Lost Battalion and, 248–52
  Marshall and, 219
  Montfaucon and, 223–30
  Pershing plan and, 215–19, 260–61
  Runyon and, 248–49

Meuse River, 183, 265

Mexico, 29, 44, 249

Minneapolis, USS (cruiser), 138

Monacacy, USS (warship), 80

Mongolia, SS (troopship), 99

Montdidier, 107

Montfaucon, 170, 205–7, 212, 217–18
  captured by 313th, 224–30, 262,
    264
  memorial at, 298

Montignies Saint Christopher,
  Belgium, 14

Moroccan troops, 109, 213, 233–34

Mortensen, Hans, 52

Mount Vernon, USS (troopship), 102,
  197–200

My Experiences in the World War
  (Pershing), 305

"My Soul Bears Witness to the Lord"
  (spiritual), 169

Nancy, 61

Nantucket, 53

Napoleon, 94, 103, 110

Navy and Merchant Marine Magazine, 60

Navy Department, 221

Navy Yard, 24

New Jersey, U-boats off, 165

New Mexico, 29

New Orleans, Battle of, 76

New York, SS (troopship), 115

New York America, 250

New York City
  flu epidemic, 139
  German spies in, 34
  outbreak of war and, 8
  Victory Parade in, 302

New York Harbor, 6–8, 72–73, 90
  after armistice, 276–77
  U-boats and, 59

New York Times, 2, 10

New-York Tribune, 6–7, 52

Nicholson, USS (destroyer), 114, 163

Ninety-Fourth Aero Squadron, 269

93rd Division, 76

Ninth Cavalry, 76

Nivelle, Robert, 215

Norris, George, 31

Northern Mine Barrage, 194

Northern Pacific, USS (troopship), 187–90, 200

North Sea, 194, 241

Northwestern University, 99

nurses, 95–99, 232, 240, 306
  battlefield hospital and, 183–85
  death of, 99

flu epidemic and, 243–46
  sail on *Leviathan,* 64, 66, 69, 125–31

O'Brien, USS (destroyer), 67, 148

Ochs, Adolph S., 2

Oise River, 106

Olympic (British liner), 9

Oman, Joseph "Buggs"
  destroyer rendezvous and, 65–68, 79–80
  Leviathan's run to Cuba and, 51–59
  Leviathan's sail to Europe, 63–65, 68–73
  removed from command of *Leviathan,* 79–80

163rd Infantry Regiment, 64

164th Infantry Regiment, 64

167th Infantry Regiment, 263

168th Infantry Regiment, 263

open field warfare, 109, 179

Order Number 40, 284

Overman, Lee Slater, 135

Overman Act (1918), 135

Paolina (US freighter), 52

Paris
  armistice and, 270–72
  Bastille Day Victory Parade and, 298–99
  bombardment of, 105, 166–67, 183
  FDR in, 193–94
  French government evacuates, 153
  German spring offensives and, 94, 106–7, 134, 153–54, 157
  Pershing in, 48–49, 105, 112, 299

Paris Peace Conference (1918–19), 276, 278–79, 293, 295
    Treaty of 1919 and, 297–98, 303
Passchendaele, Battle of, 46
Patton, George S., 44
Pennsylvania, USS (battleship), 276
Pennsylvania (German liner), 8
Perry, Oliver Hazard, 76
Pershing, Helen Frances Warren "Frankie," 42–43, 261
Pershing, John J. "Black Jack"
    armistice and, 267–72
    background and family of, 42–43
    Brest and, 94
    Château-Thierry and, 156–57
    death of, 305–6
    FDR and, 192–93
    flu epidemic and, 247
    German spring offensives and, 105–12, 153–58
    illness of, 248
    Lost Battalion and, 251
    MacArthur and, 295
    memoirs of, 305
    Meuse-Argonne Offensive and, 215–19, 228, 240, 247–48, 251, 260–61, 263–66, 305–6
    Mexican campaign and, 44, 248–49
    moves troops to France, 61, 110–11, 156–59
    nickname "Black Jack" and, 43
    open vs. trench warfare and, 179
    Paris and, 48–49, 105, 112, 299
    Paris Treaty and, 297–98
    Pétain and, 155
    postwar career of, 305
    promoted by Wilson, 300–301
    regiments turned over to France by, 120
    returns to US on *Leviathan*, 299–302
    romance with Micheline Resco, 48–49, 112, 160, 270–72, 299, 300, 305
    sails to Europe with US entry to war, 38–42, 44–49, 82
    Saint Mihiel and, 202, 204
    son Warren and, 293, 298
    Victory Parades and, 299, 302
Pershing, Warren, 43, 293, 298–99, 301
Pétain, Philippe, 94, 106–7, 109, 153, 155, 215–16, 218, 271, 288
Phelps, Susie, 222
Phelps, William
    armistice and, 273–75
    becomes captain of *Leviathan*, 200, 220
    court-martial of, 221–22
    final trips at end of war, 257–60, 275–78
    flu voyage and, 230–32, 241–46, 252–55
Philadelphia, flu epidemic and, 221
Philippine Islands, 42, 80–81
Picardy, 108–10
Pittoni, Giovanna Battista, 3, 37
Plunkett, Charles, 194
pneumonia epidemic, 116, 138–41, 191, 200, 241–42, 245, 254, 290
Pocahontas, USS (troopship), 141–42
Pont-à-Mousson, 202

Pontanezen Barracks, 103, 118, 177–78, 245

President Grant, USS (troopship), 117

presidential election of 1916, 31, 84

President Lincoln, USS (troopship), 8, 102

sinking of, 161–63, 166, 176, 181

Prinzess Irene (German liner), 8

Prinz Joachim (German liner), 8

Punitive Expedition, 44, 249

Q-ship (armed raider), 144

Queenstown, Ireland, 64–66, 126, 193

Rade Abri, 101

Rainey, Paul J., 2

Rankin, Jeannette, 32

rats, 203, 205

Rawson, John, 241–42

Red Cross, 14, 168, 175

Reims, 17, 170

Rembercourt, 121, 123, 169

Remy, Walter, 144–45, 147–49, 162, 166

reparations, 266–67

Republican Party, 26, 31

Resco, Micheline, 48, 112, 153, 160, 270, 299–300, 305

Revenue Cutter Service (*later* US Coast Guard), 21

Rhine River, 266

Richards, Charles, 221

Richelieu, Cardinal, 101

Richthofen Squadron, 262

Rickenbacker, Eddie, 112, 219, 269–70, 308

Ripont, 233–34, 236

Ritz, César, 3

Roberts, Needham, 171–72

Rockefeller Institute for Medical Research, 185

Rogers, Will, 306

Romagne, 217–18

Rome, 195

Rommel, George, 102

Roosevelt, Eleanor, 26, 59, 195, 200

Roosevelt, Franklin D.

affair with Mercer, 200

becomes assistant secretary of Navy, 26, 59

early life of, 59–60

Leviathan commissioned as troopship by, 60–61

Leviathan voyage and flu of, 195, 197–200, 220

Paris Peace Conference and, 278–79

presidency of, 308

U-boats and, 59

visits front, 192–95

Roosevelt, Theodore, 60, 294

Ross, Lloyd, 263

Rough Riders, 60

Rubin, Edgar, 191

Runyon, Damon, 44, 248–52, 308

Russia

Civil War, 280

outbreak of war and, 5, 7–9

Revolution of 1917, 48, 61

separate peace of 1917, 61

sabotage, 33–34

Saint Gervais and Saint Protais, Church of, 167

Saint Mihiel, 109, 216, 219
    offensive, 184, 192, 202–13
Saint-Nazaire, 118–19
Saint Paul, SS (liner), 12
Sambre River, 15
San Francisco, 139
San Juan Hill, 76
San Quentin prison, 137
San Salvador, 56
Santa Olivia, USS (troopship), 281
Santiago, Cuba, bombardment of, 80
Sarcus, 155–56
Saturday Evening Post, 11, 84
Schlieffen plan, 13
Scotland, 5, 194
Second Army, 265, 268
Second Division, 108, 155–57, 159–60
Second Naval District, 80, 81
Secret Service, 24
Sedan, Battle of (1870), 264
Sedan-Mezieres line (German
    defenses), 217–18, 264, 266
segregation, 74–75, 117–19, 123–24,
    290, 306–7
Serbia, 5
Seven Days Leave (film), 98
Seventh Cavalry, 30
Seventh Machine Gun Battalion, 155
Seventy-Seventh Division, 250
79th Division, 132, 179–80, 230, 262
Sims, William, 47, 79, 152, 189, 191,
    197
Sioux, 30
Slotkin, Richard, 251
Smith, John, 123
Smythe, Donald, 40, 48–49, 112, 218
Soissons, 154–55, 168–70, 305

Somme, 106
    Battle of (1916), 46
South Dakota, 29–31
Spain, flu epidemic, 140
Spanish-American War, 43, 53, 60, 80
Speaking of Operations (Cobb), 84
Springfield rifle, 121
Spring Offensives
    first (March 21-April 5), 93–94,
        105–8, 116, 134, 167
    second (April 9–29), 111–12, 116,
        134, 140
    third (May 21-June 11), 153–57
Stenay-Le Chesne, 218
Stevens (destroyer), 259
Stowers, Freddie, 74–77, 117–23,
    169–71, 207–13, 219, 233–40, 285,
    289, 307
    death of, 239–240
    Medal of Honor, 307
Stowers, Pearl, 74
Summerall, Charles, 262
surgery, 184–85
Sweezey, Claude, 134, 226, 228

Taft, William H., 76
Tailly, 265
Tamines massacre, 19
Taylor, David, 60
telescope, German high-powered, 206
Tenth Cavalry, 76
Texas, 29
Third Division, 155, 156, 159
Thirty-Second Division, 261
313th Infantry Regiment, 225, 287
    Champlitte and, 178–80
    Leviathan trip to France, 175–78

313th Infantry Regiment (*cont.*)
Meuse-Argonne Offensive and, 223–30
Pontanezen Barracks and, 177–78
Saint Mihiel and, 201–7
training of, 131–35, 170–71, 179–80
369th Infantry Regiment (New York African Americans)
Cobb visits, 171–73
Croix de Guerre and, 171–72, 285
Meuse-Argonne Offensive and, 234
371st Infantry Regiment (South Carolina African Americans), 73–76, 117
attached to French 157th Division, 120–22, 207–13
casualties and, 209–10, 289
Cobb visits, in Rembercourt, 169–73
Croix de Guerre and, 285–86, 288
Hill 188 memorial and, 307
Meuse-Argonne and Hill 188 and, 212–13, 233–40
night patrols and, 210
postwar welcome in France and, 283–88
postwar return to US on *Leviathan* and, 288–91
sails for France, 117–18
Saint Mihiel and, 203, 207
Thanksgiving and Christmas meals and, 284–85
train to Rembercourt, 119–24
training of, 122–24, 208–13
white officers and, 119
wine rations and, 123
372nd Infantry Regiment

arrive in France, 118
French command and, 120
racial tensions and, 118–19
Titanic (ocean liner), 1, 4
Tour Tanquy, 101
trench warfare, 117, 122–24, 179, 205
tuberculosis, 98
Turkey, surrender of, 259
Tuscania, SS (British troopship), 83, 85–87
Twentieth Machine Gun Battalion, 188
Twenty-Sixth Infantry (Yankee) Division, 140
Twenty-Eighth Infantry Regiment, 155

U-53, 27
U-58, 114–15
U-77, 85
U-90, 144–45, 147–52, 161–62, 166
U-151, 165–66
U-boats, 27, 29, 40–42, 47, 52, 55, 57–58, 142, 176
Brest and, 94, 127
Covington and, 181
cruise range and, 55
eastern seaboard and, 165
FDR and, 59–60
German POWs from captured, 113
Germany recalls fleet, 259
Justica and, 190, 191
Leviathan and, 60, 64–68, 72, 90, 92–93, 173, 241
Lincoln and, 181
Lusitania and, 25
Mount Vernon and, 197–99

Pocahontas and, 141–42
  Tuscania and *Baltic* attacked by,
    82–87, 89
Universal Service, 249
University of Pennsylvania, 95–97
US Army Medical Corps, 138
US Army Nurse Corps, 95–99
US Coast Guard, 21
US Coast Guard Academy, 22
US Congress, 221, 306
  declaration of war and, 23, 26–32
US House of Representatives, 23, 26,
  32, 132, 306
US Marines, 159–60
US Naval Academy (Annapolis), 53, 81
US Naval Intelligence, 81
US Naval Radio School, 138
US Navy
  Bureau of Construction and Repair,
    60
  flu epidemic and, 138, 140
  Vaterland refurbished by, 36
US Senate, 23, 32, 134
US Supreme Court, 26

Vaterland, SS (German superliner;
  later *Leviathan*)
  charity ball of 1916, 25
  in Hoboken at outbreak of war,
    1–9, 21–23
  luxury design of, 3–4, 37
  refurbished as troopship, 35–38
  renamed *Leviathan*, 38
  sabotage attempts on, 33–34
  seized by Coast Guard, 22–25,
    33–34
  speed of, 58

Vaux, 156
venereal disease, 241
Verdun, 124, 193, 215–16
  Battle of (1916), 155, 206, 215–16
Verriers, 265
Versailles (Paris) Treaty of 1919,
  297–98, 303
Versailles Treaty of 1871, 297
Vesle River, 154
Victoria, Queen of England, 41
Vigilancia (steamship), 27
Villa, Francisco "Pancho," 44, 249
Vosges Mountains, 283

Wadsworth, USS (destroyer), 163
Walke, USS (destroyer), 176
Walker, William, 206
War Department, 187
War of 1812, 76
Warren, Francis E., 42
Washington, DC
  Naval Conference of 1918, 197
  Victory Parade of 1919, 302
Waterloo, Battle of (1815), 110
Weaver, Anna, 95
Weaver, Cortland Scott, 96
Weaver, Emma Elizabeth, 95–99,
  127–31, 182–85, 306
Weaver, Moses, 95
"When the Boys from Dixie Eat the
  Melon on the Rhine" (song), 172
"Where Do We Go from Here,
  Boys?" (song), 87
Whistler, James, 279
White Star Line, 1, 9, 38
Whittlesey, Charles, 248–51
Why Not Marry (film), 98

"Why We Are at War" (Taft), 76

Wilhelm II, Kaiser of Germany, 3, 5, 8, 41, 105, 267, 280–81

Wilhelm, Crown Prince of Germany, 206

Wilson, Edith, 38

Wilson, Woodrow, 41, 134, 261
    declaration of war and, 23, 26–32
    election of 1916, 31, 84
    emergency war powers and, 134–35
    FDR and, 60
    Paris Peace Conference and, 276
    Pershing promoted by, 300–301
    stroke, 300
    troops moved to France and, 61

U-boats and, 47
    Victory Parade and, 302

Woodward, Vincent, 51–52, 55–56, 58

World's Work, The, 10

World War I
    armistice, 266–72
    casualties of, 291
    outbreak of, 5–8
    US enters, 26–32, 40, 44–47

Yacona, USS, 220

Ypres, 46, 98

Zeppelin bombers, 105

Zimmermann telegram, 29

ABOUT THE AUTHOR

PETER HERNON is the author of five books, including the *New York Times* bestseller *Under the Influence: The Unauthorized Story of the Anheuser-Busch Dynasty* (with Terry Ganey). Hernon worked as an editor at the *Chicago Tribune*, and before that was an investigative reporter for the *St. Louis Post-Dispatch*. He lives in St. Louis, Missouri, with his wife.